The Private Lives of Private Eyes, Spies, Crimefighters, & Other Good Guys

NICK

The Private Lives of Private Eyes, Spies, Crimefighters, & Other Good Guys

by Otto Penzler

Grosset & Dunlap
A Filmways Company
Publishers • New York

NOTE: The books in the bibliographies are first American editions, and filmographies are complete for English language sound films.

Published simultaneously in Canada
Library of Congress catalog card number: 77-80370
ISBN: 0-448-14325-9 (hardcover)
ISBN: 0-448-14326-7 (paperback)
First printing 1977
Printed in the United States of America

For Chris
The beautiful princess of my fairy tale.

Acknowledgments

It is impossible to attempt a book of this type without the comforting assurance that help will be available when you need it. I needed it. The time required to read again and cull information from every book in which these great detectives appear would have been immeasurable—or roughly the size of the debt owed to those who helped so much with the monumental research involved in this project.

The risk of listing the names and acknowledging the assistance of those whose efforts were instrumental in the production of this book is that some will be inadvertently omitted, but it must be taken in order to give credit and thanks to Bill De Andrea, Charles Shibuk, Norman S. Nolan, Jon L. Lellenberg, Marvin P. Epstein, Diane Nolan, Barbara Fortunato, Faith Franck, Jane Paznik-Bondarin, Phoebe J. Epstein, Marvin Lachman, Chris Steinbrunner, Carol Brener, J. Randolph Cox, Peter O'Donnell and Kenneth Millar.

Also Joyce Frommer, Joan Brandt and Marie Reno, who must share the blame for getting me into this in the first place.

O.P.

Introduction

Sherlock Holmes struggles in a titanic battle to the death with the unconscionable Professor Moriarty.

Nero Wolfe gambles his life when he matches wits with the villainous Arnold Zeck.

James Bond risks the fate of the world in his encounters with the insidious Ernst Stavro Blofeld.

And, on a less epic scale, all great detectives, in all their cases, fearlessly don suits of white armor for their confrontations with the black forces of evil.

This duel forms the essence of every detective story ever written. It is, in fact, the most basic concept in all fiction—permeating virtually every story conceived, tracing its origins all the way back to the Bible. There the struggle between Good and Evil, God and Satan, is on the grandest of all levels, infinite and eternal.

Good may be portrayed in various forms, as God, or as a god, or a mythical hero, an armored knight, a musketeer, a cowboy or a private eye. Evil is sometimes the Prince of Darkness himself, or an ogre, a dragon, a barbarian, an Indian or a criminal. Sometimes, in a slightly more subtle or complex form, Good takes the guise of honor, love, humility, devotion or the state. Evil may be seen as any of the apocalyptic horsemen, cruelty, arrogance, hate or, of course, the state.

The Bible pitted these diametrically opposed forces against each other in their purest forms. Mythology gave us titanic gods, overwhelmingly endowed with either positive or negative attributes, but with a trace of human frailty—neither perfectly Good nor invulnerably Evil. The heroic knights of medieval epics were still more flawed than the Olympian gods, and their dragons and Saracens more capable of being destroyed. The dilution of powers on both sides of the wall of morality has continued to the present day.

Always, however, there is someone to defend Good, even if he sometimes seems ill-equipped for such a burden, and always there is an adversary riding the coattails of Evil. Never are the positions more clearly defined than in the detective story.

The first genuine detective of literature, Edgar Allan Poe's C. Auguste Dupin, did not appear until 1841. The major reason for the absence of detective stories before that time is that there were, of course, no detectives.

While it may be difficult to comprehend in retrospect, it is nonetheless a fact that there was no organized police force, or crimefighting organization, until the nineteenth century. François Eugène Vidocq, an active thief, informer and all-around blackguard, offered his dubious services to Napoleon in 1809, after being released from jail, and became the head of the first police department in the world: the famous French Sûreté.

Soon after, Scotland Yard was organized, as well as the first police departments in America, sharing the level of achievement common to all law enforcement agencies at that time—hopelessly inept. This is less than shocking when one recalls that virtually all police officials had been criminals in the past, and they were reluctant to abandon their original careers. Bribery, blackmail and corruption flourished.

It is in this atmosphere that Dupin was born, and it requires no exhausting exercise of the imagination to understand his contempt for the official police, an attitude later shared by Sherlock Holmes—and just about every private eye and amateur detective who followed.

Initiating a tradition which still blazes today, Dupin viewed himself as an instrument of justice, a defender of Good, and a foe of Evil. Consciously or not, a similar role has been assumed by other detectives so regularly and naturally that anything else would rob them of that title.

The greatest crimefighters of all ages have certain other characteristics in common, else they would be unfit to wrap themselves in their cloaks of invincibility. While it is impossible to pinpoint precisely what these shared traits are, the most vital is a philosophical certitude in the *rightness* of Good and the *wrongness* of Evil. It has a simplistic ring to it, but consider the rarity of that viewpoint and it ceases to be astonishing that so few fictional entities (not to mention real-life ones) are capable of carrying the banner.

To determine exactly how these great detectives have come to be immortal, it is possible to say only that no single road has had to bear all the traffic.

Modesty Blaise came through the alleys and prison camps of the Mideast, Father Brown through a seminary, Nick and Nora Charles from a lifestyle of urban sophistication, Miss Marple from a sleepy village, Dupin from poverty, Archer from the middle class, Vance from great wealth, Poirot from Belgium, Mr. Moto from Japan, Nero Wolfe from Montenegro and The Shadow from who knows where.

Wolfe will not leave his house except under extreme provocation; an earthquake might qualify. Mike Hammer does not like Communists; to deal with them, he suggests, "Kill, kill, kill, kill!" Holmes kept his unanswered correspondence transfixed to his mantle with a penknife. Chan loathes Japanese, Moto loathes Chinese, Drummond loathes Germans, Bond loathes Bulgars.

Is there a connecting link to these eccentricities, a universal factor possessed by all the great detectives to indicate that they are marble hewn from the same quarry, awaiting only the artists' hands to assure their immortality? Of course not, but they are the first of the many clues that will present themselves in the biographies that follow. One fact is certain: each of the crimefighting heroes or heroines whose lives are here described is a unique and colorful personality, with an appeal that extends to every literary and cinematic taste.

Only three factors connect the towering figures whose lives are examined in this book. All twenty-five are crimefighters, whether private eyes, official policemen, spies, or amateurs. All twenty-five are extraordinarily successful; even their rare failures do them credit. All twenty-five are possessed of fascinating personalities and life histories.

A few years ago, the Republic of Nicaragua issued a special series of stamps to commemorate the fiftieth anniversary of Interpol. A poll conducted by **Ellery Queen's Mystery Magazine** named the twelve greatest detectives of all time, and portraits of those private eyes and other crimefighters illustrated the stamps. Those twelve (Brown, Chan, Dupin, Holmes, Maigret, Marlowe, Mason, Poirot, Queen, Spade, Wimsey, Wolfe) are portrayed in this book, together with an additional thirteen (appropriately, since that number is shrouded in magic and mystery) heroic characters, to comprise a compendium of the *crème de la crème* of crimefighters.

The Private Lives of Private Eyes, Spies, Crimefighters and Other Good Guys is the first attempt to provide in-depth profiles of all these great detectives. The minutiae of the life and personality of, say, Perry Mason, could heretofore be learned only by reading the eighty-one books about him. Most of the material gathered in this volume has been culled directly from the books about the private eyes and other good guys, but it is often supplemented with information gathered from motion pictures, radio and television shows, essays and studies written by the creators of the characters—anything that helps to provide the most fully rounded portrait possible. Infrequently, these hard data have been augmented with inferential trivia. Details of Holmes' relationship with Irene Adler, for example, although largely unchronicled, seem clear enough in retrospect.

These character sketches may serve as reminders of those charismatic qualities that have made their subjects the best-loved detectives of all time. More significantly, they may impel readers to become more familiar with them by reading again—or for the first time—the adventures of some of the most vital literary creations of the past century and a half.

Since its inception, the detective, or mystery, story has been the most widely-read form of fiction to grace the printed page, and the favorite motion picture genre of several generations.

Even people who claim to have no affection admit to powerful positive feelings for such works as Dostoevsky's **Crime and Punishment,** Faulkner's **Intruder in the Dust** and **Sanctuary**, Dickens' **Bleak House,** Hugo's **Les Misérables,** Chesterton's **The Man Who Was Thursday,** Twain's **The Man That Corrupted Hadleyburg,** Collins' **The Woman in White,** Balzac's **Père Goriot** and Dreiser's **An American Tragedy**—all excellent works of crime, mystery, suspense or detection.

There is an appeal to the detective story that is irresistible to those of us who are helplessly optimistic, who believe in the inevitable triumph of truth and justice, who love beautiful princesses and stalwart heroes, who can accept nothing less than a happy ending. In other words, those of us who still love fairy tales, and for whom a great detective is the reassuring signpost that, in the end, the wicked will be punished and the deserving will live happily ever after.

New York
June 1977

Otto Penzler

Contents

Lew Archer

Lew Archer is an anachronism thrust into the twentieth century and unable to syncopate his rhythm with anyone else's. Totally unafraid to display his outdated code of ethics, his huge reservoir of old-fashioned values, he is a prisoner of his virtues, trapped in a philosophy which he considers inviolable. Applauded by some, ridiculed by others, it is immutable, revealed in all its brilliance, and sometimes in all its drabness, for anyone who cares to look.

In an era when many are willing to sell their souls, their existence, not to mention their bodies or their talents, to the highest bidder, Lew Archer persists in his quixotic search for justice. He never relaxes his willingness to help those in need of it and inexorably pursues truth—even if he will realize no profit, either financial or spiritual, when he ultimately succeeds in his quest.

Archer is a direct descendant of the hard-boiled detectives of the 1930s, with many of the characteristics of such heroes as Sam Spade, Philip Marlowe and Mike Hammer. He is, actually, a contemporary of the latter two. (It is sometimes difficult to remember that the first Archer novel was published only ten years after the first Marlowe novel and two years after the first Hammer.) All are private detectives and somewhat over-dedicated to their profession. Although they often hurt themselves (Spade sends a woman he loves to jail, Hammer and Marlowe endure terrible beatings, Archer refuses enormous fees), they have a single-minded purpose once they have committed themselves to a client, and nothing can deter them. They employ different methods, to be sure (Marlowe and Archer are basically gentle men, Spade and Hammer are less concerned about violence), but they bring similar ethical viewpoints to a case.

None of them will ever abandon a client, or turn their backs on anyone who needs help, unless they feel they are being used or tricked. They will never drop a case because they are threatened or bribed. They will sacrifice everything—fees, professional reputation,

A handsome and hard-boiled Lew Archer appears on the cover of The Name Is Archer *(1955).*

physical well-being—for abstract ideals of honor, truth or justice. Their definitions of those terms may not always coincide with other people's and their idea of ethical conduct often transcends the bounds of strict legality, but those highly personal guiding forces remain clear and inflexible to the private eyes.

Many common elements link the tough private detectives of fiction. Without exception, they are American. Beginning in the pulp magazines of the 1920s, the "hard-boiled" private eyes began, and have remained, the most recognizably American of all literary figures, their banner surehandedly carried today by Lew Archer.

A film producer once asked Macdonald if Archer is based on any real person. "Yes," Macdonald answered, "myself." Although he had known many real-life private detectives and admired them and their work, "Archer was created from the inside out," he explained. "I wasn't Archer, exactly, but Archer was me."

Although changed to Harper for the film representations of some adventures, Archer's name has an honorable genesis: it was taken from Sam Spade's partner, Miles Archer, who is murdered in **The Maltese Falcon**.

Paul Newman's portrayal of Harper is superb, an enduring contribution to the private eye genre in film, but he remains separate and distinct from Ross Macdonald's literary figure. While much of Harper is Paul Newman, much of Archer remains Ross Macdonald.

His name came from Dashiell Hammett, his values from Ross Macdonald, but the early Lew Archer was patterned after Philip Marlowe in almost every other way. Only with the writing of **The Galton Case** did Archer take on the enduring qualities of his own full personality, just as Macdonald's style became more personal and distinctive. One major similarity which continues to exist in the adventures of the two private eyes is the southern California locale of the tales, not merely as a backdrop but as a vital element in the cases. (The problems in need of solution in southern California seem not to exist anywhere else on the surface of the planet.)

Macdonald described the early similarity between Archer and Marlowe in this way: "Chandler's Anglo-American background and my Canadian-American one gave our detectives a common quality: the fresh suspicious eye of a semi-outsider who is fascinated but not completely taken in by the customs of the natives."

Archer may be a derivative detective, but he is unique in several ways, not the least of which is that he is the only true detective hero who has every appearance of simultaneously being an anti-hero.

An automobile glides under the unblinking southern California sun, steered by a solitary figure. The man is a private detective hired by a wealthy family to locate a missing, possibly kidnapped, child. In all likelihood he will discover the child has run away, not been abducted, and the disappearance will be followed by at least one murder as closely and surely as a solitary figure's inexorable shadow on a lamplit street. After a close examination of the relationships between the child, who is probably in the late teenage years or early twenties, and its parents, the murder or murders will be solved by the discovery of a seminal event from the distant past.

Clearly, this is a Lew Archer case. No other detective so frequently finds himself in the position of family counselor and social worker, and none would have the sensitivity and patience actually to help. And Archer does help, often patching torn relationships between parents and their emotionally distant children, though the rift is sometimes too great to be closed. Murders have occurred, and someone will have to go to jail, and lives will be shattered despite new understandings and forgivings. Like life, Archer's cases are inevitably complex and too rarely result in simple, happy conclusions.

Because Lew Archer narrates his own exploits, everything—individuals, relationships, landscapes, even such abstractions as justice and morality—is seen through his eyes, colored by his personal philosophy. There is no pure objectivity in his stories, although he strives to be fair and succeeds, sometimes. Good intentions don't make Archer much more fair than most everyone else, but he is intelligent and kind, almost virtuous, so if he presents portraits with warts for the sake of accuracy, the ugliness will be softened with shadows for the sake of compassion.

Basically lonely, somewhat disappointed with the world, and seldom happy, it is a trifle surprising to find Archer remaining compulsively just. It would be so much easier to be bitter.

Once, someone suggests to Archer, "You have a secret passion for justice. Why don't you admit

Unflamboyant and gentle, Brian Keith was a surprisingly good choice to portray Archer, *the very short-lived NBC series.*

it?"

"I have a secret passion for mercy," he replies. "But justice is what keeps happening to people."

Still, justice is important to him, and he sometimes works only for the sake of it. Intensely loyal to his clients, whether or not they deserve loyalty, he refuses to accept their orders if he feels to do so would compromise his own standards of morality. He has been fired more than once for his strong-mindedness (some would call it obstinacy, if not out-and-out mulishness) but has continued his investigations anyway—purely to resolve the problem and arrive at the truth. He knows that no fee will be forthcoming, but he sometimes cares about the people in the case too much to turn his back on them.

"The problem," he once said, "was to love people, to serve them, without wanting anything from them. I was a long way from solving that one." Maybe, but he comes closer than any other detective.

It is impossible for Archer to remain detached or aloof. He simply cares too much, and his sensitivity makes him vulnerable to pain. He has experienced it often enough to be exhausted from it, and he lives his lonely years as an outsider, peering into the hopeless pains of others, trying somehow to relieve them. He stands apart from society in general, but he is even more removed from his particular region because it has so much unreality for him.

He lives in Hollywood, specifically West Hollywood, and works out of an office on Sunset Strip. Although he is an alien in his environment, he is accused of being "Hollywoodish," at which he grins, calling it his "protective coloration," his way of blending into his surroundings.

"Hollywood started as a meaningless dream, invented for money," he says. "But its colors ran, out through the holes in people's heads, spread across the landscape and solidified. North and south along the coast, east across the desert, across the continent. Now we were stuck with the dream without a meaning. It had become the nightmare that we lived in."

He may not love it, but Hollywood is Archer's home. A friend to many in the movie business, he often uses his contacts in the pursuit of information, even posing once as a literary agent.

Now in middle age, Archer spent ten years as what he describes as a "Hollywood peeper," handling divorce cases. He feels mildly guilty and embarrassed by having earned his living as "a private eye at the keyhole of illicit bedrooms" but he was reluctant to consider giving it up entirely. Perhaps he knew he did his job well, or perhaps he had finally decided to stay with something.

Much of his life has been composed of uncompleted ventures which had beginnings and endings but lacked in-between substance. His unhappy marriage to Sue, whom he loved, ended in divorce because of his total dedication to his job and because, Archer admits, "she didn't like the company I kept." In his riper years, he wanders from one relationship to another, though not promiscuously. While he may be genuinely moved by a new woman, the duration of their relationship seems to be measured only by the amount of time required to solve a case. When the case ends, so does the romance. There is little continuity of people, places or things beyond the specific requirements of Archer's profession.

He does not often mention his parents, though he once traveled to Canada in an attempt to trace his father, who had been missing for twenty years. There were no

Paul Newman was perfectly cast as the famous private eye. He used the name Harper for two films: Harper *(1966) and* The Drowning Pool *(1975).*

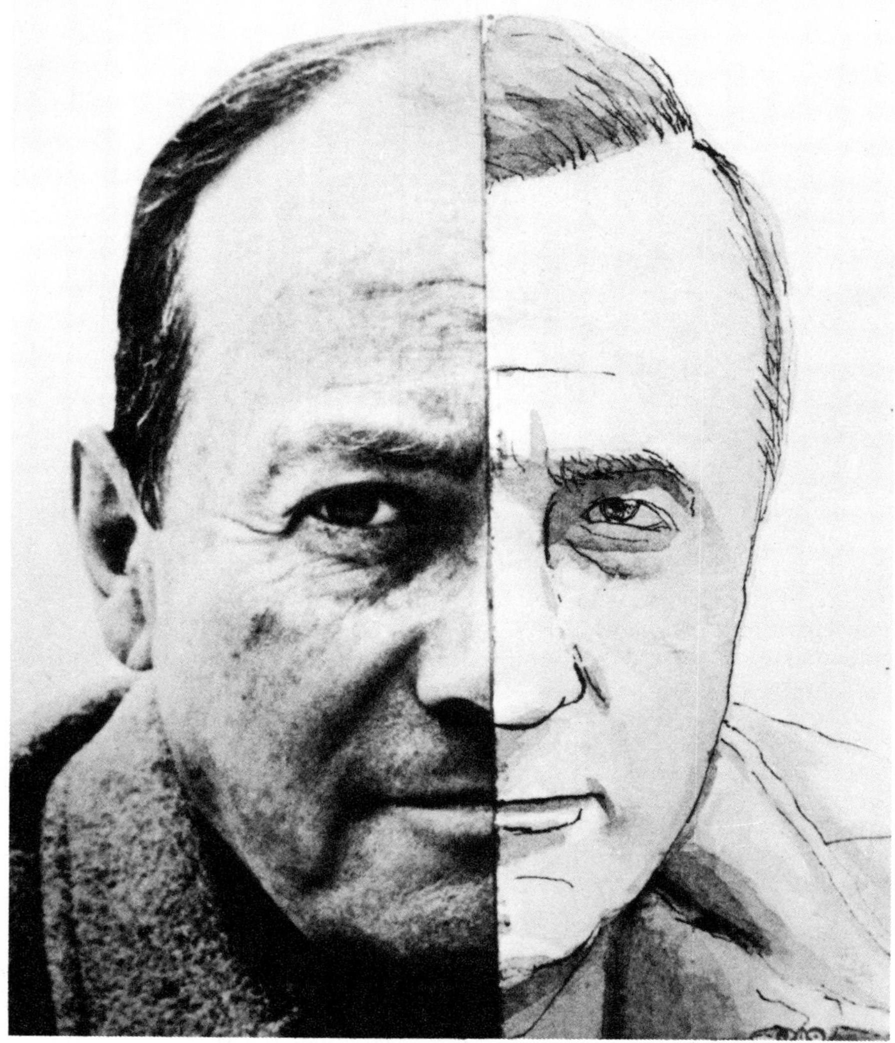

This composite illustrated the cover of On Crime Writing *by Ross Macdonald. His photo is on the left; Archer is on the right.*

children in his marriage. No brothers or sisters. No long-time pals or lovers. No faithful secretary or consistent housekeeper. Archer is as free and uncommitted as it is possible for someone to be, yet one has the feeling that he hopes for something permanent. He has no life of his own. All his energy and emotion are devoted to his clients and the salvation of some part of their troubled lives. Yet, when a case is concluded, he collects his fee, if he is able, and moves on, as uncompleted and solitary as when he entered the lives of those involved in the mystery he had been hired to solve.

He has been solving other people's problems for a long time. Before receiving his license as a private investigator he was a member of the Long Beach police force. The overbearing necessities of the life of a policeman turned the profession sour for Archer because he viewed the administration as corrupt and felt incapable of doing anything to change it. He decided to continue his quest for justice privately.

It had been a boyhood fascination with a motion picture detective hero which had initially made him determined to become a cop. As a youngster growing up in Long Beach (he was born in 1913), he had regularly attended Saturday afternoon matinees and been much impressed with the exploits of "Inspector Fate of Limehouse." Years later, Archer remembered his former screen idol and was impelled to emulate him as closely as possible by becoming a private eye, in which profession he has remained — except for the time he spent in intelligence work during World War II.

Archer is good-sized, over six feet tall, and a

tough professional. Although he isn't anxious to use his gun or his fists, he does know how to handle himself: "When he came after me, I shifted my attack to his head, jabbing with the left until he was off balance on his heels. Then I pivoted and threw a long right hook which changed to an uppercut. An electric shock surged up my arm. Devlin lay down on the green tiles, chilled like a side of beef."

But he is no impetuous, death-defying fool. Held at gunpoint, he considers his alternatives. "I swallowed anger and nausea, estimating my chances of knocking the gun to one side and taking him barehanded. The chances seemed pretty slim. He was heavier than I was, and he held the automatic as if it had grown out of the end of his arm. You've seen too many movies, I told myself."

Unlike many private detectives, he seldom uses his gun, regarding it less as an ever-ready equalizer against the gigantic forces of evil that seem to permeate his existence than as a "moral weight" against an immoral society.

It is Archer's sense of morality which lifts him above most of the people he encounters. He is aware of his ethics and describes them in a low-key style. "Most good policemen," he says, "have a public conscience and a private conscience. I just have the private conscience, a poor thing but mine own."

Having set his own standards of morality, he tries to live with them and up to them, without trying to cram them down the throats of others. Those standards occasionally seem eccentric to outsiders but Archer is fairly certain of his own rightness.

His unusual dedication to morality is always tempered with compassion. He tends to find himself on the side of the underdog more often than with those in power, whether the relationship is parent to child, master to servant, policeman to fugitive. His initial sympathies lie with those least able to control their fates. Although he takes sides in virtually every situation in which he finds himself, he does not hopelessly offend those with whom he is at odds. Not many people hate him. He can talk with anyone and make them feel listened to—the wealthy, their servants, their inevitably unappealing sycophants, policemen, blacks, youngsters, artists and human derelicts. At least once, Archer can get them to talk and reveal something of themselves or throw light in a dark corner.

Although not fanatic about it, Archer criticizes overabundance—whether of wealth, power or consumption—and progress, particularly with regard to the world of business and technology. Fast cars, big houses, fast-paced living and the other trappings of big money leave him cool, if not unwaveringly icy.

"You can't blame money for what it does to people," he says. "The evil is in the people, and the money is the peg they hang it on. They go wild for money when they've lost their other values."

Archer speaks disparagingly of money and is generally distrustful of the rich, but he is not a revolutionary. Some of his views are shared by those toward the left of the political spectrum, but a philosophy cannot choose its followers. He is essentially apolitical, his personal values determined more by morality and compassion than politics or theology.

He does not attend church services and doesn't rely on God to run the universe, but he doesn't deny His existence, either. "What's the use of praying?" he rhetorically asks, then answers, "It keeps the circuits open. Just in case there's ever anybody on the other end of the line."

Archer is more acutely aware of the environment than any detective since November Joe, "the detective of the woods" about whom Hesketh Prichard wrote more than half a century ago. Few crimes outrage him more than those against nature, and he constantly notices the results of thoughtless industry or individuals in the form of oil-blackened beaches, ruined birds, and smog-thick air. He was interested in, and knowledgeable about, ecological matters before they became political issues, often displaying his love of nature and ability to identify and appreciate flowers, birds and trees.

Nature is only one of the areas in which he is educated (he attended college but did not graduate). Intelligent and articulate, he loves to tell stories—perhaps a characteristic of most lonely people. He also enjoys reading and art; a personal favorite is the Japanese artist Kuniyoshi. Perhaps his artistic sense is responsible for his frequent use of imagery as he narrates his adventures. His sensitivity makes that imagery singularly effective, and no one has ever used similes and metaphors more colorfully or correctly.

While Archer's conjured images are sometimes amusing—"He smiled like a corpse in a deft mortician's hands"—and his wit is rapid and omnipresent, he is not basically a humorous man. He seldom laughs and is never frivolous. He is, in fact, too serious to be truly likable for a long stretch of time. Still, men enjoy his rough-and-ready manner and like to drink with him; women are quickly and strongly attracted by his masculinity. And everyone seems to enjoy one particularly winning trait of the best private detective in southern California: he is less interested in himself than in the subject in which they are primarily interested—themselves. He cares, he is often able to help, and he is there with advice when needed.

ROSS MACDONALD (pseudonym of Kenneth Millar, 1915–   ) He was still an infant, when his family moved from Los Gatos, Calif., to Canada and shortly thereafter broke up, permanently affecting his life and the theme of his literature. His first novel, **The Dark Tunnel** (1944), and the next three, all mysteries, were published under the name Kenneth Millar. To avoid confusion with his wife's books (she is the famous mystery novelist Margaret Millar) he adopted the pseudonym John Ross Macdonald, only to be confused with another mystery writer, John D. MacDonald, and he changed it again to the familiar Ross Macdonald name. One of the finest stylists active today, he is a rarity among writers of detective fiction in that critics regard him as a major novelist, irrespective of the subject matter of his fiction. He has received the Grand Master Award of the Mystery Writers of America.

FILMOGRAPHY

1966 **Harper** (Warner Brothers) with Paul Newman (as Lew Archer, renamed Harper for this film version), Lauren Bacall, Julie Harris, Arthur Hill, Janet Leigh, Robert Wagner, Pamela Tiffin, Robert Webber, Shelley Winters; directed by Jack Smight.
1975 **The Drowning Pool** (Warner Brothers) with Paul Newman (again using the name Harper), Joanne Woodward; directed by Stuart Rosenberg.

BIBLIOGRAPHY

1949 **The Moving Target** (Knopf)
1950 **The Drowning Pool** (Knopf)
1951 **The Way Some People Die** (Knopf)
1952 **The Ivory Grin** (Knopf)
1954 **Find a Victim** (Knopf)
1955 **The Name Is Archer** (Bantam)
1956 **The Barbarous Coast** (Knopf)
1958 **The Doomsters** (Knopf)
1959 **The Galton Case** (Knopf)
1961 **The Wycherly Woman** (Knopf)
1962 **The Zebra-Striped Hearse** (Knopf)
1964 **The Chill** (Knopf)
1965 **The Far Side of the Dollar** (Knopf)
1966 **Black Money** (Knopf)
1968 **The Instant Enemy** (Knopf)
1969 **The Goodbye Look** (Knopf)
1971 **The Underground Man** (Knopf)
1973 **Sleeping Beauty** (Knopf)
1976 **The Blue Hammer** (Knopf)
1977 **Lew Archer, Private Investigator** (The Mysterious Press)

Modesty Blaise

It would not be difficult to count on the fingers of three hands the total number of beautiful female crimefighters in literature. Not wives of patient, understanding, exasperated but amused young men who have to rescue their fair damsels from the clutching fingers of sneering villains; not naive young things whose innocent curiosity inevitably causes their lives to be threatened in the next-to-last chapter as they think to themselves: "If only I had known yesterday what I know now, these twenty-seven grisly murders would not have been committed during the past horrible weekend"; and not precocious teenagers or old-maid great-aunts—just honest-to-goodness beautiful female crimefighters. And today, it would be possible to count on the thumbs of one hand all the beautiful female crimefighters who are effective, famous and enduring. Her name is Modesty Blaise.

Like Wonder Woman, Modesty began as a comic strip character (in 1963), then appeared on the screen, but she also was the subject of several novels and short story collections by her creator, Peter O'Donnell. Furthermore, she required only normal human gifts and powers to accomplish her business, unlike her predecessor, Wonder Woman, who enjoyed the advantages of having the beauty of Aphrodite, the wisdom of Athena, the strength of Hercules and the speed of Mercury. While Modesty often appears to have the same superhuman powers as the glamorous Amazon princess of Paradise Isle, they are actually skills which could have been developed by anyone. Well, almost anyone.

In many ways, Modesty is one of the first truly liberated women of mystery fiction, although it is doubtful that she ever thought of herself in those terms. Her creator has, however, and denies that he has created every man's sexual fantasy.

"I don't know that the idea of this very attractive, but at the same time very tough, woman would appeal to most men. I'm trying to think how I would react myself. It'd be a bit daunting for a man, wouldn't it? I suppose if I were being objective about it I would see her as rather a dominant female, except that I don't paint her that way when she's between the sheets."

While Modesty acknowledges that she likes men in general and needs one specifically (Willie Garvin) to assist in her adventures, both she and Willie understand that she is in control and guides their relationship. Interestingly, Willie does not feel "threatened" by his role.

It has been said often, and correctly, that Modesty Blaise is the female James Bond. Just as he works outside the law as a zealous and patriotic protector of Great Britain's interests, so does she. Just as 007 is irresistible to the opposite sex, so is Modesty. Just as he possesses a range of physical talents and intellectual resources a step beyond those of ordinary men, so does Modesty possess them beyond the capabilities of ordinary women—*and* men.

One major difference between Bond and Blaise is that, while he is a member of British Intelligence, described merely as a civil servant, she is a freelancer with a criminal background. As the leader of **The Network**, a highly efficient criminal organization, Modesty earns a fast and vast fortune, retiring while still young. Although she has everything she ever wanted, and is safely beyond the reach of the law in her high-class and spotless retirement, she is successfully recruited to perform high-risk deeds for the government because Sir Gerald Tarrant of British Intelligence shrewdly realizes that she craves the adventure and peril of her past life. When he provides her with the opportunity to relive the excitement of her criminal years, she cannot resist.

Modesty's extraordinary background is so vague and undocumented that most of the information contained in her dossier at Intelligence is a loose concoction of guesses, theories, deductions and unconfirmed "facts."

She is known to have been a refugee in the Middle East shortly after World War II, a dirty little urchin growing up and struggling to survive among the narrow black alleys of Turkey and Persia. Her kindergarten had been in a prison camp in Greece. Parentless, homeless, stateless, she manages to save the life of an old man called the "professor," also a refugee. Years later, when talking of her childhood and recounting the meeting with the old man, she is asked if he looked after her.

"No," she says, "I looked after him. In and out of half a dozen refugee and displaced persons camps for about five years."

The old man had been a professor of philosophy at Budapest and spoke five languages. To repay the little girl's kindness, he taught her. For six hours a day, every day, he tried to teach her everything he knew. At first, she hated the lessons but pretended to listen so that she wouldn't hurt his feelings.

"And that was strange," she said, "because I was as hard as nails with anyone else." She gradually became interested in the things he told her until her knowledge became extensive and her appetite for more of it insatiable. "That old man knew everything," she recalls, "and he knew how to teach. But he'd let the food be stolen out of his hands. He'd have starved without me." Although only twelve at the time, she would fight anyone to protect their meager supply of food and what other possessions they had. She felt no trepidation about taking on a fully grown man.

"It wasn't so hard," she remembers. "For one thing, I wasn't scared. I'd had all that burned out of me a long time before. For another thing, I had the right attitude, the right frame of mind. Most people scare easily. They're afraid of getting hurt, even by something small, if it's fierce. So they have to work themselves up to a certain pitch before they'll risk fighting." But not Modesty. "There's a point where you're committed," she continues, "and from there on it's dangerous to pussyfoot around. You have to throw the switch. Go in like a ball of fire and finish it as quick as you can."

It is the old professor who wryly gave her the name "Modesty"; she chose her own last name from the tutor of Merlin the magician in the Arthurian legends.

At one time during these early years of deprivation, while lost and wandering in the desert, she was taken in by Sheik Abu-Tahir, ruler of Malaurak. "Her wearing is rags," he reminisces to Sir Gerald, "and she has hunger. But not fear. She is very *fierce*, like small wild animal. She not asking help—but I give. I take her into our tents. Tell women to give food." Modesty stayed with him for half a year, reminding the sheik that, in that time, she had become "the best goat-herd of all your people."

The official British Intelligence dossier first

Monica Vitti plays the title role of Modesty Blaise *(1966), thus far the only film of her adventures. Terence Stamp is Willie Garvin.*

Willie Garvin keeps a watchful eye on the beautiful Modesty throughout their adventures. This illustration for the script of a (still unproduced) film has never before been published.

makes note of her at the approximate age of seventeen (she admits that even she doesn't know her precise age since she was unable to trace any authoritative records), working in a small gambling house in Tangier. The establishment was controlled by a modest criminal organization headed by Henri Louche. When he was assassinated by a rival gang in the following year, Modesty assumed control of the group, immediately expanding its size, strength and resources at a remarkable rate. This more successful organization became known as **The Network** and operated on a grand scale in every extremity of the world. Among the crimes in which it specialized were art and jewelry thefts, gold and currency manipulations, smuggling and an espionage service. Modesty assures Sir Gerald that at no time did **The Network** trade in secrets belonging to Her Majesty's Government, although the reason seems not to have been patriotic fervor or Anglophilia. The adventuress had decided to settle in Great Britain when her illicit career ended and had no desire to be considered "undesirable."

Modesty's group totally abstained from trafficking in two potentially lucrative areas—drugs and vice—she found them repellent. It is reported, in fact, that **The Network** actually gave valuable information to the United States Bureau of Narcotics on two separate occasions.

Approximately two or three years after organizing **The Network**, she was joined by Willie Garvin, who remains "a close associate." **When Modesty and Willie retired, The Network** was split up among its top officers—"branch-managers," British Intelligence calls them—in various countries. She called it quits at the age of (about) twenty-six when she had acquired the half-million pounds (considerably more than a million dollars at the time) which she had set as her goal at the age of seventeen. Willie bought the pub he had always dreamed of owning. Comfortably settled in England, they led exemplary lives, with their fabulous wealth the only explanation offered by British Intelligence for their failure to engage in illegal activities.

In 1962, Modesty had married and promptly divorced a derelict Englishman in Beirut in order to gain British citizenship. When James Fraser, Tarrant's assistant, suggests that it seemed to be purely a financial arrangement, she responds, "Yes. Very purely." Her chastity is of considerably less concern to her on numerous other occasions and in various situations, when she finds it convenient or necessary to spend time between sheets with a man for reasons other than personal enjoyment. Her beauty makes it a simple task for her to seduce men, and her ample physical attractions ensure that they rarely mind the fact that they have been, well, tricked.

Modesty does not possess the perfection of the classic beauties of history, but she takes the breath away. Each of the deviations from the ordinary standards of beauty seems essential to her unique composition. Tarrant is baffled by her compellingly exquisite loveliness and appraises her in his mind.

"The face was smooth and calm with high cheekbones under dark, contemplative eyes. She would be five foot six, but with the black hair drawn up into a chignon on the crown of her head she appeared taller. Her skin held a soft, matte tan that would have made a fortune for any man who could get it into a bottle." Her mouth intrigues Tarrant. "Studied in isolation it was a touch too wide, but in the totality of her features a smaller mouth would have been wrong. Her neck, he decided, though magnificent, was definitely too long, but then again, that wonderful poise of the head would have been marred by a shorter neck. Her legs—no, dammit, they weren't too long. He wasn't going to fall into the same trap again. This girl was made to be looked at as a whole—and as often as possible, for preference. He was surprised to find that he had an urgent wish to see her smile." When she rewards Tarrant's wish, her smile, he notes, "is rich with delight, completely without restraint, and holding a gamin touch of mischief."

Although Tarrant is *almost* too much of a gentleman to notice, or to admit (even to himself) that he does notice, Modesty has large, firm breasts which have an unfailing penchant for straining mightily against flimsy sweaters.

Feminine charms are not the only weapon in Modesty Blaise's arsenal. She is fearless in physical action of a more violent kind, having mastered several forms of the martial arts, and has an impressive ability to handle firearms, although she prefers archery. So that she can keep her eye sharp, Willie has provided a firing range for her. While she seldom carries a handgun, and uses it even less frequently, she maintains that "However rarely you use a gun, when the moment comes you're either ready or you're dead." In order to become ready, she practiced for fifteen hundred hours—two hours a day for two years.

Although she is unlikely to need her gun in a hurry, she has a favorite—a Brevete, a small and light automatic. When it is suggested that the gun is merely a toy, she replies, "It's adequate—if you are." To fill a more urgent need, her preference is for a Colt .32. She is unable to carry it in the traditional shoulder holster because her breasts get in the way, so she wears a snap-holster belted at the back of the hip, covering it with a short jacket that she clears out of the way by using the FBI draw. The indispensable Willie produces special bullets to cut down on the noise.

Willie hates guns but is an expert at knife-throwing and has a collection of strange, barbaric weapons, each with its own specialized use. He can spin a blackthorn staff (which he calls "the finest non-explosive hand weapon ever devised") so fast that the eye is incapable of watching it. But it is the knives on which he most frequently and confidently relies. Inside the left breast of his jacket, a lightweight windbreaker with a zipper front, he has stitched a double sheath of thin but stiff leather which holds two knives. He sometimes carries them in a harness sheath beneath his shirt, but he clearly prefers the jacket. Willie is as fast and as lethal with a knife as others are with a revolver. And his knife is far from ordinary. A five-and-a-half-inch steel blade is honed to perfect razor sharpness for its entire length, which is a slightly asymmetrical curve up to the point. It has no cross-guard, only a small fillet of brass to protect the hand. The brass is preferable to steel because of what Modesty calls "the Bowie principle": when guarding against a thrust, steel would enable the other knife blade to skip off too easily; with brass, a softer metal, the other blade nicks in and catches. Tarrant regards knife-throwing as a mere circus trick until he sees Willie in action. He is now convinced of its efficacy.

When Modesty met Willie Garvin (in Saigon, during the early years of her rise to power as head of **The Network**), he was dirty, scruffy, uneducated and a bit too earthy for most people's tastes. His loyalty, as well as other attractions, soon brought him to the position of right-hand man to Modesty, whom he worshipfully calls "Princess." Since those early times, he has acquired the air of a born gentleman. Fraser describes him as "a rough diamond, but remarkably well polished in parts. His manners are impeccable."

Garvin is big, about six foot one or two, a few years older than Modesty, with blue eyes, generally tousled blond hair, and a heavily muscled body. On the back of his huge right hand is a big scar shaped like an incompleted "S." It was made with the red-hot knife blade of a villain named Suleiman. The "S" remained incomplete because Modesty sneaked up behind the torturer and snapped his neck.

After retirement from the criminal life, Willie is, like Modesty, unable to resist the temptation to return to action. "It's one way of knowing you're alive," he says. He is captured and, instead of fearing his apparently inevitable death, he thinks of Modesty while in his cell and of how angry she would be if she knew that he had allowed himself to be caught. That thought frightens him.

Even Sir Gerald, who calls him "an uneducated criminal with a record as long as your arm," admits Willie has certain "curious skills" but is surprised to learn of one in particular. "He can sense trouble coming," Modesty tells him. "His ears prickle." To this revelation, Tarrant responds in the only sensible way. "You're joking," he says. But she isn't. "No," she insists, "it's saved my life twice. I don't know how many times it's saved his."

Garvin retains a heavy cockney accent which immediately relegates him to a lower social class, but he is able to drop it and adopt a variety of alternative accents at will. Modesty explains that he prefers not to lose the cockney because it fits a niche he has found for himself, and he likes the niche. A voracious reader, he reads history, biography, technical books and science fiction—almost anything except general fiction and travel. He has almost total recall and argues intelligently on a wide range of subjects, even with his revered Modesty. His knowledge of the arts is limited, but detailed within those limits. His sharp mind would have taken him anywhere, Modesty claims, if he had just had a different start. He is a terrible cook.

Modesty admits to being a good cook, though not excellent, and freely concedes other shortcomings. She can neither sew nor do crossword puzzles, and her thumb is not green. "Whatever I plant is doomed," she says. She cannot sing, "even in the bath, because my range is about half an octave," and she plays no musical instrument. Her palate for wine is nonexistent—she prefers a rough Algerian red to a vintage claret—and she is unable to understand modern sculpture. Not a shortcoming, but seemingly quite out of character, is her proclivity for crying after a tough job. Quietly and unhysterically, she trembles, sobs and weeps unashamedly (but in front of Willie only—none other), then puts it behind her. It is a release of tension having no connection whatever with fear. Although she conquered fright at an early age, she later practices yoga to help stifle her imagination when the situation requires clarity of thought.

The yoga is useful, but almost superfluous, because she has always had the ability to block unpleasantness from her mind. This exceptional gift has been useful on more than one occasion. She was raped twice, the first time by a peasant near Baalbeck when she was twelve. When she was unable to fight any longer, she simply made herself unconscious—a rare feat of self-induced faint. The second time, she was about twenty-two, in Beirut. Again, she passed out and had no memory of it. Willie went after the rapist and killed him, angering Modesty. She has little regard for personal revenge and didn't want him to take unnecessary chances. Willie doesn't much care about revenge, either, considering it an indulgence, but this was different, to him. He didn't like the idea of the man's boasting that he had had Modesty.

Although he would give his life for Modesty without hesitation, and holds her in higher regard than anyone or anything in his world, he has shared every intimacy with her except sex. A lusty womanizer, he feels no jealousy when she goes off with another man and he has no inclinations toward or fantasies about Modesty. "It would be a liberty," he claims.

Although Willie and Modesty no longer work together when **The Network** is disbanded, they stay in touch. After a short time with the pub of his dreams, The Treadmill, on the side of the Thames river, he is bored and longs for the thrills of years past. He gets the needed opportunity when Modesty declares him indispensable as an aide for her first job for the British government.

After her many years as a successful criminal, followed by a year of luxury in her penthouse, indulging her hobbies (which include gem-cutting), she is approached by Sir Gerald Tarrant of British Intelligence to provide the type of service which cannot be handled through normal channels. Her blazing desire to taste again the adventure of her previous career needs only the smallest prodding to flare anew. She accepts an assignment (ironically, guarding a multi-million dollar diamond shipment) on which her life is staked and for which she cannot

Another illustration for the same film script displays Modesty at the top of her athletic form. This artwork helps maintain the comic strip's great popularity in most parts of the world.

possibly gain any profit beyond the fun of endangering her continued existence. She receives no payment, but has to take no orders, being free to conduct the escapade in whatever fashion she considers most appropriate.

Tarrant uses Modesty to accomplish a difficult task that could have been done successfully by no one else. Her life is risked, an undeniable fact that Tarrant loathes and regards as the worst part of his job. Yet he knows he will call on Modesty again, and risk her life again. He has a job to do and must use the best instruments available—even if they happen to be human instruments. He will use Modesty again, he says, "if she'll let me, because she's unique. You can take a girl from University or the typing pool; if she's got the right potential you can put her through Intelligence and combat training, and produce a damn good agent. *But you won't produce a Modesty Blaise.* It took a rare potential and 20-odd years of hard conditioning to do that...all her life, for as far back as she can remember."

PETER O'DONNELL (1920-) Born in London, O'Donnell dropped out of Catford Central School at the age of sixteen. Not long thereafter, he joined the British Army for seven years of war-related service. While in the Signal Corps in Persia, he saw refugees from many countries struggling to freedom through the mountains. They made a deep impression on him and, years later, he used the experience in his formation of Modesty Blaise, a comic-strip heroine, who had a background similar to the one endured by those refugees. She saw the first light of the journalistic day in 1963 and now appears in sixteen languages throughout the world. She is also the heroine of eight books and a disastrous film, for which the author deserves no blame. Only one line in the entire film is his.

BIBLIOGRAPHY

1965 **Modesty Blaise** (Doubleday)
1966 **Sabre-Tooth** (Doubleday)
1967 **I, Lucifer** (Doubleday)
1969 **A Taste for Death** (Doubleday)
1971 **The Impossible Virgin** (Doubleday)
1972 **Pieces of Modesty** (London: Pan; not published in the U.S.)
1973 **The Silver Mistress** (London: Souvenir; not published in the U.S.)
1976 **Last Day in Limbo** (London: Souvenir; not published in the U.S.)

FILMOGRAPHY

1963 **Modesty Blaise** (Twentieth Century-Fox; British) with Monica Vitti (as Modesty Blaise), Terence Stamp, Dirk Bogarde, Harry Andrews; directed by Joseph Losey.

James Bond

Approximately a quarter of a century ago, Ian Fleming, an English journalist with an extensive background in espionage, wrote the first of a series of thrillers featuring the deadly and sophisticated secret agent, James Bond, also known as 007.

Casino Royale, published in 1953, was merely the first of the successful series that enjoyed public favor during the next decade. Then, in the early 1960s, two events occurred which ensured that the Bond books would forever be regarded as classics in their field.

John F. Kennedy, then the popular president of the United States, candidly disclosed that he was a devotee of the books. In 1963, **Dr. No**, the first motion picture involving Bond, was released. Two more films were released the following year, and the flood was on.

Not since Mickey Spillane's books about Mike Hammer in the late 1940s and 1950s had a series character enjoyed such enormous popularity. Sean Connery captured the spirit of James Bond perfectly in his cinematic portrayals, and the books themselves had a rare flavor of authenticity, due in large measure, no doubt, to Fleming's long (if vague and unpublicized) connection with the British secret service.

James Bond quickly became the best-known spy in history. His popularity remains considerable today, although slightly diminished from its apex of a decade ago.

Almost all of the fourteen Bond books have sold more than a million copies each, and the motion pictures have a remarkable durability; although Connery tired of the role, other actors have come forward to fill the breach, notably Roger Moore in the most recent productions. There have also been James Bond coloring books, toys, puzzles, games, trading cards and a line of 007 toiletries, not to mention the countless imitators, parodists and pastichists. The television series "The Man from U.N.C.L.E." has obvious derivative elements from the Bond saga, and Fleming himself contributed the concept and several scripts to the program.

Simplistic attempts to explain the enormous popularity of the resourceful agent attributed his success to a happy combination of "sex, sadism and snobbery."

While the handsome Bond has many sexual

adventures, there is no graphic depiction of them in any book or film, and the limited descriptions that do occur are in such euphemistic language that few could be offended (or, for that matter, be entirely certain of exactly what is happening). The language of both the author and Bond is restrained, the text of the entire series containing not a single word that could shock—or titillate—any but the most puerile reader.

What sadism transpires in the books is directed at Bond by the various fiends into whose hands he invariably falls. The act which comes closest to sadism on Bond's part is his failure to rescue a thug from a pool of barracuda—a decision which is arguably more prudent than sadistic.

The question of snobbery is, perhaps, one of definition. Certainly Bond enjoys the fruits of his perilous efforts. He knows what he likes and insists upon getting it. He is familiar with "brand names" and refuses to accept anything second-rate.

The Bond books and films are not entirely realistic, and that may be the chief clue to their continued success. They have the elements of adult fairy tales. Bond's world is populated with beautiful maidens (well, beautiful women, anyway) and unconscionable monsters with superhuman powers and villainous hordes at their command. Instead of the pure-hearted princes of fairy tales, the hero in these fantasies is an educated, well-trained man of the world, who has a few tricks of his own.

Just as in the fairy tales, the hero destroys the monster and wins the beautiful princess. And they live—if not happily ever after—for a couple of weeks in sensual ecstasy.

Although James Bond's father was a Scot (a Highlander from the area near Glencoe) and his mother a Swiss, his British patriotic zeal is a prime motivating force in his life. While still in his teens, he joined the British Secret Service in 1938 or 1939, and immediately at the outset of World War II joined the navy, rising to the rank of Commander (a title by which he still is sometimes addressed) by the end of the conflict.

Because both his parents had been killed in a climbing accident when he was eleven, leaving him an independent annual income of £1000, he spent an adolescence of unusual freedom. He attended Eton for a year, then Fettes, a preparatory school in Edinburgh, but devoted just as much time to nonformal educational pursuits. On one of his trips to the continent, at the age of sixteen, he lost both his wallet and his virginity in Paris.

A flat in King's Road, Chelsea, is Bond's home, kept tidy for him by May, a true gem of a maid, who also cooks for him when he is in town. The Scottish May "would call no man 'sir' except English kings and Winston Churchill" but shows her regard for Bond by addressing him as "Mister James."

The apartment is mainly a place for Bond to eat and sleep between assignments. He keeps his books there—volumes about golf, about cards, John F. Kennedy's **Profiles in Courage,** titles by Raymond Chandler, Eric Ambler and Rex Stout.

While he occasionally entertains his "few close friends" at the flat, he rarely brings women home with him. It is not that Bond lives a celibate life; it is merely that he spends his times of intimacy with them elsewhere.

He is extremely attractive to women. Approximately six feet, one inch tall, he weighs about 170 pounds. He has blue eyes, and was once described as resembling a young Hoagy Carmichael. Bond has a "dark, clean-cut face...the eyes were wide and level under straight, rather long black brows. The hair was black, parted on the left, and casually brushed so that a thick black comma fell down over the right eyebrow...the longish straight nose ran down to a short upper lip, below which was a wide and finely drawn and cruel mouth. The line of the jaw was straight and firm."

According to the SMERSH dossier on him, he also has a five-inch scar running down his right cheek, and another on his left shoulder. There are traces of plastic surgery on his right hand, where an identifying mark carved by a SMERSH agent has been removed.

A careful dresser, Bond favors comfortable, well-tailored suits, with which he wears a black knitted-silk necktie. He never uses a Windsor knot and dislikes at first sight a man who does. For more casual wear, he favors "island" shirts and sandals. At night, Bond wears only pajama tops or long, comfortable, nightgown-type garments—if he wears anything at all.

Sean Connery is so closely identified with James Bond that the artist for this Swedish paperback used the actor's face for his portrait of 007.

Ostensibly, Bond works in London in some indeterminate middle-executive capacity for an enterprise called Universal Export (which later changes names to become Transworld Export). When he is not out of town on an assignment, he works a traditional eight-hour (10 A.M. to 6 P.M.) day; he is paid £1500 a year in 1955.

In fact, Universal Export is, of course, a front for the British Secret Service. One full-time employee devotes all his energy to ensuring that the company loses the exporting contracts which it might ordinarily obtain. When Bond is summoned to his boss' office, the topic is not likely to involve commerce.

James Bond's superior is M (Admiral Sir Miles Messervy, telegraphic code name Mailedfist), an elderly gentleman who grew up "with the certain prospect of becoming Fifth Sea Lord" but elected instead to head Universal Export, at a salary of £5000 a year. M lives in a house known as the Quarterdeck, likes marrow bones, smokes two cheroots a day, reads Rex Stout (also a favorite of Bond), wears bow ties and has "frosty, damnably clear, grey eyes."

M and Bond have a father-son relationship. M expresses gruff concern for his favorite agent's excessive drinking (a half-bottle a day), smoking (sixty cigarettes a day, a Balkan-Turkish blend made especially for him by Morlands of Grosvenor, identifiable by their three gold bands) and womanizing. For his part, Bond has a strongly affectionate regard for his boss, saying he "loves and obeys" M's voice and once telling someone that he is "married" to M.

When the security light (which changes color from time to time, going from green to red to blue) outside M's office is switched on, Bond is referred to only as "double-oh-seven." Outside the office, or on personal business, M familiarly refers to Bond as "James"; Bond calls him "Sir" at all times.

It has been said that M has "an exaggerated faith in Scotsmen," which may explain why he relies so heavily on Bond. On at least two occasions, he asks for and receives personal favors from Bond: the avenging of the murder of two of M's friends, and the teaching of a hard lesson to Sir Hugo Drax, who has been cheating at cards in M's beloved Blades Club.

While it may at times seem as if they are, Bond and M do not form the entire British Secret Service. There have been eleven agents in history who have merited the "00" prefix, licensing them to kill in the line of duty. Only 007, 008 and 0011 remain alive.

Among the office staff is Miss Moneypenny, M's superbly competent personal secretary. The 00 section also rates a secretary: Loelia Ponsonby, leaving to get married, is replaced by Mary Goodnight, who functions as the major heroine in one recorded adventure.

Major Boothroyd, the armourer of the Secret Service, issues to Bond his many and varied weapons. Bond used to carry a .25 Beretta automatic in the holster under his left shoulder, but Boothroyd dismissed it as a "lady's gun," replacing it with a Walther PPK 7.65 mm. in a Burns-Martin triple-draw holster. At one time or another, Bond has also used a .38 Colt Police Positive, a .45 Colt automatic, a .38 Smith and Wesson Centennial Lightweight (all handguns), as well as a Savage 99F rifle with a Weatherby 6 x 62 scope.

Bond is an expert shot (often practicing at the Maidstone Police Range) and a skilled knife-thrower (he carries a knife strapped to his left forearm); he is also able to use a razor effectively. He wears steel-capped shoes, for kicks with a little extra zap, is an expert boxer, and has mastered the Oriental martial arts of judo and karate.

Before going on a special mission, he hones his skills and brushes up on every form of combat or special knowledge which he is likely to need.

One of his endlessly valuable talents is his assurance and dexterity behind the wheel of an automobile. He admires other good drivers (and is especially attracted to women who drive well) and he knows and likes good cars. He once owned "one of the last of the 4-1/2 litre Bentleys, with the supercharger by Anherst Villiers" but later changed to a Mark II Continental Bentley.

Bond also knows and likes good food and drink. While he may not rate as a first-class epicure, he has a well-developed palate and he orders quite carefully—almost ritualistically. Still, for breakfast he prefers simple scrambled eggs and orders them (a double portion) almost daily. He prefers hard liquor to wine, though he knows and appreciates good vintages, and has a particular affection for champagne. His favorite drink is, however, a vodka martini, made from grain (not potato) vodka, and shaken, not stirred.

Another of Bond's special abilities lies in the area of gamesmanship. He has a well-merited reputation as the best gambler and cardsharp in the Secret Service, a skill exploited by M on at least two separate occasions. He is also adept at golf, swimming and skin diving.

The most vital of Bond's skills, and he has no illusions about it, is his ability to kill. That is

No peril intimidates the adventurous, Latin-appearing Bond (this picture illustrates a Colombian edition).

part of what he is paid to do, and his own life depends upon how well he is able to do it. "It was part of his profession to kill people," he knew. "He had never liked doing it, [but] he did it as well as he knew how."

Agent 007 approaches his job with dispassionate professionalism. He is entirely aware that the espionage agents of other, hostile, nations function according to a different set of laws, and he is willing and able to operate under the same rules. When enemies of England live outside the law of the country, he believes that "since no other law was available, the law of the jungle should be visited on [them]. In no other way could justice be done."

Because espionage is, by definition, an international undertaking, Bond frequently leaves England on missions, and has the opportunity to work with agents of governments friendly to England. His most active contact (he appears in half of Bond's recorded adventures) is Felix Leiter of the CIA and, later, the Pinkerton Detective Agency. The sandy-haired American spy works mainly in the United States and in the Caribbean. Other foreign allies include the Frenchman René Mathis, the Japanese Tiger Tanaka, and the lusty Turk, Darko Kerim.

Bond's enemies are, universally, foreigners. Auric Goldfinger, born an Englishman, holds a foreign citizenship; Hugo Drax, born German, has been naturalized (and knighted) by the British. They are the nearest any of Bond's adversaries come to sharing his national heritage. More typical of his enemies are Ernst Stavro Blofeld, the half-Polish, half-Greek founder of SPECTRE (an essentially multinational agency, the name of which is an acronym for the Special Executive for Counterintelligence, Terrorism, Revenge, Extortion), and the Soviet spies working for SMERSH (an acronym for the Russian *SMERT Spionam*—"Death to Spies").

Like the villains brought to justice by Dick Tracy, the foes of James Bond are physically hideous. Dr. No has steel pincers for hands. Goldfinger looks as if he were constructed from leftover parts, and his chief henchman, Oddjob, is a giant Korean whose cleft palate makes it impossible for him to produce intelligible speech. Mr. Big has gray-black skin, and an "enormous football of a head" with eyes so far apart that it is difficult to see them both at the same time. Hugo Drax has slick orange hair and repulsive burn scars on his ugly face. Blofeld, the ultimate Bond villain, while not hideous, is capable of changing his appearance so completely that he is a frightening and menacing figure.

The excessive depravity of their appearance is matched only by the imaginations of Bond's enemies. Goldfinger plans to rob Fort Knox. Drax wants to destroy downtown London with a nuclear missile. Mr. Big employs a voodoo cult to carry out the policies of SMERSH. Bond is so successful at foiling SMERSH's plans that he becomes the target of one of its operations. The sinister Rosa Kleb and Donavan Grant plan to murder Bond in a way that will bring disgrace to the British Secret Service, but they fail. Most inventive of all Fleming's villains is Blofeld, whose capers include an attempt to blackmail the West with two stolen nuclear devices, a plot to introduce crop and livestock diseases into the British Isles to cripple the nation, and an act of personal villainy which assures him of a permanent place among the worst men in the world.

Of all the women he has known and bedded, and who have loved him, Bond loves only one enough to marry. An hour and a half after the wedding ceremony, in a treacherous act of vengeance and indecency, Blofeld murders her.

Unfailingly attractive to women, Bond has no adventures in which the softer sex do not play a role. His reputation is immense, with no account too far-fetched for his fellow agents to accept. When Soviet spies attempt to lure Bond into a trap, they leak the story that a beautiful Russian girl has fallen in love with his *photograph*, and is willing to disclose secrets to him. No one in the British Secret Service is in the least suspicious at this.

While women of all types seem to be attracted to him, Bond has his "type." They are generally tanned, have good legs and full breasts, let their hair fall naturally, wear little or no makeup, have short, unpainted fingernails, and tend to wear wide belts and flaring, pleated skirts.

Actively interested in lovely women, he likes to think that he is able to put his job first. "Women were for recreation," he believes. "On a job, they got in the way and fogged things up with sex or hurt feelings...one had to look out for them and take care of them."

Because of a sincere sense of chivalry, that philosophy haunts him. The phrase "a bird with one wing down" is used more than once to describe the women with whom Bond becomes involved. A physical or emotional shortcoming is often present, and Bond finds it endearing. He is fond of Honey Rider's broken nose (and regrets her intention to have it "fixed"); is attracted to Domino Vitale's limp; and has enjoyed the success of his tenderness, which has defrosted the frigid Tiffany Case, freed the repressed Solitaire and converted the lifelong lesbian, Pussy Galore. Because he feels a certain responsibility, he is prepared to marry on two separate occasions, although he is rescued both times by changing circumstances.

There is more than a trace of male chauvinism in Bond. "Those blithering women who thought they could do a man's work," he explodes, "why couldn't they stay at home and mind the pots and pans and stick to their frocks and leave men's work to men?"

Still, most of the women he comes to know earn a living—even if it is a career as the mistress to a villain. Other occupations which Bond's women have pursued include clairvoyant, spy, soldier, shell collector, policewoman, showgirl, gangster, trapeze artist and fisherwoman.

Two of the most important women in Bond's life, however, do not work. Vivienne Michel is so deeply affected by her encounter with Bond that she contacts Ian Fleming, the author of his adventures, to relate to him a story of her escapade with 007. She tells the story in the first person and is given credit as a collaborator on the title page of **The Spy Who Loved Me**. Tracy di Vicenzo is the daughter of Marc-Ange Draco, the head of the Union Corse, a Corsican version of the Mafia. Fabulously wealthy, she has no need to work, but that doesn't guarantee that she will be happy. She attempts suicide and, when Bond prevents it, her father offers him £1,000,000 to marry her, but he refuses.

In the tradition of many other British spies, Bond has his share of prejudices. He goes to bed with Kissy Suzuki, who is Japanese, and Solitaire, who is at least partially black, and has friends of other nationalities, but he is not without a trace of xenophobia.

His prejudices are somewhat unusual, being centered largely on ethnic groups about whom negative remarks are rarely heard in either England or the United States. He is particularly antagonistic towards Bulgars, for example.

He has affection for only England but he thinks well of America—at least as much as he is able to considering that it is a foreign country. The United States, he admits, grudgingly, is a "civilized country. More or less."

Although he lacks the class snobbery of many of his predecessors, there can be no denying that James Bond carries with him an aura of superiority. Still, if one considers that he has a roster of skills that would be the envy of a regiment, that he has bedded some of the world's most beautiful women, and that he has saved Britain often, and the world more than once, it may be possible to excuse the merest trace of arrogance. He is, after all, superior.

IAN FLEMING (1908-1964) Born in London, Fleming was educated at Eton, the Royal Military Academy at Sandhurst, and the Universities of Munich and Geneva. He served as the Moscow correspondent for Reuter's and was a reporter for the **London Times**. During his journalistic career, he also served (unofficially) as a secret service agent, and later was the personal assistant to the Director of Naval Intelligence. It is his extensive background in espionage work that lends such an air of authenticity to his novels about James Bond, the superspy who is very much an idealization of Fleming himself.

BIBLIOGRAPHY

1953 **Casino Royale** (Macmillan)
1954 **Live and Let Die** (Macmillan)
1955 **Moonraker** (Macmillan)
1956 **Diamonds Are Forever** (Macmillan)
1957 **From Russia, with Love** (Macmillan)
1958 **Dr. No** (Macmillan)
1959 **Goldfinger** (Macmillan)
1960 **For Your Eyes Only** (Viking)
1961 **Thunderball** (Viking)
1962 **The Spy Who Loved Me** (Viking)
1963 **On Her Majesty's Secret Service** (New American Library)
1964 **You Only Live Twice** (New American Library)
1965 **The Man with the Golden Gun** (New American Library)
1966 **Octopussy** (New American Library; also published in paperback by Signet in 1967, with an additional story)

FILMOGRAPHY

1963 **Dr. No** (United Artists) with Sean Connery (as James Bond), Joseph Wiseman, Ursula Andress, Jack Lord, Bernard Lee, Lois Maxwell; directed by Terence Young.
1964 **From Russia with Love** (United Artists) with Sean Connery, Daniela Bianchi, Pedro Armendariz, Robert Shaw, Lotte Lenya; directed by Terence Young.
1964 **Goldfinger** (United Artists) with Sean Connery, Gert Frobe, Honor Blackman, Shirley Eaton, Harold Sakata; directed by Guy Hamilton.
1965 **Thunderball** (United Artists) with Sean Connery, Claudine Auger, Adolfo Celi, Luciana Paluzzi, Rik Van Nutter; directed by Terence Young.
1967 **Casino Royale** (Columbia) with David Niven (as James Bond), Deborah Kerr, Orson Welles, William Holden, Charles Boyer, John Huston, Peter Sellers, Woody Allen, Joanna Pettet; directed by John Huston, Ken Hughes, Val Guest, Robert Parrish and Joe McGrath.
1967 **You Only Live Twice** (United Artists) with Sean Connery, Akiko Wakabayashi, Tetsuro Tamba, Mie Hama, Karin Dor, Donald Pleasance; directed by Lewis Gilbert.
1970 **On Her Majesty's Secret Service** (United Artists) with George Lazenby (as James Bond), Diana Rigg, Telly Savalas, Ilse Steppat; directed by Peter Hunt.
1971 **Diamonds Are Forever** (United Artists) with Sean Connery, Jill St. John, Charles Gray, Lana Wood, Jimmy Dean; directed by Guy Hamilton.
1973 **Live and Let Die** (United Artists) with Roger Moore (as James Bond), Yaphet Kotto, Jane Seymour, Clifton James, Geoffrey Holder; directed by Guy Hamilton.
1974 **The Man with the Golden Gun** (United Artists) with Roger Moore, Christopher Lee, Britt Ekland, Maud Adams, Herve Villechaise, Clifton James, Richard Loo; directed by Guy Hamilton.
1977 **The Spy Who Loved Me** (United Artists) with Roger Moore, Barbara Bach, Curt Jurgens; directed by Lewis Gilbert.

Father Brown

One of the essential characteristics of great detectives is a well-developed deductive talent, an ability to gather obscure data and, from them, arrive at irrefutable and ultimately inescapable verities. Father Brown does not abundantly possess this talent. In fact, he does not possess it to even the smallest degree. His detectival method is intuitive; that is, he seems to "just know" who committed a crime, or how it was committed, or why, because he has some sort of vague, indefinable "feeling." It is not as easy or as infallible as it sounds. One must first be a brilliant psychologist, have remarkable insights into human motivations, and be gifted with unusual sensitivity. These traits Father Brown has in profusion.

Ellery Queen, the foremost authority on short detective fiction for half a century, once described Father Brown as one of the three greatest detective characters ever invented (Holmes and Dupin being the other two). Barnaby Ross, who is also Ellery Queen under a different pseudonym, said of Father Brown: "If there is one character in detective fiction who possesses the innocence and wisdom to sit beside the immortal Holmes, it is that apotheosis of incredulity."

G.K. Chesterson's wondrous cleric appears in fifty-one short stories. As in all the best of Chesterton's fiction, paradox abounds, and the chief delight of the stories is in beholding the absurdities which are presented, the apparently motiveless actions by the most innocuous characters, the seemingly supernatural occurrences—all of which turn out to be perfectly natural, easily understood and disentangled by the most commonplace explanations.

The kindly little priest was patterned after Father (later Monsignor) John O'Connor, a real-life curate with whom Chesterton became friendly and who was partially responsible for the famous writer's conversion (in 1922) to Roman Catholicism. Although he bore no physical resemblance to the fictional clergyman,

The only significant portrait of an unspectacled Brown illustrates The Wisdom of Father Brown *(1914).*

Father O'Connor planted the seed in Chesterton's mind for a combination detective-man of God. O'Connor had a prodigious familiarity with the criminal mind because of his many hours in the confessional, listening to the narratives of sinners. He was amused by those who believed priests were cloistered and unworldly. Chesterton was shocked when O'Connor told him of the perverted practices he had heard about from his flock. "I did not imagine that the world could contain such horrors," he later wrote. This sudden realization that an apparently innocent curate could teach, to those who considered themselves sophisticated, a great deal about sordidness convinced Chesterton of the validity of a priest-detective.

Father O'Connor, writing of his role as the prototype for Father Brown, explained: "We discussed...that unnoticed paradox of the Gospel. Professional saints are scolded and threatened, whilst professional sinners are bidden to hope. This is all that I can honestly claim as a title to the character of Father Brown."

Can a man be a detective who does not respect the law? Is there a way for a man to pursue criminals and then, having apprehended them, set them free again? Is it possible for a man to claim to be combating crime while siding with those who commit crimes, rather than with those who would punish criminals? The answer to these questions is, of course, simply and emphatically: No. Unless that man is Father Brown, unarguably the gentlest and kindliest, but also one of the most effective, detectives in literature.

An idealist and a visionary, Father Brown believes in the essential goodness of people. No matter how many crimes a thief may have committed in the past, the good padre believes it is possible to salvage his soul. Surprisingly, he is enormously successful, often causing men who have devoted their entire lives to the perpetration of crime to change their ways—merely by talking with them for a few minutes. There are some, in fact, who say that such radical transformations border on the miraculous.

Catching robbers (often with the stolen goods on them) is Father Brown's specialty. Then, having seen through the culprit's disguise, or anticipating his plans for escape, he has his felon cornered. Rather than turning him over to the police, the priest reasons with him, explaining the inevitability of failure and the loss of joy that the criminal is doomed to experience. This appeal to the intellect often results in an astonishing transmutation from villainy to goodness.Turning a criminal over to the official police does not hold much interest for Father Brown, although he has done it several times. Jail does not impress him as a valuable or effective method of dealing with those who have strayed. To him, the sight of a robber wearing handcuffs on his way to the local prison provides no heartwarming glow of satisfaction for a happily concluded case. In fact, he views it as a failure. A repentant criminal, one who vows to change his ways, on the other hand, is great cause for joy. In Father Brown's philosophy, a wrongdoer is a soul in need of salvation, not a criminal to be ground by the wheels of justice.

The thief who represents Father Brown's greatest triumph is Flambeau. The magnitude of the clergyman's success is doubly great because of the awesome stature of the famous French felon—a living legend, a criminal of almost mythical proportions and achievements—as well as the completeness of his repentance and reformation. After outsmarting Flambeau (that is not his real name) for the second time, someone suggests to Father Brown that he has caught a dangerous criminal. While he has, indeed, forestalled his adversary's nefarious plans, the priest admits to having been successful and at the same time allowing Flambeau to escape. "I caught him," Father Brown says, "with an unseen hook and an invisible line which is long enough to let him wander to the ends of the world, and still to bring him back with a twitch upon the thread." He has redeemed a soul, and basks in the very human radiance of pride in his considerable accomplishment.

In the first encounter with Flambeau, Father Brown bests him on several counts, but the most damning and conclusive evidence is the least expected by the crook. Disguised as a priest, Flambeau has ambled across the deserted countryside discussing religion with the genuine priest. Father Brown knew his companion to be a fraud, he later explains, because Flambeau "attacked reason; it's bad theology."

While possessing an uncommon mind, Father Brown has every other appearance of being ordinary, as unremarkable as any man could be.

This unsigned jacket illustration for The Secret of Father Brown *is reminiscent of Frederic Dorr Steele.*

"His chief feature was to be featureless"; "his conspicuous quality was not being conspicuous." It is valuable for him to be generally regarded as dull-witted, and so he allows that misconception to flourish. It helps him catch criminals off-guard, and even his friends and beneficiaries accept as a truism that the man of religion knows little of the world, being cloistered from evil, human passions and frailties. His relative silence and unobtrusive manner enable him to spring at the last possible moment, much to the astonishment of all concerned, many of whom are, until then, virtually unaware of his presence.

Physically, he is as undistinguished as his mind is sagacious and subtle. Short, stumpy, "a small figure with a foolishly large head," he has "a face as round and dull as a Norfolk dumpling; he had [gray] eyes as empty as the North Sea; he had several brown paper parcels which he was incapable of collecting; he had a large, shabby umbrella which constantly fell to the floor." He has close-cropped brown hair, moon-like spectacles, a round snub nose, and a complexion dark enough to be mistaken for Mexican. Shy and awkward, he is so clumsy that he constantly drops things and loses sight of them, finally blinking about in a near-futile attempt at their recovery. His appearance has been unkindly described as "second-rate" and his black clerical clothes as "muddy"—less a reflection of recent difficulties with weather and

The dust wrapper of the first English edition of The Incredulity of Father Brown *(1926) portrays the round-faced, innocent cleric.*

environment than an indication of a general lack of interest in fastidiousness. His broad-brimmed shovel hat is "clerical but not common in England." Not quite as ascetic as he looks, Father Brown enjoys drinking beer and smoking his large-bowled pipe or a cigar, and he particularly relishes an occasional sumptuous meal, partaken of in a friend's home or a good restaurant.

If a name can provide insight to a personality, then two sides of the gentle cleric are revealed by his. It would be difficult to imagine any name that is more commonplace, more human or more harmless than the good, simple English name of Brown; that is a very real part of his makeup. But, as a contrast from the simple, there is the matter of the complex enigma, the impenetrable mystery, the inexplicable question of his first name. In "The Sign of the Broken Sword" he is referred to as "Paul," but in "The Eye of Apollo" (both adventures published in 1911) he is "the Reverend J. Brown, attached to St. Francis Xavier Church, Camberwell." There is no explanation of this blatant discrepancy, which must remain an unsolved problem.

In addition to his time at St. Francis Xavier, Father Brown has been connected with St. Mungo, in a northern suburb of London; served in the seaside resort town of Scarborough in Yorkshire; had a position near London's theatre district; been employed at St. Dominic's; worked as a prison chaplain in Chicago; and done missionary work on the northern coast of South America.

When he solves those problems with which he inevitably comes into contact—no matter where he is located—the eccentric priest predictably uses unorthodox methods. He does not employ data as pieces of a jigsaw puzzle, neatly pressing each into its predetermined position. He does not gather bits of evidence, the physical clues of which the official police are so enamored. He does not make lists of all the essential elements of a case and apply a massive and rational intellect to sorting them all out, logically and calculatingly. To Father Brown, the minutiae of scientific evidence are nothing; intuition is everything. He relies on an "uncommonly keen" animal sense that enables him instinctively to recognize the odor of evil. He has a profound understanding of human behavior, particularly if it is aberrant, having been confronted with personalities of the most extreme type while in the confessional. Although he would have been unable to define it, and quite likely would have denied it, he uses a psychological approach to detection—one of the first detectives to apply it.

Father Brown explains his unique method of unmasking a killer in this way: "I try to get inside a man, moving his arms and legs; but I wait till I know I'm inside a murderer, thinking his thoughts, wrestling with his passions; till I have bent myself into his hunched and peering hatred; till I see the world with his bloodshot and squinted eyes, looking between the blinkers of his half-witted concentration; looking up the short and sharp perspective of a straight road leading to a pool of blood. Till I am really a murderer. And when I am quite sure that I feel exactly like the murderer myself, of course I know who he is."

Achieving the solution to a case is simplicity itself, when one knows how to do it, according to Father Brown. Although faced with strange, apparently inexplicable puzzles, he neither anticipates nor discovers difficulties. Anyone can accomplish the same thing he does, he explains, except they don't. "It isn't that people cannot see the solution," he says, "it is that they cannot usually see the problem."

The trick, and it is a decidedly difficult one, is to recognize that a problem exists—almost

Walter Connolly as the gentle priest endures an acerbic Una O'Connor in Father Brown, Detective. *There have been only two Brown films, both based on the same story, "The Blue Cross".*

Alec Guinness brought the perfect blend of eccentricity, credulity, and wisdom to the role of the crime-solving clergyman in The Detective *(released in England as* Father Brown*).*

before it actually does. On one occasion (which the modest prelate would admit to having been a singular stroke of luck) he hears some queer footsteps in a passage and pauses to consider their eccentric cadence. Because of that small act, he is able to avert a crime and, more important to him, save a soul.

On a different occasion, he prevents a major crime (the theft of a priceless cross) by hurling a bowl of soup against a restaurant wall, switching the salt and sugar in their containers, upsetting a table of apples, and smashing a window. These somewhat obscure clues are effectively followed by Aristide Valentin, chief of the Paris police, and the principal nemesis of Flambeau, resulting in the frustration of his scheme to steal the bejewelled cross. In this, the case of "The Blue Cross," as in all other cases, the gentle cleric uses his intuitive faculties to learn the identity of the criminal. Since all his detective work is done in this fashion, his degree of success is remarkable when one considers the amount of deductive skills generally required for this line of work. Sherlock Holmes and Dr. Thorndyke would be positively aghast at his explanations and methods for obtaining results. Father Brown sees nothing remarkable about his success. He has help.

Just as Holmes has Dr. Watson, and as Thorndyke has Polton, Father Brown has his own indispensable assistant—God. Although He does not make personal appearances in the stories, there can be no doubt that His assistance is often called upon and absolutely essential to the attainment of a satisfactory conclusion. At one point, bitterly frustrated at having a solution within his grasp but unable to make sense of it, Father Brown cries for help.

"I see half," he says. "Will God give me strength? Will my brain make the one jump and see all? Heaven help me! I used to be fairly good at thinking. I could paraphrase any page in Aquinas once. Will my head split—or will I see? I see half—I only see half."

Surely Father Brown's assistant is the most impressive in detective fiction, and the most effective. There is no other explanation for the clarity with which the little Essex clergyman is able to peek through the obfuscatory fog of veiled villainies.

An instance in which Father Brown's associate quite obviously played a major role occurred when the innocuous prelate "lost his head." Still, he believed, "his head was always most valuable when he had lost it. In such moments he had put two and two together and made four million. Often the Catholic Church (which is wedded to common sense) did not approve of it. Often he did not approve of it himself. But it was real inspiration—important at rare crises—when whosoever shall lose his head the same shall save it." It seems evident that more than human forces are at work here—forces beyond the power of even the greatest of master criminals.

God does not act as Father Brown's ally for the sport of it. He merely assists the holy man in his unorthodox method of achieving his principal goal as a member of the Church—the salvation of souls. If those methods are bizarre, and the souls in greater need of salvation than most others, and this particular priest a rather unlikely instrument of redemption—what of it? There are no commonly accepted methods of reformation. All souls require attention. And it would be a grievous mistake to believe that it is possible to predict who can and who cannot illuminate the path to repentance.

G. K. CHESTERTON (1874-1936) Born in London, Gilbert Keith Chesterton became involved with numerous intellectuals at an early age, becoming one of the most influential and prolific writers of his time. He wrote thousands of books, short stories, poems, essays and critical reviews on a wide variety of subjects, almost all of which reflect his good sense of humor and philanthropic nature. While much of his work is no longer read today, he has created several masterpieces, notably **The Man Who Was Thursday** (1908), a bizarre allegory of anarchy, and the often reprinted Father Brown stories.

BIBLIOGRAPHY

1911 **The Innocence of Father Brown** (John Lane)
1914 **The Wisdom of Father Brown** (Dodd, Mead)
1926 **The Incredulity of Father Brown** (Dodd, Mead)
1927 **The Secret of Father Brown** (Harper)
1935 **The Scandal of Father Brown** (Dodd, Mead)
1951 **The Father Brown Omnibus** (Dodd, Mead; contains all 51 stories about Father Brown, including the previously uncollected "The Vampire of the Village," which was first published in book form in 1948 in **Twentieth Century Detective Stories**, edited by Ellery Queen, World)

FILMOGRAPHY

1934 **Father Brown, Detective** (Paramount) with Walter Connolly (as Father Brown), Paul Lukas, Gertrude Michael, Halliwell Hobbes; directed by Edward Sedgwick.
1954 **The Detective** (Columbia; British. British title—**Father Brown**) with Alec Guiness, Joan Greenwood, Peter Finch, Cecil Parker, Bernard Lee; directed by Robert Hamer.

Nick Carter

Nick Carter is one of the curiosities of detective fiction—a famous character about whom everyone has heard but few have read. There are good reasons for this, not the least of which is that his adventures originally appeared in dime novels, those flimsy pamphlets of a bygone age which have long since disappeared from the shelves of bookshops and libraries.

Dime novel(s) is a generic term used to describe the paper-covered books of sensational fiction published for mass audiences in the United States from 1860 to about 1915. The largest publishing houses, Beadle & Adams and Street & Smith, produced more hundreds of millions of volumes than anyone could estimate with a hope of reliability. The few dozen titles in the Horatio Alger series alone, for example, exceeded 250,000,000 copies; the house of Beadle & Adams produced 3,158 titles, excluding reprints.

Well in front of the pack as the most successful detective in dime novel history is Nick Carter. The first three books about him were written by John Russell Coryell. (**The Old Detective's Pupil**, the serial in which Nick is "born" as Sim Carter's protegé, beginning in the Sept. 18, 1886, issue of the **New York Weekly**, was the first. Ormond G. Smith, the son of the founder of Street & Smith, provided Coryell with the basic plot outline.) After Coryell resumed his other writing tasks, numerous authors took over the series, all of which was published under three pseudonyms: "by the author of Nick Carter," "by Sergeant Ryan" and, finally, "by Nicholas Carter." The most prolific of these writers was Frederic Merrill Van Rensselaer Dey, who produced nearly 1,000 novels in the series, beginning with **Nick Carter, Detective** (1891). Each story is a little longer than 20,000 words, and Dey wrote all but the first few in precisely three days apiece—a total of more than 20,000,000 words.

The first dime novel detective story, **The Bowery Detective**, ran in the **New York Fireside Companion** (1870); the first series detective was Harlan Page Halsey's Old Sleuth, the Detective,

The cover of The Best Detective in the Country (Nick Carter Weekly *#187, July 28, 1900)*

who made his debut in the same publication in 1872 (this was the first known use of the word "sleuth" to connote a detective; its original definition was "bloodhound"); the first dime novel weekly devoted exclusively to detective fiction was the **Old Cap. Collier Library** (beginning April 9, 1883 and running for more than 16 years to Sept. 9, 1899); and the first dime novel weekly to feature exclusively the adventures of a single detective hero was Street & Smith's **Nick Carter Library**, which began August 8, 1891 and went through several changes of title and format, finally dying as a pulp magazine called **Detective Story** with the issue of Summer 1949—qualifying Nick Carter as the longest-running series detective in American history and the solver of the greatest number of cases; only England's Sexton Blake surpassed him on both counts.

Today, Nick Carter is the hero of a popular series of paperback novels, but he is no longer the clean-cut boy of the dime novels; now he is a sophisticated secret agent in the James Bond tradition.

The dime novel, despite its incredible popularity, had a bad reputation, although strong language, sex, gambling, drugs, tobacco, liquor and indolence were either not mentioned at all or were shown in the worst possible light. Regarded as lurid fiction, they were banned by many parents, therefore suffering the same fate later endured by pulp magazines and comic books. Essentially written to formulae, designed to entertain rather than educate, dime novels provided harmless pleasure for millions of young readers of all ages—the first form of literary "popular culture" in the United States. Incomparably evocative of a past era, they can be enjoyed today if read with a reasonably uncritical eye and the proper spirit of nostalgia.

The first truly authentic American detective hero, Nick Carter, always young, always successful, always just, endured as a crimefighter for more than sixty action-filled years. Edgar Allan Poe's Auguste Dupin preceded his first appearance by a half century but he was French, and Anna Katherine Green's Ebenezer Gryce is neither heroic nor remembered. Nick, perhaps the least idiosyncratic detective of the nineteenth century (although he did like to carry $1000 in cash with him in case he unexpectedly needed money in a strange city), was the idol of millions for several generations.

Among the more commonplace advantages which Nick possesses, to the envy of his countless fans, are a handsome face, an ability to stay perpetually young, a perfectly proportioned body and an acute mind. His unique talent, unmatched by any detective before or since, lies in the world of disguise. Within moments, he can change from being a tattered hobo to a Japanese prince—in appearance, manner, dress and correctly accented speech. Although his own features are clean cut, with a Roman nose, steely eyes, square jaw, resolute chin and well-trimmed, slightly curly hair, he is rarely seen without some type of disguise. In 1904, he adopts a regular costume consisting of a blue-gray suit, white vest, red bow tie and white homburg hat—but wears it thereafter only when making no attempt to keep his identity a secret.

In **Nick Carter, Detective**, an unusual event occurs—he is viewed without disguise! "Nick Carter was at home when the inspector called, and he received him as he would have received no other man in the whole city of New York: in his proper person. One of the cardinal points of Nick's faith in himself was that by keeping himself entirely unknown to everybody his various disguises were rendered absolutely impenetrable."

One of Nick's most confounding habits is to disguise himself, not merely as someone unrecognizable, but as another person involved in the case. He thus frequently appears to be the person he is trailing, or who is trailing him.

To further guarantee anonymity when he requires it, Nick assumes another identity, popping in and out of it as circumstances dictate. Just as The Shadow often takes on the mantle of Lamont Cranston, so does Nick Carter become Thomas Bolt, also known as Old Thunderbolt. With his makeup ability he is thus able to maintain a job and an office as a different entity, an older man, keeping his true name and appearance from all but his closest associates. To prevent the arousal of undue interest, Nick is also able to facilitate his occasional disappearance by calling on an important Wall Street figure and stepping into his identity.

In order to effect his many disguise changes, Nick carries with him at all times a large variety of paints, dyes, mustaches, beards and wigs. He can turn his clothes inside out and transform himself in a minute from a monocled gentleman

There have been three theatrically released Nick Carter sound films, all starring Walter Pidgeon. This seedy barroom is located in Panama, the setting for Phantom Raiders.

to an African queen. The disguises are not merely fast and dramatic, but entirely expert; he fools his own father regularly. He is able to change his visage drastically without the use of even a dab of makeup if the situation calls for exceptional haste: "And his handsome face could, in an instant, be distorted into any one of a hundred types of unrecognizable ugliness."

The mutability of his voice and familiarity with languages serve him well on numerous occasions. Not only is he able to resemble physically an endless assortment of diverse characters, but he is also adept at imitating the speech of a French government official, a Russian spy, a cowboy and a Japanese nobleman, among others. "His rich, full voice could run the gamut of sounds, from an old woman's broken, querulous squeak to the deep, hoarse notes of a burly ruffian." Nick can speak several tongues fluently. "Languages were imparted to me at first hand," he says, "while I was still a boy in years, and I was not permitted to undertake the study of a new one until the last had been thoroughly mastered." A related and impressive accomplishment is Nick's ability to read lips in three languages, making him one of the world's foremost eavesdroppers.

Nick has other advantages, of course, notably his tremendous strength. "Giants were like children in his grasp. He could fell an ox with one blow of his small, compact fist. Old Sim Carter had made the physical development of his son one of the studies of his life."

This rather startling power, particularly eye-opening in someone of average stature (to be generous) impels one of Nick's old enemies, the

Each issue of the New Nick Carter Weekly *featured this handsome portrait of Nick.*

oily Arabian crook Sindahr, to call him "The Little Giant," a sobriquet which sticks with the detective through hundreds of recorded adventures. His diminutive physique does not prevent him from taking on, and defeating (on more than one occasion), as many as twenty or thirty ruffians singlehandedly—surely the mark of a man who is familiar with the arts of self-defense, as well as one of unusual courage. Both his valor and strength are tried in enough cases to exhaust any but the fittest of young men. But Nick is, indeed, fit. "The small fist took the fellow under the jaw, fairly lifting him off his feet, and hurling him senseless on the floor."

Though he prefers to knock his opponents senseless, he is also "the best marksman in the world" and always carries at least two revolvers with him—which he is not afraid to use. "It was an unwritten law with the master detective never to use two hands for anything if he could possibly manage with one. This was because there were so many times in Nick Carter's life when he couldn't use one hand, because it had a gun in it."

He is able to handle other weapons, too, in the most extraordinary fashion. "From under his vest he drew a flat case about an inch wide and eight inches long, which he fastened in a slide in his handkerchief pocket. The case contained a knife with a short, broad blade, the sharpness of which was simply incredible. With one whirl of that little knife, Nick could cut in two a floating sheet of tissue paper, and then penetrate a two-inch oak plank."

His athletic abilities are invaluable to Nick, enabling him to perform gymnastic feats of untold wonder and giving him resiliency beyond measure. During his youthful experiences as a crimefighter, he is drugged literally hundreds of times, and knocked unconscious (generally by a blow from behind) just as often. When he has been surprised, or weakened, or hopelessly outnumbered, he is beaten mercilessly by the most vicious thugs and bullies. Yet, within a matter of hours, or, at the worst, a few days, he is as strong and sprightly as ever, showing no marks, bruises or lessening of nerve. Every conceivable method of inventive torture and attempted murder is directed at Nick. He is bound and gagged and thrown from speeding trains and wagons and automobiles, or into raging rivers and bottomless oceans. He is bitten by poisonous snakes, thrust unarmed into a den of ferocious beasts, and attacked by virtually every known species of carnivorous wildlife. He is pushed partway into a blazing furnace, and forced to endure the bitterest sub-Arctic temperatures. He is lashed to the conveyor belt of a whirring, high-speed, steel-bladed buzz saw in a scene worthy of Pearl White. Even the special skills that make Nick the finest boxer, wrestler, marksman and swordsman in the world are of little avail in these precipitous situations, and still he manages to escape unscathed, ultimately to wreak justice and vengeance. He is Superman without tights.

A seemingly endless assortment of powers, some of which border on the fantastic, are not enough. Nick still needs help to combat the veritable army of villains with whom he is perpetually confronted. The most important and influential person in his life is, beyond question, old Sim Carter, his father. "To my father," Nick once says, "who was a detective before me, is due the credit for whatever ability I possess. He began, as soon as I was old enough to understand, to train me for the profession I have followed. I was trained in athletics and in all that word comprehends, with the same care and diligence that was bestowed upon my mental equipment; my muscles and my brain received the same care and attention in my

A master of disguise, a Mexican-looking Nick binds a foe "until he had the appearance of a mummy" on the cover of Nick Carter at Hellion City *(*Nick Carter Weekly *#117, March 25, 1899).*

development, and I was taught to use them together. There were times when I thought my father a hard task-master, but now I daily find occasion to bless his memory for the strict rules he laid down for me to follow."

Perhaps the next most essential ingredient to Nick's continued success is his early meeting with Chick Valentine, who quickly becomes Nick's most trusted assistant and a regular participant in the cases—as much a part of Nick's professional life as Polton is in Dr. Thorndyke's and Bunter is in Lord Peter Wimsey's.

Their first meeting shows Nick to have a well-developed sense of humor, although it doesn't shine as frequently or as brightly as one might wish. In **One Against Twenty-One**, Chick is described as "a shock-headed,ragged fellow, but his eyes shone with unusual brightness, and his face was intelligent beyond his years, which could not have numbered more than seventeen. 'Hello, boy!' said Nick. 'Who are you?' 'Chick.' 'Chick, eh? Well, who is Chick?' 'Me.' 'You don't say so!' " In **Nick Carter's Sealed Crime**, that first meeting is recounted more fully. "Chick, as a boy, had been a homeless waif in Nevada, when Nick Carter had an opportunity one day to save him from a situation of desperate peril. It was an occasion which gave the detective a chance to note that the youth was not only of proved physical courage, but possessed unusually bright mentality. So Nick asked the lad if he would care to enter his service. There was a ready and delighted acceptance. It was not long before Nick Carter adopted him as a son, and he became known as Chickering Carter."

Chick leads an active life, not excluding a certain amount of contact with the fair sex. In 1891, he marries Bertha Mortimer, only to have his pretty young wife killed by one of Nick's worst enemies—Zelma, the Female Fiend. Despite Nick's initial objection, Chick later marries Leila Loring, whom Nick once thought was guilty of a crime. (Nick would never have given the liaison his blessing if he had continued to think her guilty of a serious wrongdoing.)

Perhaps the most wholesome detective in history, Nick declines to smoke cigarettes (until the pulp era), although he does enjoy cigars; and he refuses to drink anything stronger than beer or wine, lie, use drugs, gamble or swear. He does go so far, however, as to find women attractive, and they frequently, but demurely, cast covetous glances in his direction. Unfailingly a gallant gentleman, he manages some romantic entanglements, particularly early in his career. An early affair of the heart involves a villainess, Princess Olga Plavatski, the tiger-chief of the Russian Nihilists. "There was a subtlety about her that, even in the shadow where he could not perceive her remarkable beauty, was as manifest as the perfume of an Easter lily." Olga eventually falls in love with Nick and kills a man to save his life. But it is not to be. With her last words on her lips, "And now—I die rather than face the consequences of my act," Nick desperately tries but fails to prevent her from taking a fatal dose of poison.

Although it seems to be in the best interests of everyone for Nick to remain romantically abstinent, he loses his heart on several subsequent occasions, notably to Clarice, the Countess Detective; to Carma, the Amazonian Queen; and to Ethel (sometimes inaccurately referred to as Edith by chroniclers of Nick's exploits), whom he marries—only to suffer the tragedy of her slaying. He also once has a fiancée but she, too, is murdered.

A character more enduring in Nick's coterie is Patsy, an invaluable assistant who has a background as a newsboy and bootblack. Early in his relationship with Nick, Patsy's last name is Murphy, which he drops to replace with the surname Garvan.

Other members of the cast of players include Ten-Ichi, a son of the Emperor of Japan who is sent to the United States to study with Nick Carter, serving as his assistant for a time. Ten-Ichi speaks flawless English and can disguise himself, presumably after Nick's tutelage, as a Caucasian. Nick's valet frequently makes brief appearances. He is generally called Joseph, but that may not be his real name because Nick whimsically calls him by a variety of names, changing them as his mood dictates. Mrs. Peters, the housekeeper in the Carters' Fifth Avenue home, turns up fairly regularly, as does Ida Jones, another assistant.

During the two year period (1897-98) in which Nick retires to supervise a school for young detectives, Trim Carter, Chick's son, is an active and successful detective. Several policemen also have recurring roles in Nick's adventures, but the best of the lot is, without question, Inspector Byrnes.

Not everyone in Nick's life is a willing helpmate, of course. Some of the most memorable characters with whom he has dealings include an array of villains that would daunt any but the very strongest of heart.

In addition to Princess Olga and Zelma, the Female Fiend, who have been mentioned, Nick has matched wits and sinew with every type of villain, ranging from mere cutthroats (singly and

A more up-to-date-looking Nick Carter is on the cover of the New Magnet Library *edition of* The Detective's Pretty Neighbor.

in mobs) to brilliant master criminals intent on world domination. The most heinous, and a recurring adversary (much like Holmes' Moriarty, James Bond's Blofeld, and Nero Wolfe's Zeck), is Dr. Jack Quartz.

"As powerful as a veritable giant; stronger than the great detective himself; as keen as a razor; as quick as a flash; thoroughly educated; noted for his skill as a physician; as perfect and adept at disguises as Nick Carter; a scholar, and a man utterly without conscience or heart, he was one to whom even the keenest of all detectives—for Nick Carter had no peer—was forced to accord the old saying: 'This is a foeman worthy of my steel.' " In **The Fate of Doctor Quartz**, the villain talks of the little things that make his life bright and cheerful: "She was beautiful. I like beautiful girls. I like to cut them up. It is my passion."

There are other strange and fearful villains. Zanabayah uses "vitic force" to send a shocking current through anyone who touches him, much in the manner of an electric eel. The Dalney family of upstate New York has members of

No longer a simon-pure hero, Nick Carter today is an espionage agent. His natty attire reflects the change in his image.

incredible physical strength—a muscular superiority that could make even Carter blanch. They enjoy—no, they relish—vivisection. Dazaar appears to combat Nick with an entire syndicate of exotic villains, including a Russian princess and a Tibetan lama. Dan Derrington is an unscrupulous gambler—an occupation which Nick finds particularly detestable. Another gambler, Cadslerg, merely has to hear Nick's name and he turns into "a beast at bay," convinced that the young detective will learn all the clouded secrets of his profitable gambling casino.

But, while it takes no more than the sound of his name to send the black of heart scurrying into a corner with fright, Nick Carter's name brings comfort, relief and hope to the helpless, forlorn victims of evil. Near to giving up, the kidnapped heiress Angela Rutherford learns that she suddenly has found an answer to her unuttered prayers: "The name of Nicholas Carter had...a magic effect. From the moment when standing with the flickering candle in her hand that name had come to her ears the situation lost its terrors."

It is difficult to pinpoint Nick's most successful method of solving cases. Physical action, deduction, and sometimes fortuitous coincidences all come into play. His amazing string of successes has confounded others. "It is often said of Nick Carter that he knows in advance just how a case is coming out. Headquarters men who have no other superstitions will declare their belief that some mysterious instinct supplies Nick with the criminal's name at the start, and that he really has nothing to do but arrest his man and prepare his evidence. They have long since ceased to be jealous of Nick's infallibility, and now they are trying to account for it." Nick denies that is so, of course, and is somewhat amused by the suggestion. "I follow a train of reasoning, and am often astonished to find where it leads me. This talk of a mysterious instinct is all nonsense."

However he accomplishes it, he has solved more cases than any other American detective.To the happily rescued Angela Rutherford, Nick Carter "was a worker of miracles, invincible, a man who never failed." Impressive—even allowing for an excited young woman's hyperbole.

NICHOLAS CARTER The byline of many Nick Carter Novels was "Nicholas Carter" (preceded by "Sergeant Ryan" and "the author of Nick Carter"). All the names, including that of the famous detective, were Street & Smith "house names" (just as "Maxwell Grant" was a "house name" for The Shadow authors). Many writers produced the stories, the most prolific being Frederic Van Rensselaer Dey (1861-1922), who is often credited with more than 1,000 stories (though some experts suggest that six hundred might be a more accurate figure). The actual creator of the Nick Carter character was Ormond G. Smith, the son of one of the founders of the publishing company, who presented his conception of the heroic detective, and the outline of the first story, to John Russell Coryell, who wrote it, developed the character more fully, and wrote the next two stories before turning the series over to Dey and dozens of other writers.

BIBLIOGRAPHY

It is unlikely that an accurate number can be arrived at for all the Nick Carter adventures, starting with the serial which began in the Sept. 18, 1886, issue of **New York Weekly**, running through hundreds of novels and short stories in the dime novels, numerous appearances in pulp magazines, and on to his reincarnation in paperback originals of the 1970s. He has appeared in more books than any other American detective, however—no less than 581.

FILMOGRAPHY

1939 **Nick Carter, Master Detective** (MGM) with Walter Pidgeon (as Nick Carter), Rita Johnson, Donald Meek, Henry Hull, Milburn Stone, Sterling Holloway; directed by Jacques Tourneur.

1940 **Phantom Raiders** (MGM) with Walter Pidgeon, Donald Meek, Joseph Schildkraut, Florence Rice; directed by Jacques Tourneur.

1940 **Sky Murder** (MGM) with Walter Pidgeon, Donald Meek, Joyce Compton, Karen Verne, Tom Conway; directed by George Seitz.

Charlie Chan

Sinister Orientals are not often used in adventure fiction today, but a half-century ago they were one of the favorite clichés of authors who needed genuinely frightening villains. The ultimate "Yellow Peril" was, of course, the insidious Dr. Fu Manchu, but he had plenty of nasty company in the early years of the twentieth century immediately following the Boxer Rebellion and continuing right up to the Second World War. The Japanese attack on Pearl Harbor took the fun out of fictional menaces from the East.

The concept of an Oriental as a hero, or even as a major benevolent entity, was a new one in 1925 when Earl Derr Biggers created Charlie Chan to serve as a detective. One account of the genesis of Chan tells of Biggers' reading a report in a Honolulu newspaper of a local murder case being cracked by Chang Apana and Lee Fook, two Oriental policemen on the island. The idea of writing mysteries about a Chinese detective struck Biggers and he immediately wrote **The House Without a Key**.

"Sinister and wicked Chinese are old stuff," Biggers wrote, "but an amiable Chinese on the side of law and order had never been used."

Although Biggers always maintained that his Chinese detective was entirely the product of his imagination, Chang Apana, who had once visited the author at his Honolulu home, was equally convinced that he had served as the model for Charlie Chan.

Like Chan, Apana was a Chinese-American (Hawaiian) detective on the Honolulu police force, but unlike Chan, who is huge (particularly in the first book about him), he was small and slender.

Chan appears in only six books by Biggers, but they were all very popular, reprinted often, and all were serialized in **The Saturday Evening Post**. It is, however, in motion pictures that Chan is best known, appearing as the hero of more films than any other detective except Sherlock Holmes. With more than fifty films produced, Chan has been portrayed by a wide variety of actors—not one of whom has been

A corpulent Charlie Chan as depicted by F.R. Gruger for a serialization of The Black Camel *in* The Saturday Evening Post *in 1929.*

either Chinese or Hawaiian. Two Japanese actors have taken the role of Chan, but the three who are most familiar are Caucasian: Warner Oland, Sidney Toler and Roland Winters.

Substantial differences exist between the Chan whose adventures are recorded in book form and the detective who appears so frequently on the screen. The infamous numbers one and two sons, constantly intruding themselves into the film investigations, do not appear except incidentally in the books.

Unlike the films, in which pieces of evidence are turned up with commendable regularity, the novels do not rely on physical clues as an ingredient vital to the development of the investigation. While some scraps of hard evidence are essential, the denouement is generally arrived at through Chan's understanding of human nature.

"If I understand Charlie Chan correctly," wrote Biggers, "he has an idea that if you understand a man's character you can nearly predict what he is apt to do in any set of circumstances."

Perhaps the greatest difference between the two versions of the same character is that the Chan of the books is presented as a more complex, three-dimensional human being than the Chan of the films, where his chief distinguishing characteristic, aside from his race, is his unquenchable penchant for spewing epigrams, almost always in pidgin English.

The gentle and philosophical Chan has grown in the affection of mystery fans through the years largely because of his humanness, although it would be a mistake to underestimate the attractiveness of those witty and pertinent aphorisms. He is one of the few detectives of literature to have been paraphrased in the speech of an American president.

"Long journey always start with one short step," said Chan in 1935.

"A journey of a thousand miles must begin with a single step," said President John F. Kennedy in 1963.

Charlie Chan devotes considerable energy to two lives, each of which are extremely important to him—his professional life and his distinguished career as a policeman, and his personal life and devotion to his large, close-knit family.

His ability and reputation as "the best detective on the force" (according to Amos Winterslip at the outset of the first of Chan's recorded cases) get him a promotion from detective-sergeant to inspector by the time of his fourth recorded adventure.

Characteristically, Chan dismisses the promotion as the result of an "upheaval in local police department, and I am rewarded far beyond my humble merits."

Nevertheless, he works hard, bringing enormous zest and patience to his investigations. "Needle can be found," he says "when correct thread located."

Although he does not discuss it to the point where it becomes intrusive, Chan obviously leads a happy and active private life with his wife and family. He has nine children in 1925 and adds two more during the next five years, "which makes for a noisy house," he says in typical understatement.

His wife, a plump, jolly-looking woman, nearly as broad as Chan, has a smiling face, calm eyes, a generally placid temperament and a warm friendliness designed to make visitors feel comfortable instantly. Like her husband, she is not a native of Hawaii, but is less comfortable with the English language than Charlie, her accent running to such mutilations as "plitty tellible thing" and "mebbe you have moah tea."

Charlie had first seen her on the gleaming sand of a beach. She was, he reminisces, "as slender as the bamboo is slender, beautiful as the blossom of the plum."

All of the Chans' children are American citizens, and Charlie fears a gulf is widening between himself and them as they become more and more Americanized, making no effort to remember the precepts of their Chinese heritage. Their language is so idiomatic and slangy that it grates on his sensitive ear.

Not all of the children (eight boys, three girls) appear in his criminal cases, and he does not often speak of them, except in a general, all-inclusive manner, but those who have made their presence felt are: Rose (the oldest girl, attending college on the mainland), Evelyn (who is fifteen in 1929), Barry (the eleventh child, at whose birth Charlie is not able to be present because he has been detained by the exigencies of an investigation), and Henry (who smokes cigarettes at the breakfast table and is constantly trying to borrow the family car).

In a moment of relaxation at home, Chan is dressed in a long, loose robe of dark purple silk, seated at a table playing chess with Henry. A

Warner Oland, previously famous for his roles as Oriental villains, became the first of the great Charlie Chan actors in 1931. This scene is from Charlie Chan in Egypt *(1935).*

visitor, one of the principal figures in a murder case, calls at Chan's house, receiving a friendly welcome.

"You do my lowly house immense honor," the detective says. "This proud moment are still more proud as opportunity to introduce my eldest son." Motioning his chess opponent to step forward, the visitor notices that he is a slim, sallow boy with amber eyes—Chan himself before he put on weight.

"Mr. John Quincy Winterslip of Boston, kindly condescend to notice Henry Chan," says Charlie. "When you appear I am giving him lesson at chess so he may play in such manner as not to tarnish honored name."

Henry bows low, impressing the visitor as one of those members of the younger generation who has a deep respect for his elders. "Your father is my very good friend," Winterslip tells him, "and from now on, you are too."

Not necessarily viewing his numerous (and often trying and burdensome) sons and daughters in the same light as everyone else may, Chan considers himself unusually fortunate to have such a family. He quotes Confucius, saying, "No man is poor who have worthy son."

His house hangs "precariously" on Punchbowl Hill. Chan likes to stand at his bedroom window, which overlooks Honolulu and the sea, and reflect on his good fortune. It is particularly gratifying to him that he was able to bring his mother from China to Honolulu, so that she could spend her last years with him. She is dead now, buried on a hillside in a Chinese cemetry.

Although the house is once referred to as a

After sixteen films with Oland and twenty-two with Toler, the Chan series concluded with Roland Winters. Here, he unenthusiastically views a corpse in Docks of New Orleans.

cottage, it is furnished beautifully, and Chan is evidently financially secure. He is a member of the Rotary Club, and in 1930 reports having a brand new car, which he refers to as a "flivver" and which he drives fast and recklessly. In that same year, he takes a round-the-world cruise.

Born in China, Charlie Chan moved to Honolulu in 1900, when he was approximately fifteen years old, working as a houseboy in the Phillimore mansion. He was well-treated by Sally Jordan, a Phillimore daughter, who helped him get his citizenship papers, and he remains loyal to her and the rest of the family, even after becoming a famous detective—as a personal favor for them, he carries some valuable pearls (a $300,000 necklace) from Honolulu to San Francisco in 1926.

Chan takes his American citizenship seriously, as he does the language. Speaking of his adopted country, in which he has lived for twenty-five years (referring to himself as a *Kamaaina*—an old-timer), he says, "On soil of democracy you are safe from persecution."

When he affects the guise of an ignorant Chinese cook to solve the case of **The Chinese Parrot** in 1926, Chan is forced to revert to using pidgin English, which distresses him greatly. "All my life," he says, "I study to speak fine English words. Now I must strangle all such in my throat, lest suspicion rise up. Not a happy situation for me."

In Winterslip's opinion, Chan's use of the English language is "dragged from the poets."

The best-known characteristic of Chan's language is his colorful and evocative use of aphoristic wit and wisdom, his ability to find a proverb to fit any situation. In his early cases, his language is merely picturesque, but he gradually changes his style, becoming more and more philosophical as his career progresses.

Typical words of wisdom from Chan include epigrams on countless subjects, including the following:

"Door of opportunity swing both ways."

"Tongue often hang man quicker than rope."

"Man who fights law always loses; same as grasshopper is always wrong in argument with chicken."

"Owner of face cannot always see nose."

"Theories like fingerprints—everybody has them."

"Man without enemies, like dog without fleas."

"Roundabout way often shortest path to correct destination."

"Each man thinks own cuckoos better than next man's nightingales."

"Mind like parachute, only function when open."

"If you want wild bird to sing, do not put him in cage."

"He who feeds the chicken, deserves the egg."

"To describe bitter medicine will not improve its flavor."

"Making bedfellow of serpent no guarantee against snakebite."

"Too late to dig well when honorable house is on fire."

"Fresh weed better than wilted rose."

"Make haste only when withdrawing hand from mouth of tiger."

"Time only wasted when sprinkling perfume on goat farm."

"Man is not incurably drowned—if he still knows he's all wet."

"Curiosity responsible for cat needing nine lives."

"Never hunt rabbit with dead dog."

"If strength were all, tiger would not fear scorpion."

"Bad alibi like dead fish—cannot stand test of time."

"Silence big sister of wisdom."

Charlie Chan's wisdom has been demonstrated in many areas, on many occasions. His reputation is both impeccable and widespread.

After the Swedish-born Oland died, the role of the Chinese sleuth was assumed by Missouri-born Sidney Toler, who discovers a chilling murder method in Charlie Chan in Black Magic.

Sir Frederic Bruce, the former head of the Criminal Investigation Division of Scotland Yard, takes it for granted that Chan excels at his job, and he remains unimpressed. "A Chinese should make an excellent detective," he says. "The patience of the East, you know."

Chan believes more than that is involved. Although he is patient, he is also highly active. When told on his first case that the criminal must be apprehended, he calmly agrees, saying, "What will be will be."

Angrily, a lady at the scene of the crime snaps at Chan, "I know—that's your Confucius, but it's a do-nothing doctrine, and I don't approve of it."

A faint smile flickers across Chan's face. "Do not fear," he replies. "The fates are busy, and man may do much to assist. I promise you there will be no do-nothing here." Gentle almost to a fault in most instances, he follows his statement with a warning that is—for him—almost bellicose. "Humbly asking pardon to mention it, but I detect in your eyes slight flame of hostility. Quench it if you will be so kind. Friendly cooperation are essential between us."

The only time Chan displays open hostility is when he attempts to deal with Japanese, against whom he is somewhat prejudiced.

In a restaurant, he scowls at the plate in front of him and sends for the proprietor, a suave little Japanese.

"Is it that you serve here unsanitary food?" Chan asks.

"Please deign to state your complaint," the Japanese responds.

"This piece of pie are covered with fingermarks," rebukes Chan. "The sight are most disgusting. Kindly remove it and bring me a more hygienic sector."

The proprietor picks up the offending pastry and carries it away.

"Japanese," remarks Chan, spreading his hands in an eloquent gesture.

Chan's assistant, Kashimo, is Japanese, and not overly bright. Small and anxious-looking, he tries to please his superior but is generally inefficient. On at least one occasion, he has lost the evidence—a pair of dice vital to a gambling case. When Kashimo attempts to be apologetic, Chan completely loses his patience.

"Be sorry out of my sight," he tells his hapless underling. "While you are in it my vision blurs and I feel my self-control under big strain."

Chan's racial prejudice toward the Japanese is humorless and bitter. He once states wearily, "Cooking business begins to get tiresome, like the company of a Japanese." At the end of a case, he uses judo on the murderer and grudgingly admits that it is the only thing he ever learned from the Japanese.

He has learned a great deal from others, however. A student of the English language, he also speaks Cantonese. Learned in Chinese philosophy, he is proud of his heritage and willingly dispenses his knowledge. He uses the abstract concept of ambition to distinguish a major difference between the Chinese and Caucasians (against whom he has no prejudice).

"Coarse food to eat, water to drink, and the bended arm for a pillow—that is an old definition of happiness in my country," says Chan. "What is ambition? A cancer that eats at the heart of the white man, denying him the joys of contentment. I fear I am victim of crude philosophy from Orient. Man—what is he? Merely one link in a great chain binding the past with the future. All times I remember I am one link. Unsignificant link joining those ancestors whose bones repose on a far distant hillside with the 10 children—it may now be 11—in my house on Punchbowl Hill...so, waiting the end, I do my duty as it rises. I tread the path that opens."

Chan feels that the success he enjoys in his career is based on "luck—always happy luck."

That assessment is, of course, far too modest. Chan does admit to being modest. "Falling hurts least those who fly low," he says. Sir Frederic concurs, saying, "And Sgt. Chan flies so low he skins the daisies."

Although that modesty may seem virtuous, it fails to explain accurately Chan's true methods of fighting crime, which have less to do with luck than with intelligence, attention to detail, and a profound understanding of human nature.

"Fingerprints and other mechanics good in books," Chan explains. "In real life not so much so. My experience tell me to think deep about human people. Human passions. Back of murder what, always? Hate, revenge, need to make silent the slain one. Greed for money, maybe. Study human people at all times."

He does not ignore physical clues, however. At the beginning of his first published case, Chan takes copious notes (possibly in shorthand) in a notebook. When the Chinese detective's superior prepares to question a witness, Chan's pencil is poised, always ready to add bits of information to his file. He describes the search for clues unpretentiously. "We grope about," he says.

When Charlie Chan gropes about, it is an amusing sight. His great bulk makes virtually any type of movement a major enterprise, al-

Two artists' versions of Charlie Chan perhaps reflect a full circle. On the left, he has the look of infinite wisdom we expect of him; on the right, he could pass for a villain.

---

though he does manage to pull it off with a certain grace. When Chan makes his entrance in **The House Without a Key**, he causes some astonished glances.

"In those warm islands, thin men were the rule, but here was a striking exception. He was very fat indeed, yet he walked with the light dainty steps of a woman. His cheeks were as chubby as a baby's, his skin ivory-tinted, his black hair close-cropped, his amber eyes slanting."

When Chan kneels to search for a clue, he is described as "a grotesque figure" who has to rise "laboriously" to his feet. When he takes a respite from the pressures of a case, he goes to the beach, presenting an enormous figure floating languidly on the water. "Little pleasant recreation," he explains. "Forget detective worries out here floating idle like leaf on stream."

In later cases, he has apparently lost weight, being described merely as "plump."

When dressed (always in western clothes, except when he is at home), Chan is entirely undistinguished, resembling every other overweight man on the island. Next to his huge stomach, his most impressive feature is his eyes.

His small, slanted eyes have the look of keen brightness that makes "the pupils gleam like black buttons in yellow light." His eyes are also the most expressive part of his face. They often "blink with pleasure," "sparkle" with amusement, shine from "some inner excitement," and widen with surprise or delight.

When he is especially pleased, his face breaks into a huge grin. Unlike the actors who have portrayed him in motion pictures, Chan wears no moustache and carefully shaves every vestige of black stubble from his cheeks.

Chan's enormous girth was not hereditary. He likes to eat, though he is generally not fond of western cooking. He enjoys drinking great quantities of tea, his favorite beverage.

In an American restaurant, he invites a visitor to join him and accept "some of this terrible provision." The coffee he calls "unspeakable" but politely offers his companion some, then grabs the check, saying, "No—pardon me—the honor of paying for this poison-tasting beverage must be mine."

Chan tries always to be polite but, he says, at times "police affairs forbid utmost courtesy."

Still, Chan is generally courteous, saying

"please" and "thank you" and bowing deeply from the waist, even as he prepares to put handcuffs on a suspect. Gentle, kind and humble, he is liked by all who know him, and he is never more charming than when he "distills the wisdom of the ages" in a new and captivating epigram.

Charlie Chan's last recorded case, **Keeper of the Keys**, ends with one of his most enduring and endearing statements: "Three things the wise man does not do," he counsels. "He does not plow the sky. He does not paint pictures on the water. And he does not argue with a woman."

EARL DERR BIGGERS (1884-1933) Born in Warren, Ohio, he graduated from Harvard University in 1907 and landed a job on the **Boston Traveler**, writing a column of humor and occasional dramatic criticism. He wrote several plays, the first of which, **If You're Only Human** (1912), was a failure; later, **Seven Keys to Baldpate** (1913) was a huge success—partially due to George M. Cohan's adaptation. Cohan also starred in the first of five film versions of the 1913 novel. After good success with several mystery novels, Biggers created Charlie Chan for a series of six novels beginning in 1925 with **The House Without a Key.** While the books were popular and successful, it is the numerous motion picture adventures of the famed Chinese-Hawaiian sleuth that have insured his enduring fame.

BIBLIOGRAPHY

1925 **The House Without a Key** (Bobbs-Merrill)
1926 **The Chinese Parrot** (Bobbs-Merrill)
1928 **Behind That Curtain** (Bobbs-Merrill)
1929 **The Black Camel** (Bobbs-Merrill)
1930 **Charlie Chan Carries On** (Bobbs-Merrill)
1932 **Keeper of the Keys** (Bobbs-Merrill)

FILMOGRAPHY

1929 **Behind That Curtain** (Fox) with Warner Baxter, Lois Moran and E. L. Park (as Charlie Chan in a minor role); directed by Irving Cummings.
1931 **Charlie Chan Carries On** (Fox) with Warner Oland (as Charlie Chan), John Garrick, Marguerite Churchill; directed by Hamilton MacFadden.
1931 **The Black Camel** (Fox) with Warner Oland, Sally Eilers, Bela Lugosi, Dorothy Revier, Robert Young; directed by Hamilton MacFadden.
1932 **Charlie Chan's Chance** (Fox) with Warner Oland, Ralph Morgan, H. B. Warner, Marian Nixon; directed by John Blystone.
1933 **Charlie Chan's Greatest Case** (Fox) with Warner Oland, Heather Angel, Roger Imhof, John Warburton; directed by Hamilton MacFadden.
1934 **Charlie Chan's Courage** (Fox) with Warner Oland, Drue Leyton, Donald Woods, Paul Harvey; directed by George Hadden.
1934 **Charlie Chan in London** (Fox) with Warner Oland, Drue Leyton, Douglas Walton, Alan Mowbray, Mona Barrie; directed by Eugene Forde.
1935 **Charlie Chan in Paris** (Fox) with Warner Oland, Mary Brian, Erik Rhodes, John Mijan, Thomas Beck; directed by Lewis Seiler.
1935 **Charlie Chan in Egypt** (Fox) with Warner Oland, Pat Paterson, Thomas Beck, Rita Cansino (Rita Hayworth); directed by Louis King.
1935 **Charlie Chan in Shanghai** (Twentieth Century-Fox) with Warner Oland, Irene Hervey, Jon Hall, Keye Luke; directed by James Tinling.
1936 **Charlie Chan's Secret** (Twentieth Century-Fox) with Warner Oland, Charles Quigley, Astrid Allwyn, Rosina Lawrence; directed by Gordon Wiles.
1936 **Charlie Chan at the Circus** (Twentieth Century-Fox) with Warner Oland, Keye Luke, Francis Ford, Shirley Deane, John McGuire, George and Olive Brasno; directed by Harry Lachman.
1936 **Charlie Chan at the Race Track** (Twentieth Century-Fox) with Warner Oland, Keye Luke, Helen Wood, Thomas Beck, Alan Dinehart, Gavin Muir; directed by H. Bruce Humberstone.
1936 **Charlie Chan at the Opera** (Twentieth Century-Fox) with Warner Oland, Keye Luke, Boris Karloff, Charlotte Henry, Thomas Beck, Nedda Harrigan; directed by H. Bruce Humberstone.
1937 **Charlie Chan at the Olympics** (Twentieth Century-Fox) with Warner Oland, Keye Luke, Katherine De Mille, Pauline Moore, Allan Lane; directed by H. Bruce Humberstone.
1937 **Charlie Chan on Broadway** (Twentieth Century-Fox) with Warner Oland, Keye Luke, J. Edward Bromberg, Leon Ames, Joan Marsh, Donald Woods; directed by Eugene Forde.
1938 **Charlie Chan at Monte Carlo** (Twentieth Century-Fox) with Warner Oland, Keye Luke, Virginia Field, Sidney Blackmer, Harold Huber; directed by Eugene Forde.

1938 **Charlie Chan in Honolulu** (Twentieth Century-Fox) with Sidney Toler (as Charlie Chan), Phyllis Brooks, Victor Sen Yung, Layne Tom, Jr., Eddie Collins, John King, Claire Dodd; directed by H. Bruce Humberstone.
1939 **Charlie Chan in Reno** (Twentieth Century-Fox) with Sidney Toler, Ricardo Cortez, Phyllis Brooks, Slim Summerville, Kane Richmond, Victor Sen Yung; directed by Norman Foster.
1939 **Charlie Chan at Treasure Island** (Twentieth Century-Fox) with Sidney Toler, Cesar Romero, Victor Sen Yung, Pauline Moore, Douglas Fowley; directed by Norman Foster.
1939 **Charlie Chan in the City of Darkness** (Twentieth Century-Fox) with Sidney Toler, Lynn Bari, Richard Clarke, Harold Huber; directed by Herbert I. Leeds.
1940 **Charlie Chan in Panama** (Twentieth Century-Fox) with Sidney Toler, Jean Rogers, Lionel Atwill, Victor Sen Yung, Mary Nash, Jack LaRue; directed by Norman Foster.
1940 **Charlie Chan's Murder Cruise** (Twentieth Century-Fox) with Sidney Toler, Marjorie Weaver, Lionel Atwill, Victor Sen Yung, Leo G. Carroll; directed by Eugene Forde.
1940 **Charlie Chan at the Wax Museum** (Twentieth Century-Fox) with Sidney Toler, C. Henry Gordon, Marc Lawrence, Marguerite Chapman, Victor Sen Yung; directed by Lynn Shores.
1940 **Murder over New York** (Twentieth Century-Fox) with Sidney Toler, Marjorie Weaver, Robert Lowery, Ricardo Cortez, Melville Cooper; directed by Harry Lachman.
1941 **Dead Men Tell** (Twentieth Century-Fox) with Sidney Toler, Sheila Ryan, Paul McGrath, George Reeves, Ethel Griffies; directed by Harry Lachman.
1941 **Charlie Chan in Rio** (Twentieth Century-Fox) with Sidney Toler, Mary Beth Hughes, Victor Jory, Cobina Wright, Jr., Victor Sen Yung; directed by Harry Lachman.
1942 **Castle in the Desert** (Twentieth Century-Fox) with Sidney Toler, Arlene Whelan, Richard Derr, Henry Daniell, Victor Sen Yung, Ethel Griffies; directed by Harry Lachman.
1944 **Charlie Chan in the Secret Service** (Monogram) with Sidney Toler, Gwen Kenyon, Mantan Moreland, Benson Fong; directed by Phil Rosen.
1944 **The Chinese Cat** (Monogram) with Sidney Toler, Benson Fong, Mantan Moreland, Joan Woodbury, Weldon Heyburn, Ian Keith; directed by Phil Rosen.
1944 **Charlie Chan in Black Magic** (Monogram) with Sidney Toler, Mantan Moreland, Frances Chan, Joe Crehan, Jacqueline DeWit; directed by Phil Rosen.
1945 **The Jade Mask** (Monogram) with Sidney Toler, Mantan Moreland, Janet Warren, Edith Evanson; directed by Phil Rosen.
1945 **The Scarlet Clue** (Monogram) with Sidney Toler, Benson Fong, Mantan Moreland, Helen Devereaux, Robert Homans; directed by Phil Rosen.
1945 **The Shanghai Cobra** (Monogram) with Sidney Toler, Benson Fong, Mantan Moreland, Walter Fenner, Joan Barclay; directed by Phil Karlson.
1945 **The Red Dragon** (Monogram) with Sidney Toler, Fortunio Bonanova, Benson Fong, Willie Best, Carol Hughes, Barton Yarborough; directed by Phil Rosen.
1946 **Dark Alibi** (Monogram) with Sidney Toler, Benson Fong, Mantan Moreland, Teala Loring, Joyce Compton; directed by Phil Karlson.
1946 **Shadows over Chinatown** (Monogram) with Sidney Toler, Mantan Moreland, Victor Sen Yung, Tanis Chandler, Mary Gordon; directed by Terry Morse.
1946 **Dangerous Money** (Monogram) with Sidney Toler, Victor Sen Yung, Willie Best, Joe Crehan, Dick Elliott, Elaine Lang; directed by Terry Morse.
1946 **The Trap** (Monogram) with Sidney Toler, Mantan Moreland, Victor Sen Yung, Tanis Chandler, Larry Blake, Kirk Alyn; directed by Howard Bretherton.
1947 **The Chinese Ring** (Monogram) with Roland Winters (as Charlie Chan), Mantan Moreland, Victor Sen Yung, Warren Douglas, Louise Currie, Philip Ahn; directed by William Beaudine.
1948 **Docks of New Orleans** (Monogram) with Roland Winters, Mantan Moreland, Victor Sen Yung, Virginia Dale, Carol Forman; directed by Derwin Abrahams.
1948 **The Shanghai Chest** (Monogram) with Roland Winters, Mantan Moreland, Victor Sen Yung, Tim Ryan, Deannie Best, Tristram Coffin; directed by William Beaudine.
1948 **The Golden Eye** (Monogram) with Roland Winters, Mantan Moreland, Victor Sen Yung, Wanda McKay, Bruce Kellogg; directed by William Beaudine.
1948 **The Feathered Serpent** (Monogram) with Roland Winters, Keye Luke, Victor Sen Yung, Mantan Moreland, Robert Livingston, Nils Asther; directed by William Beaudine.
1949 **Sky Dragon** (Monogram) with Roland Winters, Keye Luke, Mantan Moreland, Noel Neill, Tim Ryan, Iris Adrian, Elena Verdugo, Milburn Stone, Lyle Talbot; directed by Lesley Selander.

Nick & Nora Charles

An attractive characteristic of the great detectives of fiction is that they inevitably have many fascinating adventures and solve an exhausting variety of cases. A factor contributing to their excellence is that they would not be content to solve a single mystery and then rest on their laurels. It is a further axiom that the creators of great detectives do not like to retire their heroes, for reasons as valid and diverse as aesthetics and economics. If a detective has a wide readership, it verges on nastiness to deprive the happy reader of additional cases in which they are involved. And it verges on foolhardiness for an author to turn his back on the wide sales assured by a popular series crimefighter.

One of the deviations from this sensible pattern is the unpredictable husband-and-wife team, Nick and Nora Charles, who appear in only one published adventure, **The Thin Man**. Although a memorable and successful series of motion pictures starring William Powell and Myrna Loy was based on the eccentric couple, Dashiell Hammett wrote only that single exploit.

Nick Charles, incidentally, is not the thin man. The titular character of the novel is a missing scientist who is described as very thin. The public identified Nick with the title, however, so the film sequels continued to use the phrase, shifting the description from the corpse to the hero.

Hammett wrote only five novels, **The Thin Man** being the last. Begun in 1930 to fulfill a contractual commitment, it was not actually completed until he desperately needed money in 1933, when it was published in **Redbook** magazine; it was published, in a slightly expanded form, in February 1934 in book form.

The published book had been significantly altered from its original conception. In its earliest state, the detective hero was named John Guild (who gave his name to a police sergeant in the finished book)—essentially a tough, hard-boiled private detective, much like the Continental Op, Sam Spade and Ned Beaumont, Hammett's other major detective characters.

William Powell and Myrna Loy played Nick and Nora Charles in the six-film Thin Man *series.*

NICK
JR

In many ways, **The Thin Man** is a reflection of the author's changing lifestyle. An acknowledged alcoholic much of his life, Hammett writes about a man and wife who give every appearance of being borderline alcoholics, too, if lovable ones. No longer interested in dedicating himself to his work, preferring to gamble and drink, Hammett records incidents in the life of a retired private investigator who was once tough and effective but who now prefers to drink, loaf and spend his wealthy wife's money.

Hammett based Nick Charles on himself to a greater degree than he had any of his previous detectives. The dust wrapper of **The Thin Man** features an illustration of a tall, slender, good-looking man posing in a manner clearly evocative of the sophisticated detective. The model for the photograph is Hammett himself.

Nora Charles is loosely based on Lillian Hellman, with whom Hammett had a famous on-and-off-and-on-again romance for thirty years, beginning in 1930 when they were both in Hollywood and married—to other people. Miss Hellman was divorced in 1932; Hammett in 1937. **By the time The Thin Man, was published, they had lived together for some time, and it is not difficult to imagine their lives together being very like the time shared by Nick and Nora.**

Miss Hellman, to whom the book is dedicated, wrote a few years after Hammett's death in 1961: "It was a happy day when I was given half the manuscript to read and was told that I was Nora. It was nice to be Nora, married to Nick Charles, maybe one of the few marriages in modern literature where the man and woman like each other and have a fine time together."

Nick Charles narrates his own adventure about "the thin man" and his first words tell a lot about him. "I was leaning against the bar in a speakeasy," he says. During the remainder of the recorded case, he (joined more often than not by his wife Nora) consumes more alcohol than a St. Patrick's Day party.

In his earlier years, Nick was a very tough private investigator for the Trans-American Detective Agency in San Francisco. He had an unusual reputation. He was not only extraordinarily successful in bagging criminals, but he managed to earn the respect and friendship of a substantial percentage of the underworld population on both coasts. Even the hoodlums he beat up (a not-unusual occurrence for the fearless private eye) and sent up the river give him a grudging respect earned by very few upholders of the law.

One crook gave him an especially warm recommendation for honesty and trust-worthiness, telling another thug: "Nick might not maybe sell his own mother out."

He has led an active and event-filled career, but Nick is not the only courageous member of the Charles family. On one noteworthy night, a desperate gangster holds a gun to Nick and Nora. Acting quickly, Nick hits his wife in the jaw, knocking her out, to get her out of the revolver's range. He jumps their assailant, getting shot in the side but nonetheless being able to subdue him after a struggle. When Nora regains consciousness, she instantly informs Nick that she is furious with him because his action, although chivalrous, caused her to miss all the fun.

Nora learns more about Nick's bravery from one of his old army friends. Although Nick modestly attempts to downplay the significance of the event, it has, for evident reasons, left an ineradicable memory with his friend, who reminds him:

"I wanted to tell you I hadn't forgotten what I owed you and—"

"Nonsense," Nick replies.

"It's not." He turns to Nora. "I don't suppose he ever told you he saved my life once in a shell-hole in—"

"He's nuts," Nick tells her. "He fired at a fellow and missed and I fired at him and didn't and that's all there was to it."

The long-lasting loyalty Nick inspires is further evidenced by the help he gets from members of the underworld when he is on a case. Gangsters are comfortable with him, and he with them. Nora loves the exhilaration of walking in dangerous neighborhoods, visiting seedy speakeasies, and meeting the unpalatable characters who inhabit them.

Once, shortly after hearing a tough use a slang expression, she asks Nick what it means. He explains that "lugs" are ears. In a logical extension, she tells her husband, "I love you, Nicky, because you smell nice and know such fascinating people."

Despite some differences, Nick and Nora get along well. At the time of **The Thin Man** (1933), Nora is twenty-six and Nick indeterminately, but substantially (although not outrageously) older. His distinguished career as an operative has come to a close and he has decided that he wants nothing more from life than to drink enormous amounts of liquor and spend his wife's considerable fortune.

They were married in 1926 when Nora was nineteen, and her father died the following year, leaving her a lumber mill, a narrow-gauge railroad and "some other things." Nick resigned from the detective agency to look after them.

Although it is obvious that his only serious interest is partying (mainly drinking), Nick does, in fact, attend to the business and seems capable.

"I had a stenographer in the next morning," he notes, "and got rid of most of the mail that had been accumulating; had a telephone conversation with our lawyer in San Francisco—we were trying to keep one of the mill's customers from being thrown into bankruptcy; spent an hour going over a plan we had for lowering our state taxes; was altogether the busy business man, and felt pretty virtuous by two o'clock, when I knocked off work for the day and went out to lunch with Nora."

In all likelihood, the Charles' concept of lunch is different from most people's idea of a nutritious diet. While most people, most of the time, eat their lunches, the Charleses invariably drink theirs. It is rare to find either Nick or Nora with their mouths closed, but they are rarely opened for the purpose of consuming anything more substantial than an olive. They drink, they smoke cigarettes, and they make wisecracks.

When Nora asks Nick, "How are you?" he answers, "Terrible. I must've gone to bed sober."

When Nick awakens and tells his wife he wants a drink, "to cut the phlegm," she suggests breakfast instead. "It's too early for breakfast," he replies.

Nick has very little trouble sleeping (that is, if he were left alone he would have very little trouble—but he is almost never left alone). Nora, on the other hand, does some of her best thinking in the small hours. To help her fall asleep, she reads Chaliapin's memoirs. When Nick dozes off, she asks him if he is asleep, to which he replies in the affirmative. When a telephone rings in the middle of the night, and Nick learns they are about to have company at 5:00 A.M., he says, "That's great. I was afraid I was going to have to go to sleep."

Both Nick and Nora possess an exceptionally sophisticated wit and are popular in the upper-crust social world of San Francisco and New York. It is not only their wealth and sense of humor which keep them high on invitation lists. They are also both physically attractive.

Two members of the Charles family are Asta and Nick, from a paperback of The Thin Man.

Nora is described as a lanky brunette with "a wicked jaw," but John Guild, the police sergeant investigating the Wynant case, is instantly smitten by Nora's charms, constantly telling Nick how lucky he is and what a fine woman Nora is. Nick goes so far as to allow that "she can smile very nicely." Although many of Nick's old friends are evidently suspicious of all women, they eventually seem to like Nora well enough.

Nick narrates his most famous case in the first

Mrs. NICK CHARLES
NICK CHARLES Jr.

person and modestly neglects to describe his physical appearance, but he is certainly tall and slender and must be remarkably handsome since Nora, a young woman of exceptional beauty, fell in love with him quickly and deeply, and most of the other women with whom he has contact make no secret of their desire to form a relationship with him which transcends the purely professional.

Although he is of Greek ancestry (his real name was Charalambides but when his father came through Ellis Island the name was "whittled down" to Charles), Nick is among the most American of detectives, being comfortable in all levels of society and familiar with the nuances of language and idiom characteristic of those levels.

A fun-loving playboy content to count and spend his wife's millions (he tells her frequently that he married her for her money, and discusses his affairs with other women with good-natured braggadocio; it is not easy to determine whether he is telling the truth or joking), he is nevertheless a man to be taken seriously. He is tough, both temperamentally and physically, despite appearances to the contrary.

A third member of the Charles family travels everywhere with Nick and Nora but does not participate in the criminal investigations. Asta, a schnauzer (not the terrier depicted in the films), is an active, frisky dog who gets excited about greeting people and is particularly fond of taking a running start before punching Nick in the stomach with its front paws.

Nick and Nora have a rare rapport among husband-and-wife teams (real-life or fictional) who work together in any profession, but particularly among detectives where the usual relationship has the husband rescuing the wife from peril brought about by her own foolishness. They enjoy life and each other.

Although they often have minor disagreements and sometimes display sarcasm toward each other (Nick once tells Nora, "I don't see how any detective can hope to get along without being married to you"—and is less than completely sincere about it), they laugh a great deal with each other and at each other's jokes and foibles. They talk to each other and listen to what the other has to say.

Neither Nick nor Nora is a paragon, but you wouldn't mind knowing them, either.

DASHIELL HAMMETT (1894-1961) Samuel Dashiell (the Americanized version of the French name DeChiel, with the accent on the second syllable) Hammett was born in Maryland, dropped out of school at thirteen, and tried a variety of jobs before becoming a private operative with the Pinkerton National Detective Agency in Baltimore, remaining with it for eight years and using many of his cases and the people involved with them for his stories. After serving as a sergeant in the Motor Ambulance Corps in World War I, he worked briefly for the agency again, then wrote advertising copy, and finally wrote detective stories, which he sold to the best pulp magazine of its time, **Black Mask**. Although Carroll John Daly invented the "hard-boiled" private eye, Hammett developed the type with such creations as the Continental Op, Nick and Nora Charles, Ned Beaumont, Sam Spade, and Secret Agent X-9, a comic-strip FBI agent. He did very little writing after 1934, most of his time and energy going to political efforts for left-wing causes.

Hammett's only novel about Nick and Nora Charles spawned one of the most successful film series of the 1930s and 1940s, even introducing a new character: Nick Jr. Asta appeared in all six.

BIBLIOGRAPHY

1934 **The Thin Man** (Knopf)

FILMOGRAPHY

1934 **The Thin Man** (MGM) with William Powell (as Nick Charles), Myrna Loy (as Nora Charles), Maureen O'Sullivan; directed by W. S. Van Dyke.
1936 **After the Thin Man** (MGM) with William Powell, Myrna Loy, James Stewart, Elissa Landi; directed by W.S. Van Dyke.
1939 **Another Thin Man** (MGM) with William Powell, Myrna Loy, C. Aubrey Smith, Virginia Grey; directed by W.S. Van Dyke.
1941 **Shadow of the Thin Man** (MGM) with William Powell, Myrna Loy, Donna Reed, Barry Nelson; directed by W.S. Van Dyke.
1944 **The Thin Man Goes Home** (MGM) with William Powell, Myrna Loy, Lucile Watson, Gloria DeHaven; directed by Richard Thorpe.
1947 **Son of the Thin Man** (MGM) with William Powell, Myrna Loy, Keenan Wynn (title role), Patricia Morison, Gloria Grahame, Jayne Meadows, Dean Stockwell; directed by Edward Buzzell.

Bulldog Drummond

Just as the cowboy is a uniquely American hero, and the samurai definably Japanese, a certain breed of adventurer is recognizably British. The robust, beer-drinking, loud, hard-fighting fellow who loves nothing so much as danger and the camaraderie of other men of the same type is epitomized by Bulldog Drummond.

Dedicated to righting wrongs, even when they have no personal interest in a situation, these romantics are unafraid to punch a villain in the nose or to take on a whole gang single-handedly. Above all, they are sportsmen and gentlemen. Once they have given their word—even if it is to an arch-villain intent on world conquest, or to the most repugnant of mass murderers—they will honor it. They would no sooner slug someone from behind than they would force their attentions on a virtuous girl.

No adventure is too wild for Bulldog Drummond, and no risk too great. The word "hopeless" is without meaning for him. So is the word "sensible."

In one instance, he hears a woman's scream in the house of his greatest adversary, the fiendish Carl Peterson. Drummond knows a trap has been set for him. An American policeman also tells him that a trap has been set. Still, he dashes headlong into the house because he simply cannot resist coming to the aid of a damsel in distress.

Drummond, in fact, comes to the aid of anybody who seems to need it. It may appear today to be a philosophy of excess, as well as being simultaneously noble and foolhardy, but it involved no intellectual decision for either Drummond or his creator. For them, it was merely the natural way to behave.

The creation of H. C. McNeile, Bulldog Drummond was based partly on the author himself, and partly on his good friend, biographer and fellow novelist, Gerard Fairlie, who continued to write the series after McNeile's death from a war-related injury.

Some similarities exist between Drummond and James Bond, neither of whom is strictly a

The dust wrapper of the first English edition of The Female of the Species *(1928) features a Bulldog Drummond who looks like the Godfather.*

detective but both of whom protect England and the world from foul, deranged, would-be rulers and subversive organizations. Both are intensely patriotic and engage in monumental struggles with powerful foreign villains. Neither Bond nor Drummond strikes the casual observer as being overly intelligent. Each is often captured by the enemy, escaping only with the assistance of such outside forces as good luck or turncoat women.

Drummond's career ranged from 1919 to 1954, during which time he gave the appearance of being in his mid-20s until the time of World War II, when he seemed to age severely. Ten of his adventures were recorded by McNeile (who used the pseudonym "Sapper"—a military slang term for an engineer) and seven by Fairlie.

Many actors have portrayed Hugh Drummond on the stage and in motion pictures, but never has he been evoked more brilliantly than by Ronald Colman—handsomer than Drummond but with the bravado and insouciance which endeared him to two generations.

In the first few adventures, Drummond's nickname is spelled "Bull-Dog" but it later is changed to "Bulldog."

"Demobilised officer, finding peace incredibly tedious, would welcome diversion. Legitimate if possible, but crime, if of humorous description, no objection. Excitement essential. Would be prepared to consider permanent job if suitably impressed by applicant for services."

This advertisement, placed by Captain Hugh Drummond, D.S.O., M.C., retired, runs in a newspaper early in 1919, in some measure as a joke but with just a hint of seriousness.

On the first day, Drummond receives forty-five responses to it, selecting from that number the problem of Phyllis Benton, a beautiful young girl concerned about her father's involvement with some evil men.

Drummond thus takes the first step down two parallel boulevards that will define the rest of his life, launching a career as an adventurer that is to last thirty-five years, and launching a romance, which will culminate in marriage to a lovely, supportive woman, that lasts equally as long.

So little is known of his past that the world could not have been prepared for Drummond, who gloried in the First World War and who emerged from it with an insatiable appetite for heroics.

He does not talk of his childhood or his family, but he has spoken warmly of his nanny, Mrs. Eskdale, who was "built like a steamroller."

During World War I, he served in France, particularly Guinchy, with His Majesty's Loamshires as a platoon leader. He was known for his incredible feats of bravery, earning him the virtual adoration of the men under his command. It was during this service that he became adept at hand-to-hand combat, picking up "two or three secrets" (probably judo, which was little known in the western world at that time), from an unidentified Japanese. At the conclusion of hostilities, he was mustered out of the service as a captain.

The devotion given to him in the army was not a solitary instance. He is a born leader. It is said that there are quite a few men in England "who acknowledged only two rulers—the King and Hugh Drummond. And they would willingly die for either."

This type of loyalty is not easily achieved. The king was born to it, but Drummond obtains it by his extraordinary courage. "As nearly as a man may be, he was without fear."

Cowardice, to Drummond, is the ultimate human weakness, if not sin. His favorite pastime, almost to the point of passion, is the pursuit of "fun"—that is, danger.

"It has been stated," one narrative explains, "that men can be divided into two classes . . . those who look for trouble, and those who do not. [Drummond] by no stretch of the imagination . . . could be placed in the second category." To further illustrate the point, it is said that he "is always ready to run his head into a noose if it offered the smallest chance for adventure."

Drummond admits that "no one is fonder of a thick-ear party then I am." Villains with whom he comes into confrontation describe him as "a young man of dash and temperament" and as having "an infinite capacity for making a nuisance of himself."

If Drummond's quest for excitement seems excessive, it is trivial compared with his obsessive need to adhere to the rules of fair play and sportsmanship. They are his religion, and he is a zealot.

Engaged in a titanic struggle with master criminal Carl Peterson and his gang, Drummond has the opportunity to rid himself, and England, of Peterson's henchman, Lakington. Drummond

Among the noted actors who have portrayed Drummond on the screen, none was more suited to the role than the dashing Ronald Colman. In Bulldog Drummond, *Joan Bennett played Phyllis.*

plans to kill him—without a trial, of course—but his conscience forbids it and he relents. Instead, he engages him in a "fair fight." He is actively opposed to murder of any sort, he maintains, because "it revolted his sense of Sport."

He once works very hard to clear an escaped convict who has been accused of murder, saying, "He may have been a swine, but we couldn't let the poor blighter swing without making a concerted effort to save him."

To Drummond, "the sense of art was synonymous with the sense of fair play." This point of view forces him to conclude that "The principal combat must be between Peterson and him—no mercy given, no mercy asked."

One of the byproducts of his dedication to sportsmanship is a highly developed sense of chivalry. "Nothing pleased him more than to defy the hectoring type of bully," it is said of Drummond; but without question his greatest joy and self-imposed purpose for living is the protection of women.

When he first meets Phyllis, whom he later marries, he vows to help her, even if it means having to thrash someone "within an inch of his life." But it is not only the beautiful Phyllis for whom Drummond would risk his life.

He likes pretty young women. "Adorable girls had always been a hobby of his." He is protective of them all, in a purely brotherly fashion.

Curiously, he has no qualms about playing up to women if a case requires that course of action. He even goes out dancing with a disguised Irma, Peterson's mistress. He is married at the time, but Phyllis raises no objections.

Drummond has no difficulty in getting close to women. They are as attracted to him in their way as men are in a very different way.

This silhouette decorates 1937's
Bulldog Drummond Double-Header.

"Slightly under six feet in height, he was broad in proportion. Not . . . goodlooking, but . . . the fortunate possessor of that cheerful type of ugliness which inspires immediate confidence in its owner." He has crisp brown hair, a large, full mouth, and a nose which was broken in the boxing finals of the Public School Heavyweights.

Perhaps his most interesting facial feature is his eyes, which are "deep set and steady, with eyelashes many women had envied, and they showed him [to be] a sportsman and a gentleman." They are also described as "honest eyes" and as "lazy eyes [that could] bore like gimlets."

Drummond knows good clothes and, while he doesn't make a fuss about the subject, he is rather dapper in a grey suit, wearing a white gardenia in the buttonhole. He carries a cigarette case filled with both Virginian and Turkish cigarettes, but often prefers to smoke a pipe.

On occasion, Drummond's voice can have a deep commanding ring to it, but most of the time it has an air of "assumed flippancy." He has considerable control of his voice, being able to adopt cockney and Southland accents well enough to fool native speakers of these dialects, but he is more limited in his repertoire of animal sounds. It is his inability to imitate any animal except an owl that leads to the selection of a hoot as the call of the Black Gang, a loosely organized association to which he belongs.

It is perhaps of greater significance to examine *what* he said. It would probably also be to his advantage to ignore the subject altogether. One of those people not enamored of Drummond suggested that some of his speech mannerisms make Philo Vance sound like Winston Churchill.

One example of an early Drummond statement, recorded for posterity, should provide the flavor of his vocabulary: "Verily, I believe that we have impinged upon the goods."

During his avid courtship of Phyllis, he woos her with such suave endearments as "Old Thing" and "Old Girl." Fortunately for them both, he simply calls her "Phyllis" after the marriage.

His language has other eccentricities. He does not use foul words, though he does go so far, once in a while, as to say "damned," but his more frequently used expletives are "Great Scot!" and Holy Smoke!" He has some command of the German language, less of the French.

When he refers to foreigners or ethnic groups, he uses such terms as "wog," "nigger," "wop," "Huns" and the like, but generally without malice. He is openly anti-Semitic, dislikes Russians, and hates Germans. Politically, he finds his enemies on the extreme right and their counterparts on the left.

Speaking of Germans, he says, "The scum wouldn't be complete without the Boche."

At the time of World War II, he echoes Churchill, saying, of Russians, that "any enemy of Hitler's is a friend of ours," but he is normally no friend of the Soviet Union. He once helps a scientist prevent a deadly poison from falling into the wrong hands—those of "Russia, ruled by its clique of homicidal, alien Jews." In other instances, once a person has been established as a Jew, he no longer refers to him by name, but only as "the Jew."

He fears and loathes Nazism, taking an intense stand for British military preparedness in 1935 as a method of averting war. He equally detests the political far left.

"Years ago," he says, "we had an amusing little show rounding up Communists and other unwashed people of that type. We called ourselves the Black Gang, and it was great sport while it lasted."

While all foreigners are viewed with some suspicion, Americans are well regarded by Drummond. In his first adventure, he meets Jerome K. Green, who is described as a member of the Police Force of the United States of America. Since no such organization exists, it is probably either a misunderstanding by Drummond or a euphemism for another crimefighting or espionage agency. Green proves himself worthy of Drummond's respect by saving his life.

That fortuitous rescue is not the only time Drummond has the good fortune to be bailed out of a seemingly impossible situation. He often needs help, due to the fact that he combines only moderate intelligence with stupendous courage, thereby finding himself up to his armpits in trouble more frequently than virtually any other adventurer in history.

He does have his talents, however, and they are considerable. He is, for example, deadly. He has always trained himself physically, so he has "enormous strength" without being clumsy. He can "move over ground without a single blade of grass rustling" and is able to "kill a man with his bare hands in a second."

Drummond's favorite target in a fight is the neck; he either snaps his adversary's neck or crushes his throat in a fight to the finish. While he kills when he has to, he feels guilty when he thinks of it; he has an active conscience.

Under great emotional stress, or in a serious fight, the veins on his forehead stand out. This is bad news for any bad guy within his range. When he loses control of himself, as occurs when Phyllis is threatened, he goes berserk and is unstoppable.

It is, therefore, not difficult to understand why "the mere mention of [his] name had struck fear into the hearts of the criminal fraternity."

Drummond is an excellent stalker, able to "make cover where none exists," and he can generally outlast his foes. He is tireless, and also able to "snatch 40 winks almost at will."

He can read tire tracks, analyze handwriting, and knows how to handle a gun. He owns a small Colt revolver and a water pistol (which he calls "son-of-a-gun") which he fills with ammonia and squirts into the faces of some thugs.

Drummond never forgets a face, although he has been fooled more than once by a clever disguise. He is adept in the art of disguise himself, and has a fairly complete makeup kit which he uses more than most crimefighters. The treacherous Irma admits that Drummond is but "little less than an expert at disguise."

Finely tuned powers of observation have proved invaluable to Drummond. He has the "ability to notice things other people would never observe in a lifetime," and can also "intuitively make a very shrewd guess at the innermost thoughts of others."

Other attributes Drummond brings to his adventures include the ability to control his facial muscles so perfectly that he ranks as "one of the best poker players in London"; a cheerful and optimistic (if somewhat fatalistic) attitude; and a reputation (ill-earned, it would seem to some) as "the soul of discretion," according to a War Office official.

Drummond is far from perfect, however, as he would be the first to admit. He has virtually no knowledge of politics, no interest in art, no talent for chess, no familiarity with economics, and only "the most sketchy ideas" of first aid. Aware of his shortcomings, he is not much concerned about them.

For all his pronounced abilities, Drummond generally cracks a case by eavesdropping on the criminals while they obligingly discuss it in complete, candid and totally detailed terms. Once he has learned the situation and its ramifications, Drummond concludes the encounter with a physical confrontation. The villains are invariably foiled, although they frequently escape (sometimes turning up again in later adventures).

The arch-fiend who turns up most often is Carl Peterson, one of the most evil criminals in literature. Even though he finally dies in his fourth recorded struggle with Drummond, his presence pervades the rest of Drummond's life. His mistress Irma is a constant reminder of the fiendish Peterson, but more important to Drummond is the memory of his enemy. He is the yardstick against which all other villains must be measured.

Carl Peterson's name is merely a convenience, a pure fiction, as are his background and nationality. Drummond continues to call him Peterson because that is the name under which he originally encountered him, but he soon learns that it has no basis in fact. He has used countless aliases, including le Compte de Guy,

Edward Blackton, Baron Darrott, Professor Scheidstrun, Franklyn, Libstein and who knows how many more.

He changes nationality as it becomes convenient, saying, "I have no nationality, or rather...I have every nationality." Languages present no difficulty for him because he is able to speak English, French, German and Spanish fluently, and can, he says, "make myself understood in Russia, Japan, the Balkan States and—America."

A master of disguise, Peterson is so accomplished in this art that it is virtually impossible to know exactly what he looks like, but he most often is described as having a "profile aquiline and stern. Eyes...cold grey blue; thick brown hair, flecked with grey, brushed back from a broad forehead," giving an overall impression of "a man of power: a man capable of forming instant decisions and carrying them through."

With an off-again, on-again beard, there is a good chance that Peterson actually looks like this, or at least that it is his favorite disguise and therefore presumably would *like* to look this way.

Peterson is certainly a man to be reckoned with, a foeman worthy of Drummond's mettle. There is "power in every line of his figure, in every movement of his hands. He might have reached the top in any profession he had cared to follow, just as he had reached the top of his present one."

In his first battle with Drummond, an American policeman testifies to Peterson's reputation in other parts of the world, admitting that the villain is "the biggest proposition we've ever been up against on this little old Earth. He's a genius. He's the goods. Gee!"

While in disguise as William Robinson, Peterson describes himself as the "King of Criminals, without mercy—a black-hearted villain."

Although he is revolted by blackmail, Peterson keeps a file on virtually everyone he has met or knows by reputation primarily for the purpose of being familiar with their weaknesses so that he can exploit them if a scheme requires it. This card file and accumulation of information is the basis of his organization, which he calls the "Brotherhood." The pay for members is very good (his secretary, Freyder, receives an annual salary of £ 10,000 in the 1920s), but failure is dealt with severely. An incompetent is not fired—he is killed.

A conscience does not trouble Peterson, nor impair his activities. He has "an inhuman passivity in the face of suffering" and an equally inhuman capacity for causing that suffering.

His favorite methods of torture include the use of thumbscrews, and pressing a victim against a red-hot stove. To assist in the acquisition of information, he employs will-deadening drugs. A hooded cobra has the run of his house at night, and a ferocious gorilla roams the grounds to keep out unwanted visitors. An acid bath is always ready to dispose of bodies. During his most sadistic acts of murder and torture, Peterson "laughs gently."

Peterson's criminal motivations are various, but a craving for power must rank at the top. In the first instance in which Drummond encounters him, Peterson has obtained the backing of two Germans and an American in a plot to foment a general strike in England designed to destroy the government, which he is prepared to take over.

A lust for wealth is also evident. He once charges a fee of a half-million pounds to suppress a process that can produce flawless artificial diamonds, then plans to make use of the process for his own benefit. The desire for money is stronger than other, perhaps more human, emotions. "Revenge," he says, for example, "is only worthwhile if it pays."

There are indications that much of the motivating force in Peterson's life is the same as that in Drummond's: the craving for excitement. He even gets bored when his plans go too smoothly and wonders what it would be like to be "respectable." He decides that if he could pull off "a really big coup...into the millions," he would give up his life of crime. His coup does not materialize and he remains a criminal, which ultimately costs him his life.

Despite Peterson's extraordinary powers (he is a genius at reading men's minds, and has such control over himself that he can take cocaine without becoming a slave to the drug—just as Sherlock Holmes maintained a mastery over it), he has some weaknesses, but he is "far too clever not to realize his own limitations."

The first of his major shortcomings is a virtually unbreakable habit of tapping his left knee with the middle finger of his left hand. This nervous tic is a dead giveaway that enables Drummond to penetrate his best disguises. Later in their perennial engagements, Irma discovers that Drummond is aware of Peterson's habit; Drummond is fooled by Peterson as they turn his knowledge against him.

Perhaps the greatest failure of Peterson's vile career is his choice of henchmen. To a man, they are without a modicum of intelligence. If they

This pulp-style illustration of Drummond appeared on the dust wrapper of Captain Bulldog Drummond, *published in England in 1945.*

were even moderately capable, they would not allow a captured Drummond to confer with fellow prisoners, nor would they constantly turn their backs on him, thus presenting him with the opportunity to escape or attack them. Thanks to them, Drummond's life and career have been longer and more successful than one would have expected.

Over the years, Drummond and Peterson develop a mutual, if grudging, respect. The villain praises Drummond's "resource...initiative...strength." Drummond, meanwhile, thinks of Peterson as "Murderer, thief, forger and blackguard generally, but what a brain! After all, [Peterson] fought a lone hand, deliberately pitting himself against the whole of the organized resources of the world."

Peterson did not play a totally lone hand, however. Irma was constantly at his side. Little is known about the background of the beautiful villainess except that she came under Peterson's influence as "a child." In polite society, they pretend to be father and daughter. It is difficult to speculate about how many people are actually fooled by this charade, but Drummond sees through it.

Irma apparently loves Peterson and remains true to his memory after Drummond causes his death, never forgetting her grudge against him and admitting that "the main object in my life"

An artist's conception of the adventurer adorns the front cover of Bulldog Drummond Double-Header.

is to avenge her protector's death by killing him.

Although she is known as Irma Peterson, that is clearly not her real name. In the first place, Peterson was not the villain's name; in the second, there is no evidence that they were ever actually married, and it is certain that she was not his daughter, although their age difference might have been adequate for that relationship to seem possible.

She may not be quite the worthy adversary that Peterson was, but Irma is as persistently evil. She carries on Peterson's hatred of England (that "dreadful country") and Drummond seems to relish his war with her. Although he agrees that she is "one of the most dangerous criminals alive today," and that she is a woman "without mercy or scruple," he admits he is fond of her "in a peculiar sort of way." Whether or not this "peculiar sort" of fondness has any relation to her great beauty is never made clear.

Drummond probably has his hands full with another beauty—Phyllis, who makes his "heart sing" so much, and so quickly, that he decides to marry her after seeing her only three times. She is daring (she smokes cigarettes), resourceful (she warms up Hugh's getaway car in the adventure in which they meet), curious (instigating her own inquiries), friendly (even servants and shopkeepers call her Phyllis) and stunning. She has "very blue" eyes, "great masses of golden brown hair," a figure that "a simple linen frock shows to perfection" and slender, lovely hands.

Some years after their marriage, Drummond retires to a pig farm and Phyllis thinks that is just fine. The whole idea is hers, and she prefers him to lead the quiet life of a pig farmer rather than risk his neck as an adventurer. When he complains that it's a dull life, she says, "the duller the better," wishing only that she and Hugh had retired to a desert island.

When World War II is in its preliminary stages, Hugh tries to join the army but changes his mind when he is informed that he would serve as a training officer. Instead, he turns his Birmingham farm over to the production of food for the military, and he becomes a platoon leader in the Home Guard.

Not long afterwards, the government requests his services for a top-secret mission in Nazi-occupied France, and Phyllis raises no objections. He finds that, since the First World War, war has changed for the worse, if that is possible, saying "Wars, both public and private, have become unpleasantly total since our day...nothing is barred, including inhumanity."

Drummond is often nostalgic about the past as he grows older. One of his warmest memories, in a general sense, is the time he used to spend drinking beer with his pals, many of whom have helped on his cases.

No one is a greater help than Algy Longworth, whose "false air of flippancy" hides his "iron nerve." For some unexplained reason, he wears "unnecessary eyeglasses." He also has a weakness for blondes, whom he chases incessantly.

At one point, he infiltrates into France, penetrating behind Nazi lines, without assistance, frustrating Irma's plans almost single-handedly. Nevertheless, the enemy persists in regarding him as an idiot. During World War II, he works on a farm and serves as a corporal in Drummond's Home Guard division.

James Denny began his relationship with Drummond during World War I, serving as his captain's batman, then as his manservant in civilian life. Phlegmatic, Denny's only overt sign of excitement is sucking his teeth. He stands at attention and clicks his heels when receiving orders from Drummond, and loves the excitement of being involved in his master's adventures. He takes care of Drummond's weaponry and admits to being unhappy about the retirement to a pig farm. Presumably his wife, a typical cockney housekeeper, is less disappointed.

Other Drummond cronies abound. Peter Darrell, who served in the army with Hugh, is his best friend, the best man at Drummond's wedding, and lives next door to him when Drummond has rooms at 60A Half Moon Street. He serves as a factory foreman and is a sergeant in Drummond's Home Guard division during World War II. Ted Jeringham, an actor, once has the chance to masquerade as a waiter and pour gravy all over Peterson. Jerry Seymour owns the Stomach Ache, a biplane which Drummond is able to use in his pursuit of Peterson. Toby Sinclair holds the Victoria Cross. Ronald Standish is the hero of several books of adventures not unlike Drummond's.

Surprisingly, considering his many adventures, there seem to be only minor disruptions and alterations in Drummond's life.

He moves from Half Moon Street to Brock Street, also in London, with little appreciable difference in lifestyle until the retirement to the Birmingham pig farm. He also owns a cottage in Goring.

His little thirty-mile-per-hour two-seater is soon exchanged for a Rolls Royce coupe, which he drives for many years. His club changes from Junior Sports to Senior Sports. He acquires three dogs in the early 1920s: a cocker spaniel named Bess, a white-haired terrier named Jock, and a bulldog named Jerry (who is killed by the bad guys about ten years later).

At the first of Drummond's meals to be described, he eats kidneys. Throughout the next three decades, he eats kidneys. He eats kidneys for breakfast. He eats kidneys with chops. He likes kidneys, in fact, as much as he likes to drink beer, and that is his favorite leisure-time activity.

Drummond undergoes few philosophical changes through the years, and remains equally comfortable with most of his original crime-fighting techniques. He prefers to work on his own, or with his friends, eschewing assistance (or interference) from the official police. Having to ask Scotland Yard for help is a sign of failure to him.

"Things have gone to the bow-wows," he says, "when the old firm have to rope in the minions of the law."

H. C. MCNEILE (1888-1937) Herman Cyril McNeile, the son of a military man (his father was a captain in the Royal Navy), also made Great Britain's armed forces his life. After studying at the Royal Military Academy, he joined the army at nineteen and served in the Royal Engineers for twelve years, retiring in 1919 as a lieutenant colonel. World War I was responsible for chronic poor health, finally causing his death in 1937. During his military career, he wrote many military adventure stories and later produced several tales in the vein of his successful Bulldog Drummond series, often about a similar character named Jim Maitland, and sometimes about Ronald Standish. He used the pen name "Sapper" for several books, deriving the term from the military slang expression for army engineers.

BIBLIOGRAPHY

(by H. C. McNeile, "Sapper")
1920 **Bull-Dog Drummond** (Doran)
1922 **The Black Gang** (Doran)
1924 **Bulldog Drummond's Third Round** (Doran; British title: **The Third Round**, Hodder & Stoughton, London)
1926 **The Final Count** (Doran)
1928 **The Female of the Species** (Doubleday)
1929 **Temple Tower** (Doubleday)
1932 **Bulldog Drummond Returns** (Doubleday; British title: **Return of Bulldog Drummond**, Hodder & Stoughton, London)

1933 **Bulldog Drummond Strikes Back** (Doubleday; British title: **Knockout**, Hodder & Stoughton, London)
1935 **Bulldog Drummond at Bay** (Doubleday)
1937 **Challenge** (Doubleday)

(by Gerard Fairlie)
1939 **Bulldog Drummond on Dartmoor** (Hillman-Curl; published in 1938 by Hodder & Stoughton, London)
1940 **Bulldog Drummond Attacks** (Gateway; published in 1939 by Hodder & Stoughton, London)
1945 **Captain Bulldog Drummond** (London: Hodder & Stoughton; not published in the U.S.)
1947 **Bulldog Drummond Stands Fast** (London: Hodder & Stoughton; not published in the U.S.)
1949 **Hands Off Bulldog Drummond** (London: Hodder & Stoughton; not published in the U.S.)
1951 **Calling Bulldog Drummond** (London: Hodder & Stoughton; not published in the U.S.)
1954 **The Return of the Black Gang** (London: Hodder & Stoughton; not published in the U.S.)

FILMOGRAPHY

1929 **Bulldog Drummond** (United Artists) with Ronald Colman (as Bulldog Drummond), Joan Bennett, Lilyan Tashman, Montague Love, Claude Allister; directed by F. Richard Jones.
1930 **Temple Tower** (Fox) with Kenneth MacKenna (as Bulldog Drummond), Marceline Day, Henry B. Walthall, Cyril Chadwick; directed by Donald Gallagher.
1934 **The Return of Bulldog Drummond** (British International Pictures) with Ralph Richardson (as Bulldog Drummond), Ann Todd; directed by Walter Summers.
1934 **Bulldog Drummond Strikes Back** (United Artists) with Ronald Colman, Loretta Young, Warner Oland, C. Aubrey Smith; directed by Roy Del Ruth.
1937 **Bulldog Drummond at Bay** (Associated British Picture Corporation) with John Lodge (as Bulldog Drummond), Dorothy Mackaill; directed by Norman Lee.
1937 **Bulldog Drummond Escapes** (Paramount) with Ray Milland (as Bulldog Drummond), Heather Angel, Porter Hall, Sir Guy Standing, Reginald Denny, E. E. Clive; directed by James Hogan.
1937 **Bulldog Drummond Comes Back** (Paramount) with John Howard (as Bulldog Drummond), John Barrymore, Louise Campbell, J. Carroll Naish; directed by Louis King.
1937 **Bulldog Drummond's Revenge** (Paramount) with John Howard, John Barrymore, Louise Campbell, Reginald Denny, E. E. Clive; directed by Louis King.
1938 **Bulldog Drummond's Peril** (Paramount) with John Howard, John Barrymore, Louise Campbell, Reginald Denny, E. E. Clive, Porter Hall, Halliwell Hobbes; directed by James Hogan.
1938 **Bulldog Drummond in Africa** (Paramount) with John Howard, Heather Angel, H. B. Warner, J. Carroll Naish; directed by Louis King.
1938 **Arrest Bulldog Drummond!** (Paramount) with John Howard, Heather Angel, H. B. Warner, Reginald Denny, E. E. Clive, George Zucco; directed by James Hogan.
1939 **Bulldog Drummond's Secret Police** (Paramount) with John Howard, Heather Angel, H. B. Warner, Reginald Denny, E. E. Clive, Leo G. Carroll; directed by James Hogan.
1939 **Bulldog Drummond's Bride** (Paramount) with John Howard, Heather Angel, H. B. Warner, Reginald Denny, E. E. Clive, Eduardo Ciannelli; directed by James Hogan.
1947 **Bulldog Drummond at Bay** (Columbia) with Ron Randell (as Bulldog Drummond), Anita Louise, Terry Kilburn; directed by Sidney Salkow.
1947 **Bulldog Drummond Strikes Back** (Columbia) with Ron Randell, Gloria Henry, Terry Kilburn, Anabel Shaw; directed by Frank McDonald.
1948 **The Challenge** (Twentieth Century-Fox) with Tom Conway (as Bulldog Drummond), June Vincent, Richard Stapley, Eily Malyon; directed by Jean Yarbrough.
1948 **Thirteen Lead Soldiers** (Twentieth Century-Fox) with Tom Conway, Helen Westcott, Maria Palmer, John Newland; directed by Frank McDonald.
1951 **Calling Bulldog Drummond** (MGM) with Walter Pidgeon (as Bulldog Drummond), Margaret Leighton, Robert Beatty, David Tomlinson; directed by Victor Saville.
1967 **Deadlier Than the Male** (Universal) with Richard Johnson (as Bulldog Drummond), Elke Sommer, Sylva Koscina, Nigel Green, Suzanna Leigh, Steve Carlson; directed by Ralph Thomas.
1971 **Some Girls Do** (Universal) with Richard Johnson, Daliah Lavi, Beba Loncar, James Villiers, Robert Morley; directed by Ralph Thomas.

C. Auguste Dupin

There may be endless arguments about who is the greatest detective, or the most eccentric, or the most popular, but there can be no discussion about the identity of the first great detective of literature. Although he appeared in only three short stories, the mantle of genesis and pre-eminence must grace the shoulders of one man, and one only: C. Auguste Dupin.

Cases have been made for the prophet Daniel in the Bible, for Sancho Panza in the second part of Cervantes' **Don Quixote**, for D'Artagnan in Alexandre Dumas' **Vicomte de Bragelonne**, Caleb Williams in William Godwin's **Things As They Are; or The Adventures of Caleb Williams**, Francois Vidocq, whose **Memoirs** are largely fictional, and several others for the honor of being the first fictional detective, and they each have some validity, but none touches Dupin for the indisputable position of being the first character whose adventures were recorded solely because of his skill at ferreting out hidden truths.

In the three stories chronicling Dupin's investigations, Edgar Allan Poe established the virtually complete boundaries of all detective stories written from that day to this. He presaged the evolution of the detective story, and the tens of thousands of examples that followed, in about one hundred pages of text—a literary achievement of such monumental proportions that it is as incredible in retrospect as it must have been at the moment of conception.

In "The Murders in the Rue Morgue," Poe created a thrilling detective story on one level, and a textbook of how to write mysteries on another. Here is the first eccentric amateur detective; the first worshipful friend, assistant and chronicler; a crime that baffles the official police force and makes the amateur's aid necessary; the innocent person charged with a crime; the locked room and "impossible" crime; the patronizing of the police by the amateur; the bafflement of the chronicler as the detective genius refuses to divulge his thoughts; the surprise ending.

Dupin, who is referred to simply as Monsieur Dupin in the first adventure but as the Chevalier Dupin in the following two tales, was probably based on a real-life person, also named Dupin. Although it is generally accepted that much of Poe's own personality is reflected in Dupin (who is both a mathematician and poet, as was Poe), and also in his anonymous friend, many of the character's more obvious characteristics were clearly derived, as Michael Harrison's research proves, from F. P. Charles Dupin, Chevalier of the Order of St. Louis, Officer of the Legion of Honor, Baron of the French Empire (1784-1873).

Dupin the detective thus takes the surname and one of the titles of the real-life Dupin, adding only a Christian name—Auguste—to the appellation of the prototype. The choice of that name presents no difficulty, since Poe evidently held the real-life counterpart of his creation in high regard, and quite likely had some affection for his character as well. The dictionary definition of the word "august" is "grand, imposing and majestic; what is worthy of respect and veneration."

Dupin the Baron was evidently perceived in this fashion by Poe. Dupin the detective was certainly all of that. Poe provides no physical description of his crime solver, attempting to stress the importance of the intellectual powers of his character, dismissing physical, emotional and spiritual considerations. Dupin, the epitome of intellect, is Poe's idealization of himself.

Details of Dupin's life are sparse, possibly because the anonymous chronicler of his criminal investigation considers them of trivial importance. Dupin is a detective; he is seen detecting, and little else.

He is described as "a young gentleman of an excellent—indeed of an illustrious family, but, by a variety of untoward events, [he] had been reduced to...poverty...".

The narrator of the tales was living in Paris "during spring and part of the summer of 18—," as written in Poe's story (sometime during the 1830s) when he met Dupin in an "obscure library in the Rue Montmartre." Because they both happened to be looking for the same volume, they struck up a conversation and became friends.

At this time, Dupin was living aloof from the world on "a small remnant of his patrimony" but, soon after this chance encounter, he moves into rooms with his new friend.

They rent "a time-eaten and grotesque mansion" at 33, Rue Dunôt, Faubourg St. Germain. While this address is quite well known, there is reason to believe it is a pun—a joke by the narrator of the exploits. "Dunôt" is not actually a French name, but a transmutation of the popular English colloquial phrase "D'you know?"

Their mode of living must be considered eccentric by any reasonable standard. The chronicler explains that, because Dupin is "enamored of the Night for her own sake...at the first dawn of the morning we closed all the...shutters...lighted a couple of tapers which, strongly perfumed, threw out only the ghastliest and feeblest of rays. By the aid of these we then busied our souls in dreams—reading, writing or conversing, until...true Darkness. Then we sallied forth into the streets, arm and arm, ...seeking, amid the wild lights and shadows of the populous city, that infinity of mental excitement which quiet observation can afford."

During their time at home, Dupin remains silent for long periods, smoking his meerschaum pipe, from which he sometimes blows a "perfect whirlwind of smoke," and sometimes reading a newspaper, even though he believes that "it is the object of our newspapers rather to create a sensation...than to further the cause of truth."

Nonetheless, newspapers play a significant role in Dupin's career as an avocational detective. In his first recorded case, "The Murders in the Rue Morgue," he reads of the brutal murder of two women in a seemingly inaccessible room.

Adolphe Le Bon, who is erroneously arrested for the murders, had once performed an unspecified service for Dupin, for which he is "not ungrateful," so the detective reviews the testimony, visits the scene of the crime, views the bodies and deduces the truth.

The solution of this case is regarded as a simple matter by Dupin because of the bizarre elements of the crime. The more *outré* the characteristics of a crime, he believes, the easier it is to solve.

Newspapers play an even greater role in Dupin's second recorded case. After M. G———, Prefect of Police, offers a sum of money to the amateur detective for his help in solving "The Mystery of Marie Rogêt," Dupin merely remains in his rooms, perusing the various Paris

---

Without question the finest portrait of Dupin was painted by Charles Raymond Macauley to illustrate Monsieur Dupin, *published in 1904.*

Another Macauley illustration of Dupin. Note that his anonymous friend is the twin of Poe.

newspapers, and commenting on the information about the crime which they provide.

By a remarkable series of coincidences (the chronicler assures us), the major facts of the case, in which an attractive young girl who worked in a *parfumerie* is murdered, parallel exactly the events leading up to and following the death of a real-life New York girl named Mary Cecilia Rogers.

The actual crime has never been solved, nor is Dupin's case concluded satisfactorily. The ending of the adventure does no more than provide a line of inquiry which Dupin theorizes would be most beneficial for the police to follow.

Sitting in his armchair, Dupin expounds on some of the many areas of knowledge in which he appears to be comfortable, including pathology, botany (informing his friend of the dubious information that grass can grow "as much as two or three inches in a single day"), hydrodynamics, philosophy, and the mathematics of probability.

While his statements on the laws of probability are widely open to question, there seems to be no field of knowledge in which Dupin is unversed. In addition to those mentioned, he seems to be a scholar of physics, both modern and classical literature (regularly quoting Chamfort, Rousseau and Crébillon), fond of using Latin phrases, familiar enough with sailor's knots to be able to identify the nationality of the man who tied the knot, and able to use a pistol "when occasion demands."

Dupin's greatest accomplishment is his use of analytical technique. There is no time, apparently, when Dupin is not observing, analyzing and deducing. He does it as naturally and as constantly as his friend breathes. "Observation has become with me," Dupin says, "...a species of necessity."

It is both a necessity for Dupin and a joy. Talking of his friend, the narrator says, the analyst "derives pleasure from even the most trivial occupations bringing his talents into play. He is fond of enigmas, of conundrums, of hieroglyphics, exhibiting in his solutions of each a degree of *acumen* which appears to the ordinary apprehension praeturnatural."

When Dupin is engaged in the process of analysis, his whole manner changes. He becomes "frigid and abstract; his eyes...vacant in expression; while his voice, usually a rich tenor, [rises] into a treble which would... [sound] petulantly but for the deliberateness and entire distinctness of the enunciation."

The chronicler understands what his roommate is doing, and says, proud of his comprehension, "It is merely...an identification of the reasoner's intellect with that of his opponent." Dupin agrees, but cautions that the practical value of this identification depends upon the accuracy with which the opponent's intellect is measured.

There is no difficulty in making observations and deductions; the trick is in doing it well, as the narrator says. The analyst, he explains, "makes, in silence, a host of observations and inferences. The necessary knowledge is that of *what* to observe."

Dupin's methods are so effective that he is able to respond to his companion's unspoken thoughts merely by observing his external behavior (a feat also accomplished by Sherlock Holmes, much to the amazement of Dr. Watson).

During the investigation of a crime, Dupin maintains that "it should not be so much asked 'what has occurred,' as 'what has occurred that has never occurred before.' "

It is essential, he feels, to seek the unique features of a case, not only because the bizarre crime is easier to solve than a commonplace one, but because "it is by prominences above the plane of the ordinary, that reason feels her way... ."

Dupin has great respect for the obvious. "Truth," he says, "is not always in a well. In fact, as regards the more important knowledge, I do believe that she is invariably superficial."

Nor is he bothered by coincidences. He regards them as "great stumbling blocks in the way of that class of thinkers who have been educated to know nothing of the theory of probability."

Providing only that it has not been influenced by some outside stimulus, Dupin has considerable respect for public opinion, feeling that it is not unlike intuition—which he calls a manifestation of individual genius.

Although he ultimately has confidence only in himself and his own genius, Dupin has some respect for the police who, he says, are "exceedingly able in their way. They are persevering, ingenious, cunning, and thoroughly versed in the knowledge which their duties seem chiefly to demand."

However, he is often condescending in his attitude toward them, and is sometimes frustrated by what he sees as their slavish

Steve Forrest portrays Dupin (inexplicably named Paul in this film) in Phantom of the Rue Morgue. *No recluse now, he is a medical student pursuing a lunatic and Patricia Medina.*

Murders in the Rue Morgue *(1932), the first film about Dupin, featured Leon Waycoff (who later became known as Leon Ames) as the detective. Bela Lugosi starred as a madman.*

devotion to routine. "There is no method to their proceedings," he says, "beyond the method of the moment. The results attained by them are...for the most part brought about by simple diligence and activity."

He decries their insistence on *relevant* facts, explaining that "a vast, perhaps the larger portion of truth arises from the seemingly irrelevant."

Perhaps surprisingly, it is the anonymous chronicler of the tales who has a lower opinion of the police than Dupin has—a curious attitude for one who is constantly baffled by his friend's vastly superior grasp of the nuances of ramifications of situations. It is M. G——— for whom he saves his greatest contempt, saying that the Prefect called "every thing 'odd' that was beyond his comprehension, and thus lived amid an absolute legion of 'oddities.' "

Dupin is not above putting the needle into M. G———. In the case published as "The Purloined Letter," he taunts the policeman by saying, "Perhaps the mystery is a little *too* plain. A little *too* self-evident."

This, the most baffling of cases for the police of Paris, was the simplest for Dupin. A compromising letter had been stolen from a "royal personage," to whom Dupin is partisan, by Minister D———, a scoundrel of the first rank.

Dupin recognizes a worthy adversary: "As poet *and* mathematician, he would reason well";

he calls the minister "that *monstrum horrendum*, an unprincipled man of genius." The detective receives a double payment for recovering the letter (and leaving a mocking note in its place)—fifty thousand francs, and the satisfaction of repaying an evil turn once done to him by the minister.

Dupin's pleasure in solving this case, and other cases, is one of the few joys of his life. He devotes almost all his energy to the solution of crimes. Young, scholarly, eccentric, romantic, aristocratic and arrogant, he is a totally cerebral being—possessor "of an excited, or perhaps of a diseased, intelligence," his chronicler admits, "but an undeniably brilliant one."

He has no friends (except his Boswell-like chronicler-roommate) and has no indulgences beyond reading only. Although poor, he manages to buy books, which he reads omnivorously, and which may have helped inspire him to try his hand at writing "certain doggerel."

His green spectacles improve his shortsighted vision, enabling him to satisfy his hunger for reading, and also permit him to observe people intently—and surreptitiously.

Those eyes, peering through their tinted shades with the sparkle of genius, must have seen a great deal. The pitiable fact that his chronicler saw fit to provide readers with only three adventures is a deprivation that all aficionados rue, d'you know?

A gorilla frightens a visitor to a carnival in Murders in the Rue Morgue. *Bela Lugosi is Dr. Mirakle, the crazed owner of the ape. Leon Waycoff is Dupin, renamed Pierre in this film.*

A melange of several Edgar Allan Poe stories and other dubious sources were used to produce Murders in the Rue Morgue *(1971). Christine Kaufman and Jason Robards starred in this Grand Guignol opus, which neither bears a resemblance to the original nor features Dupin.*

EDGAR ALLAN POE (1809-1849) Born in Boston, Edgar Poe was orphaned at the age of two and adopted (though not legally) by John Allan and his wife, and the youth took his benefactor's name. After being expelled from West Point, he wrote a great deal of poetry, as well as some short fiction and criticism, and edited several literary magazines, though he was forced to spend most of his life in poverty. In many respects, he is the most important American literary figure, having created memorable poetry, brilliant and perceptive criticism, and tales of the macabre that remain unsurpassed for their evocation of terror and dark mood. He defined the short story and developed it into the form by which it is generally recognized. With the publication of "The Murders in the Rue Morgue" he invented the detective story and with the creation of C. Auguste Dupin produced the first great detective in literature.

BIBLIOGRAPHY

1843 **The Prose Romances of Edgar A. Poe, No. 1** (Graham; the first book publication of "The Murders in the Rue Morgue," which was originally published in the April, 1841, issue of **Graham's Magazine**)

1845 **Tales** (Wiley & Putnam; the first book publication of "The Mystery of Marie Rogêt," originally published in **Snowden's Ladies' Companion,** the issues of November and December, 1842, and February, 1843, and "The Purloined Letter," originally published in **The Gift** for 1845— which was actually published before October 1844)

FILMOGRAPHY

1932 **Murders in the Rue Morgue** (Universal) with Leon Waycoff (as "Pierre" Dupin), Bela Lugosi, Sidney Fox; directed by Robert Florey.

1942 **Mystery of Marie Roget** (Universal) with Patric Knowles (as "Paul" Dupin), Maria Montez, John Litel, Lloyd Corrigan, Maria Ouspenskaya; directed by Phil Rosen.

1954 **Phantom of the Rue Morgue** (Warner Brothers) with Steve Forrest (as "Paul" Dupin), Karl Malden, Claude Dauphin, Patricia Medina; directed by Roy Del Ruth.

1971 **Murders in the Rue Morgue** (American International) with Jason Robards (as the Dupin character), Christine Kaufmann, Herbert Lom, Adolfo Celi, Michael Dunn, Lilli Palmer; directed by Gordon Hessler.

Mike Hammer

Mickey Spillane, the author. Mike Hammer, the private detective. The books written by one about the other form one of the great literary controversies of the middle of the twentieth century.

Beginning with **I, the Jury** in 1947, Spillane's novels about the tough private eye enjoyed a rage of popularity unequaled in the history of detective fiction. Each of Spillane's first seven novels roared onto the best-seller lists and remained permanently cemented there until the next was published. When a survey was taken of the all-time best-selling American fiction, all seven of Spillane's books ranked in the top ten.

While it is not uncommon for popular appeal and critical acclaim to have only the slightest coincidence, it is likely that the gap has never before or since been wider than with Spillane's books. Although the incredible popularity of his novels declined in the 1960s and 1970s, they are still regularly reprinted for a large and receptive readership.

But the appraisers of culture, even the normally mild-mannered ones and the generous ones, virtually choke with rage when the names of Hammer and Spillane are mentioned. The books have acquired a reputation for sex, sadism, vulgarity and violence that is so firmly entrenched and so repellent to sensitive critical tastes that all discussion is effectively prevented, as if the name of the Marquis de Sade were uttered in church.

Ironically, there is far less graphic sex in the Mike Hammer books than one has been led to expect. In the early novels particularly, all but the most innocuous sex acts occur off-stage, if at all, and the strongest language would fail to bring a blush to the cheeks of even the most chaste; the words euphemistically referred to as "four-letter" do not appear at all.

Those scenes generally singled out as sadistic depict Hammer enjoying the administration of a physical beating to a villain who has repeatedly and enthusiastically committed heinous acts of depravity throughout the case. The violence of these confrontations is intense, but no scenes of gratuitous torture, which abound in many much-praised contemporary novels, are present.

Ayn Rand, the novelist and objectivist

philosopher, once compared reading Mickey Spillane to hearing a military band in a public park. There is an undeniably attractive simplicity to his work, providing a clear-cut division of good and bad, without much concern about middle or neutral ground.

A romantic hero, Mike Hammer has a straightforward morality and code of honor that were more prevalent in the nineteenth century than they are today. He is a vigilante. He knows right from wrong, and takes it upon himself to see that the white forces of good survive the black onslaughts of evil. He doesn't care much for the law, which he views as a device used to circumvent justice, not to administer it.

"I'm not letting the killer go through the tedious process of the law," he says. "The dead can't speak for themselves...this time I'm the law, and I'm not going to be cold and impartial."

Philosophically, he is an individualist, although he places enormous importance on his country, his city, and other people, especially his friends. He repeatedly risks his life and good health for friends, whether long-standing or newly made, and is particularly receptive to pleas of help from those unable to protect themselves against a more formidable foe. When he locates the villains, whether gangsters or Communists, he delights in ridding the world of their menace.

The Mike Hammer character was originally conceived by Spillane as a comic book feature entitled **Mike Danger**. Spillane wanted to publish the book himself on a profit-sharing plan with other writers and artists. Mike Roy of Timely Comics (where Spillane had been an editor before World War II) drew the unpublished strip, which was essentially an outline for **I, the Jury**. It never became a reality, so Spillane turned instead to writing novels and, eventually, portraying Mike Hammer in a motion picture (**The Girl Hunters**)—the only author ever to portray his own detective on film.

If one word could be used to summarize Mike Hammer's method as a detective, it is intimidation. Violence or, more often, the threat of violence, proves remarkably effective as a means of extracting information from hitherto unwilling informants.

Getting answers to questions is an essential function of any detective, private or public, and Hammer will do almost anything to obtain those answers. He impersonates an officer several times, blackmails a recalcitrant withholder of information, and picks locks. He also thinks. "My mind can pick up threads and weave a whole cloth," he says.

But, in his quest for clues and other necessary data required to crack a case, his most valuable asset, apart from a strong right arm, is his knowledge of human personalities. His instinct for knowing people, when to believe them and when to mistrust them, his ability to make them like and willingly share their secrets, are his stock in trade. "Fingerprints and stuff are for technical men," he says. "I deal with motives and people."

He also depends on hunches, which are not to be confused with guesses. "There's a lot of experience and know-how that lies in back of what people call hunches," he maintains.

Unlike other detectives, Hammer feels that the primary responsibility of a private eye is not the detection of the perpetrators of crime, but their punishment. He is totally committed to that punishment, and never doubts that he is right when he administers his brand of justice.

"There's no shame or sin in killing a killer," he says. "David did it when he knocked off Goliath. Saul did it when he slew his tens of thousands. There's no shame to killing an evil thing."

Those Biblical references are not unique in Hammer's life. He believes in God and prays on several occasions. Secure in his conviction that he is committing a moral act when he shoots a murderer, he is also certain that God approves of the end he seeks, as well as the methods he employs to attain them. He almost thinks of himself, in fact, as an emissary of God.

"I lived only to kill the scum and the lice that wanted to kill themselves. I lived to kill so others could live. I lived to kill because my soul was a hardened thing that reveled in the thought of taking the blood of the bastards who made murder their business. I lived because I could laugh it off and others couldn't. I was the evil that opposed other evil, leaving the good and the meek in the middle to live and inherit the earth!"

Clearly, Hammer has no compunctions about killing evildoers. When he is asked how he manages to get away with killing so often, he explains, "I can work the bastards up to the point where they make a try at me, and I can shoot in self-defense and be cleared in a

Biff Elliott as Mike Hammer in I, the Jury *vows to avenge the murder of an army buddy who once saved his life. The film was shot in the short-lived 3-D (three-dimensional) process.*

court of law."

That method is not without its difficulties. It presupposes faster reflexes and a steadier hand and eye than the enemy. Mike Hammer has them. When he is asked how good a detective he is, he answers:

"I've killed a lot of men...I remember because I don't want to remember. They were too nasty. I hate the bastards that make society a thing to be laughed at and preyed on. I think fast, I shoot fast, I've been shot at plenty. And I'm still alive. That's how good a detective I am."

He has a nice assortment of weapons with which to do the shooting. He carries with him a Colt .45 automatic with walnut grips and a six-bullet clip in it; it has extra barrels and firing pins to keep the ballistics experts guessing. He calls it variously "old ironside," "old junior" and "old Betsy." He also has a .32 hammerless automatic in a boot between the front seat and door of his car; a .30-caliber Luger in his apartment; and a .24-caliber automatic in the bottom of his office filing cabinet. Loose shells for the .45 are carried in his jacket pocket.

If he is neither forced to shoot someone nor able to justify it, he uses other weapons, primarily his fists (although he does carry a razor blade, seldom used, in a pocket in his belt). When he fights, he does not observe the Marquis of Queensberry rules. He punches, kicks, gouges and elbows. He favors as targets the lower belly and groin, or the face, primarily the nose and mouth.

He has a philosophy of the technique of

fighting. "The judo bit is great if everything is going for you," he says, "but a terrible right cross to the face can destroy judo, karate, or anything else, if it gets there first."

Only when the odds are overwhelming does Hammer lose a fight, and even then the outcome is not a foregone conclusion. His fights generally begin as self-defense, but he often gets the upper hand quickly. Only rarely does he engage in cold-blooded sadism solely for the pleasure of it. Although he enjoys dishing out a thorough beating to a hood or punk who has been beating up on him or someone unable to defend him- or herself, Hammer seldom provides gratuitous injuries after his adversaries have stopped fighting. The exception occurs in **The Big Kill**, in which Mike is unusually miffed:

"The little guy stared too long. He should have been watching my face. I snapped the side of the rod across his jaw and laid the flesh open to the bone. He dropped the sap, and staggered into the big boy with a scream starting to come up out of his throat, only to have it cut off in the middle as I pounded his teeth back into his mouth with the end of the barrel. The big guy tried to shove him out of the way. He got so mad he came right at me with his head down and I took my own damn time about kicking him in the face. He smashed into the door and lay there bubbling. So I kicked him again and he stopped bubbling. I pulled the knucks off his hand and then went over and picked up the sap. The punk was vomiting on the floor, trying to claw his way under the sink. For laughs, I gave him a taste of his own sap on the back of his hand and felt the bones go all to splinters. He wasn't going to be using any tools for a long time."

Despite his noteworthy abilities in the art of self-defense, Hammer says, "I'm no athlete," which is overly modest. He has the physical attributes of the athletic type, though the only time he tries to play tennis he fails miserably. He is big, at least six feet tall, and his weight is normally between 190 and 205 pounds, though it drops all the way down to 168 by the end of a seven-year alcoholic binge.

He describes himself as "ugly" and gets no argument. A girl tells him, "You can be called ugly if you take your face piece by piece and look at it separately. You have a brutal quality about you that makes men hate you, but maybe a woman wants a brute." His secretary, Velda, calls him ugly, and so does another girl who makes it seem all right by telling Hammer he is "so ugly you're beautiful." Another character calls him "Banana Nose."

His eyes are not "blue or brown, but tiger eyes" and his favorite facial expression is a grin, which he uses in a multitude of moods. He grins when he is being defiant, taunting or enigmatic, and when he feels at peace with the world, as well as when he is under the greatest stress, referring to it as "my own kind of grin, that happened automatically when an enemy was in front of me, [I] felt my eyes in a half squint, and had a funny relaxed feeling across my chest."

Despite the fact that he was raised in New York City, his voice is without regionalism and he is able to pose successfully as someone from Des Moines, Toledo and Philadelphia.

Hammer constantly wears a felt hat (once described as battered), sometimes even leaving it on his head indoors. When he is busy on a case he sometimes goes for several days without a shave or change of clothes, but otherwise he is a good dresser. He always wears a suit and tie, and the suits are expensive, being custom-tailored to hide the bulge of the shoulder holster in which he carries his .45. He likes to walk in the rain and wears a trench coat when he does.

Although he does not discuss it, Hammer does fairly well financially as a private detective. He wears a Rolex watch, and his somewhat active lifestyle requires frequent purchases of expensive suits. As far back as 1950, he charges $50 a day (including expenses) and receives checks for $1,000 and $10,000.

In that year he moves to an apartment (9D) in a building with a doorman. A gimmick on his door lets him know if anyone has tried to get in or has otherwise tampered with the door or lock. He gets along well with his neighbors, some of whom worry about him when he stays away too long. One, who lives downstairs, is a retired nurse and helps Mike babysit (and gets knocked unconscious by a murderer for her trouble).

His office is a two-room suite, number 808, in the Hackard Building in New York. The anteroom holds a desk and typewriter for Velda, his secretary. It also contains two captain's chairs and an antique bench for waiting clients. Mike's office has a desk, in which he keeps a change of clothes, a newsclipping file, a leather swivel chair, a filing cabinet in which he keeps the spare gun, a trick lamp for hiding important documents, a washbowl and a leather couch for napping—and other more strenuous activities, in which he has participated at least once.

There is nothing fancy about the building itself, but it is convenient. It has a parking garage in the basement, good security (visitors must register to enter, and the offices have pick-

Author Mickey Spillane plays a surprisingly convincing Mike Hammer in the 1963 screen version of The Girl Hunters. *Newspaper columnist Hy Gardner aids Hammer's anti-Red battle.*

proof locks), and a good manager, Nat Drutman (who keeps the office intact when Mike takes seven years off to be a bum).

The official name of Hammer's business (which is incorporated) is "Hammer Investigative Agency" and his business cards are imprinted "Michael Hammer, Investigator." Despite the formality of the card, he is uncomfortable being called "Mister," much preferring to have everyone call him "Mike." Snobbishness is not a part of his personality, probably because of his upbringing on the unfashionable Upper West Side of Manhattan in the area of Broadway and 110th Street.

Hammer seldom talks of his early years, and little is known about them. Born in 1917, he went to school with Lipton (Lippy) Sullivan, with whom he later remembers fighting the "Peterstown Bunch"; Lippy is killed in **Survival...Zero**. Hammer says he "grew up watching Georgia Southern, Gypsy Rose Lee, Ann Corio and the rest" on the stage of the old Apollo and Eltinge Theatres.

While he does not discuss his education, it is evident that it was fairly extensive, if not necessarily formal. He is one of the few people who invariably uses the word "whom" correctly, and his familiarity with literature is profound enough to enable him to quote comfortably from Shakespeare and Clement Clarke Moore, though he is never pedantic. He prefers fiction and men's magazines (**True, Cavalier**) to newspapers, in which he reads only the comic strips.

On one case, he is able to recognize first editions and priceless manuscripts instantly. He knows and appreciates the works of Tchaikovsky, Dvořak and Beethoven, and often uses music as a metaphor for his emotions.

There is no cultural arrogance about Hammer. He specifically says that he does not like fancy French cuisine, preferring corned beef (he calls it "corn beef"), chicken, rare steak, knockwurst and sandwiches. His most exotic drink is sherry, which he shares with Velda, but he usually drinks beer (Pabst Blue Ribbon), rye (Four Roses) mixed with water or ginger ale, and he accepts an occasional nip of bourbon from Pat Chambers, his policeman friend. He also drinks countless cups of coffee, which he likes strong and hot, with milk in it instead of cream. Until giving up cigarettes when he went on the bum, he smoked Lucky Strikes.

Shortly after establishing his private detective agency in 1939 or 1940, World War II erupted and he joined the armed forces, receiving desert training and "phase" training, then fighting the Japanese in the jungles of the Pacific.

Hammer emerged from the war without a scratch, though his friend Jack Williams saved him from being bayoneted by a Japanese soldier, losing his arm in the process. After the war, Williams is killed and Hammer vows to avenge his friend's death by killing the murderer. When he finally tracks down the killer, he eschews the legal process and shoots the murderer, with whom he has become friendly, in cold blood. The stunned and dying killer asks Hammer, "How could you?" He replies, "It was easy."

Once his agency is set up, Hammer quickly establishes a friendship with Chambers, a captain of the New York Police Department, as well as a close working relationship and rapport with the official police. Although strained from time to time, Hammer's relations with the police department are closer and warmer than those of any other private detective.

"Cops are dedicated professionals," he says. "They're in a tough underpaid racket with their lives on the line every minute of the day. They get slammed by the public, sappy court decisions and crusading politicians, but somehow they get the job done."

In 1944, out of the service and back on the job, Hammer hires Velda to work for him. She had been on assignment with the OSI in London during World War II, where she met an American spy named Richie Cole. Her experience qualified her for a private investigator's license, which she obtained before going to work for Mike.

Velda is beautiful, courageous, loyal and smart. Inexplicably, it takes Hammer six years to realize he is in love with her. Although they are engaged in 1951, he does not make love to her until 1964—twenty years after meeting her and fourteen after falling in love with her. She has been in love with him from the outset. Their courtship may not have lasted quite as long as that of Perry Mason and Della Street, but it surely remains unconsummated so many years that only the strongest-willed man could have remained in control of his passions.

A fairly large woman with big breasts and "million-dollar legs," she has big brown eyes, lush, full lips, an impish grin, a face that can register "the extremes of emotion" and coal-black hair in a long page-boy style. When she returns after a seven-year absence, the color has been changed to auburn but the style remains the same.

Much more than an ornamental sex object, Velda proves to be invaluable on many cases. "She has a brain that can figure angles," Hammer says, "while mine can only figure curves."

Once, close to a crook on a case, she is willing to sleep with him to get the damning evidence. She also dresses up as a prostitute to gain information and as an effective disguise for trailing a suspect.

Like Hammer, Velda is sentimental, crying when he temporarily loses his license and she becomes the boss of the firm. She is willing to help anyone who needs it. "She was always picking up wet birds in the street," Hammer says of her.

When he finally falls in love with Velda, Hammer worships her, saying often that she is the "only decent thing in my life" and describing her as "perfume and beauty and all the good things of life."

Fearless and irreplaceable on important assignments, she shoots and kills criminals with the .32 automatic she carries in her purse or in a shoulder holster under a specially tailored suit. In 1951, the year of her engagement to Hammer, she is captured by Communists and tortured, a fate which she incurs again four years later.

Sent out on an apparently routine case to protect some jewels, she recognizes someone on whom she had spied during the war. She and the client are found out and abducted by Russian agents. Taken surreptitiously to Eastern Europe, they are presumed dead by Hammer, Chambers and everyone else in the West.

The grief-sticken Hammer goes berserk and massacres a group of unidentified thugs whom he believes guilty of Velda's death. The shooting costs him his gun permit and private detective license. He hits the skids, becomes an alcoholic and a bum, and spends the next seven years filled with remorse, despair, guilt and liquor.

Chambers finally locates him and pulls him out of the gutter with the news that a dying man has information he will impart only to Hammer. The man is Richie Cole, Velda's old friend, who tells Mike that she is still alive but up to her scrumptious neck in trouble. The news, plus the ministrations of Dr. Larry Snyder, a friend of Pat's, bring Mike around. Temporarily hired as a federal agent, he gets his license and gun back, and then gets down to some serious work.

"The Dragon," a Soviet assassin involved in the case, has the misfortune of being tracked down by Hammer who, surprisingly, doesn't kill him. Instead, Hammer decides it will be more painful for "The Dragon" to await execution through the normal procedures of justice, and is content merely to nail his hand to the floor.

Velda, after an absence of seven years, returns to Mike, and they continue their crusade against Communism together. Hammer's loathing for Communism is philosophical rather than political.

No one, and no thing, causes the bitter hatred in Hammer inspired by Communists. He calls them "vomit...rot...they had a jackal look of discontent and cowardice, a hungry look that said you kill while we loot, then all will be well with the world."

Later, he says, "Sure, it's great to be a Commie...as long as you're top dog. Who the hell is supposed to be fooled by that crap?"

He has a suggestion for the most effective method of dealing with them: "Go after the big boys. Oh, don't arrest them, don't treat them to the dignity of the democratic process of courts and law...Do the same thing to them that they'd do to you. Treat 'em to the unglorious taste of sudden death. Kill 'em left and right, show 'em that we aren't so soft after all. Kill, kill, kill, kill!"

Hammer has a fantasy for himself. "Maybe some day," he dreams aloud, "I'd stand on the steps of the Kremlin with a gun in my fist and I'd yell for them to come out and if they wouldn't I'd go in and get them and when I had them lined against the wall I'd start shooting until all I had left was a row of corpses that bled on the cold floors and in whose thick red blood would be the promise of a peace that would stick for more generations than I'd live to see."

Assisting Hammer and Velda in the struggle against Communist infiltration of important positions in the United States is Hy Gardner, a columnist for the **New York Herald-Tribune** who quotes extensively from **Alice in Wonderland**. An anti-Communist ("I hate those Commie punks as much as you do," he tells Hammer), he was involved in some undiscussed and vaguely alluded-to espionage activities during World War II. His chief role in connection with Hammer's cases is to discover background information by using his international journalistic connections.

Once, when Hammer feels he is slowing down, and that "this racket is getting too much" for him, he wonders why he doesn't get out of it, "like Hy Gardner did."

"I don't know much about politics," Hammer admits, "except that it's a dirty game from any angle." Although he is far to the right of center, he is not active in politics of any kind. "I haven't voted since they dissolved the Whig party," he says. His assessment of bureaucrats might find support from most points along the political spectrum. They are, he says, "nonsense, tax-happy, self-centered socialistic slobs who think the public's a game you can run for your own benefit." Vocally conservative, he refers to liberals as "knotheads," dismissing those who prefer to be "red than dead" as "slobs."

Captain Pat Chambers has political views not unlike Hammer's, but he still manages to function under the rules and regulations of the police department's bureaucracy. He calls Mike crazy, but almost always offers support, obviously envying his friend's freedom. Chambers has a running feud with the District Attorney, a politician, and once threatens to punch a State Department official in the mouth.

Described as a gentleman-around-town, Chambers appreciates attractive women, and is secretly in love with Velda for many years. When she is captured by the Communists, he blames Hammer, his bitterness causing him to hate his former friend; they effect a reconciliation when Velda safely returns.

Friendship is extremely important to Hammer. He thinks it perfectly natural to risk his life for a friend but is not unrealistic about the parameters of friendship. "A guy can still be your friend, even when he's teed off at you," he says.

Among the many people he befriends is Bobo Hopper, a mental deficient, treating him in an almost fatherly way. He generally has little affection for minorities, however, and his

Ralph Meeker is a physically accurate portrayer of Hammer in Kiss Me Deadly. *Director Robert Aldrich does not let the audience know if Mike and Velda survive a climactic fire.*

friends do not come from among their ranks. He is prepared to react violently when approached by a homosexual, even though he is sitting in a gay bar and realizes that an advance is almost inevitable. He refers to gays as "pansies" and "fags," and feels they have "twisted complexes."

He is friendly towards blacks who "know their place," calling him "Mistuh Hammuh" while he calls them by their first names. Those with whom he is unfriendly he calls "Jigs" and "Bogies." He also uses such terms as "Spics" and "Wops," though without hostility.

Despite his individual prejudices, Hammer has an unusual degree of civic responsibility. "I live here, see?" he says about his city. "I got a damn good right to keep [the town] clean, even if I have to kill a few bastards to do it."

He cares about his community, and wants to make it better. "I'm getting so goddammed sick of the things that happen in this town," he says. "I have to take a bath every time I stick my head out the door... Christ, what a place to live."

"The People," he feels, are a little slow to understand what is happening to them and even slower to react to it, but he believes in them. The public, he says, "might be simple enough to let themselves be bullied around, and their government rot out from underneath them, but it would only go so far. An indignant public is like a mad bull."

His feelings towards humanity in general, and his community in particular, are protective, but he feels his greatest responsibility toward the underdog and toward women. "*No* dame can take care of herself," he says. And, referring to a white slave recruiter, he says, "That kind of guy should be hunted down and strung up by his thumbs. I'd do it personally."

Hammer's attitudes towards patrons of a sex show are not much different. He says of them that they were "rich jokers of both sexes who liked smut and filth and didn't care where they got it. A pack of queers who enjoyed exotic, sadistic sex."

Among the most puritanical of all private detectives, Hammer refuses to go skinny dipping and, although he enjoys sex with beautiful women who make themselves available to him, he won't sleep with the gorgeous Velda because "we're engaged."

Virtually all the women with whom Hammer comes in professional contact throw themselves at him. Generally tall, broad-shouldered, big-breasted and with terrific legs, they eventually flaunt their luscious naked bodies at him, but he claims not to be thrilled by the inevitable turn of events. "I like to do some of the work myself," he says, "not have it handed to me on a silver platter."

He prefers mature women, in their late

twenties and thirties; only one of his women (aside from Velda) is a virgin when she offers herself to him. He rarely refuses the offers. He loves women. Merely seeing them, clothed or naked, makes "things" run up and down his back, forces his tongue to grow thick, or causes his heart to beat faster. His preference is for large women ("I like 'em husky," he says), but hair color is of no importance—although he has been highly stimulated by the contrast between dyed head hair and natural pubic hair.

Once, in the 1940s, he fell in love with a beautiful woman whom he later discovered to be a murderer. Having promised vengeance to a dead friend, he shot and killed her in cold blood—an act which was to haunt him for years. "When she died, I died, too," he says.

Many of the women in his life take care of him and nurse him after a beating. Velda most often, but other women, too, give him tenderness which transcend sex, and he is touched by them—in more ways than one. Despite all the women, and many close friends, Hammer is often lonely and introspective. During one of the many periods of depression, he says, "Any time I touch anything, it gets killed."

Although there are many instances in which he is filled with self-doubt, his depression reaches its nadir when he is overcome by Velda's presumed death. He gives up completely, and even when he returns in later years (much as when Sherlock Holmes returned from Tibet), he is never quite the same.

His long bout with the bottle had mellowed Hammer to the point where he is even friendly with a pot smoker, and he lets a dealer in marijuana get away with no more than a warning. He wonders if he is too old to continue the active life of a private eye, and he remains softer and more tentative than in the early days. The post-gutter Hammer simply is incapable of screaming *"Kill, kill, kill, kill!"*

But at the peak of his career, Mike Hammer has no problems about self-assurance. "I was me," he says, "and I couldn't be anything else. I was all right. The world was wrong."

MICKEY SPILLANE (1918-   ) Born Frank Morrison Spillane in Brooklyn, N.Y., the author shares many of the characteristics of his famous private eye hero, Mike Hammer. Tough, straightforward, and masculine, the resemblance has been close enough to allow Spillane to portray Hammer on dust jacket photographs and in a motion picture, **The Girl Hunters.** With time out for World War II duty as a trainer of fighter pilots and the flier of combat missions himself, he was an active writer of comic strips and books, helping to develop Captain Marvel, Captain America, and others. He also performed on the trampoline for the Ringling Brothers, Barnum and Bailey circus, worked with the Federal Bureau of Investigation to help break a narcotics gang (receiving two bullet wounds and a knife stab during the investigation) and wrote the Mike Hammer novels, which became the publishing sensation of the 1950s. His other major series hero, Tiger Mann, is much like Hammer, but is mostly involved in espionage work, while Hammer usually combats more localized villainy.

BIBLIOGRAPHY

1947 **I, The Jury** (Dutton)
1950 **Vengeance Is Mine!** (Dutton)
1950 **My Gun Is Quick** (Dutton)
1951 **The Big Kill** (Dutton)
1951 **One Lonely Night** (Dutton)
1952 **Kiss Me, Deadly** (Dutton)
1962 **The Girl Hunters** (Dutton)
1964 **The Snake** (Dutton)
1966 **The Twisted Thing** (Dutton)
1967 **The Body Lovers** (Dutton)
1970 **Survival . . . Zero!** (Dutton)

FILMOGRAPHY

1953 **I, the Jury** (United Artists) with Biff Elliot (as Mike Hammer), Preston Foster, Peggy Castle; directed by Harry Essex.
1955 **Kiss Me Deadly** (United Artists) with Ralph Meeker (as Mike Hammer), Albert Dekker, Paul Stewart, Marian Carr, Maxine Cooper, Cloris Leachman; directed by Robert Aldrich.
1957 **My Gun Is Quick** (United Artists) with Robert Bray (as Mike Hammer), Whitney Blake, Jan Chaney, Richard Garland; directed by Phil Victor.
1963 **The Girl Hunters** (Colorama) with Mickey Spillane (as Mike Hammer), Shirley Eaton, Lloyd Nolan; directed by Roy Rowland.

Sherlock Holmes

There are two principal theories about the life and recorded adventures of Sherlock Holmes, the world's greatest detective, and equally valid, acceptable and reasonable arguments support each of those mutually exclusive theories.

The essential difference between the theories is as basic as life and death. One camp, and by far the larger, maintains that Sherlock Holmes is a fictional character, the creation of the brilliant imagination of Arthur Conan Doyle. A much smaller coterie, but one with a more rabid and vociferous position, unequivocally states that Holmes is an actual historical entity, a real-life personage who still lives a reclusive old age in Sussex, England.

Each theory is supportable with *almost* conclusive evidence, but each leaves several questions unanswered. An objective report of the available information follows, with no conclusion offered.

In 1885, a young physician named Arthur Conan Doyle occupied a small practice in Portsmouth. The trickle of patients was so slight that he turned to writing in his abundant free time. He wrote stories on a wide range of subjects and enjoyed some success, deriving a modest supplement to his puny income.

When he began the composition of a detective novel, he wanted as his central character a new kind of sleuth, not a dull policeman or the miching type of private inquiry agent about whom he used to read. For his protagonist, Doyle took as his model Dr. Joseph Bell, his former professor at Edinburgh University.

Dr. Bell had a remarkable, almost awesome, gift for observation and inference from small details. Doyle's detective employed similar talents in his criminal investigations, developing an innovative scientific technique that was as new to real-life police work as it was to literature.

The novel, **A Study in Scarlet**, eventually was published in **Beeton's Christmas Annual** for 1887, but it received little attention and even less remuneration; all rights were sold for £ 25. When the second Sherlock Holmes novel, **The**

Artist Bruce Stark conceived of Holmes just as an entire generation sees him: as Basil Rathbone.

This silver coin issued by the Scandalous Bohemians of New Jersey is the first to honor a detective.

Sign of Four, was published more than two years later, in **Lippincott's Magazine**, it was a bit more profitable but still rather disappointing in terms of public response.

Then, in 1891, Doyle began to contribute a series about the world's first consulting detective to an ambitious new periodical, **The Strand Magazine**. The effect upon the public, beginning immediately with the first story, "A Scandal in Bohemia," was electric.

Almost overnight, Sherlock Holmes and the series of narratives about him acquired a huge and enthusiastic following in Great Britain and the United States. Interest quickly became so intense, in fact, that Doyle suddenly realized that he had lost control of his own energies to his creation. Despairing that the incessant demand for stories about Holmes was dragging him away from what he believed to be more important work, Doyle killed Holmes in 1894.

Professor Moriarty, Holmes' immensely powerful adversary, had engaged the detective in a titanic struggle at the edge of the Reichenbach waterfall in Switzerland, a battle recorded in "The Final Problem."

Public outcry was enormous, and the once-beloved Doyle was loudly criticized and became the object of vehement, even bitter, protest. He remained firm for the rest of the decade, writing about the Middle Ages, medical stories, and Napoleonic tales, while increasing his interest in and devotion to spiritualism.

As public and editorial pressure to resurrect Holmes increased, Doyle finally relented and permitted Holmes to make a posthumous appearance in **The Hound of the Baskervilles**, perhaps the best known and most read mystery novel ever written.

Soon, a new series of stories about Holmes began to run in **The Strand**, in which it was learned that Holmes had not perished after all. By the time Doyle published his last Holmes exploit in 1927 (three years before his death at the age of 71), he had produced four novels and fifty-six short stories in the immortal series that has come to be known as The Canon.

If Doyle owed a literary debt to Edgar Allan Poe's Dupin, his own effect upon succeeding mystery and detective writers has been immeasurable. Sherlock Holmes has cast a shadow over the development of the mystery genre that persists to this day: the image of the amateur detective as an eccentric loner, in the use of scientific method and abstruse knowledge supported by physical ability and energy, and in the role of a modern-day knight to whom the

Frederic Dorr Steele's illustration for "The Adventure of Wisteria Lodge" (Collier's, *Aug. 8, 1915).*

humblest may appeal for help and protection.

To the reading public, Sherlock Holmes has assumed the proportions of a mythic hero—the most familiar person, real or fictional, living or dead, in the world.

Sherlock Holmes stories are read almost eveywhere books are found; in the history of publishing, only the Bible has outsold his adventures, which have been translated into more languages than Shakespeare—or the work of any other writer.

Additionally, there have been about two hundred motion pictures, dozens of stage productions, and countless hundreds of radio and television programs devoted to the sleuth of Baker Street. More has been written about Holmes than about any character in literature. Even people who have never read a Sherlock Holmes story know his name and recognize him instantly from the objects which have come to symbolize him: the deerstalker cap, the magnifying glass and the calabash pipe.

New editions of his adventures continue to appear in many languages, each year brings new plays, motion pictures and television programs, the scholarly and critical writings about Holmes flow in an endless stream, and there are more than a hundred societies devoted to him scattered throughout the world, led by the Baker Street Irregulars in New York and the Sherlock Holmes Society in London. Thousands of distressed or admiring people in many countries each year write letters addressed to his famous lodgings at 221B Baker Street in London. To them, and to countless others, Holmes is more real, more vital, than most next-door neighbors.

Despite all the interest in his life and career, much biographical information remains unknown, the only authoritative data being those which are contained in the sixty recorded cases. Since almost every one of these tales is narrated in the first-person by Holmes' long-time friend, roommate and chronicler, we have to rely on the reports of Dr. John H. Watson for details on the life of Sherlock Holmes.

Watson has provided a wealth of information, but there are several reasons for the frequent *lacunae* encountered in the serialized biography which was published sporadically over a period of forty years.

Holmes did not come from a distinguished family and was, therefore, seldom expansive about his relatively obscure background and antecedents. Even Watson had lived with Holmes for several years before he learned of the existence of an older brother who lived not three miles away from their rooms in Baker Street.

Furthermore, Holmes placed emphasis upon the science of deduction rather than personal glory through publicity. He often accepted anonymity, and reproached Watson on more than one occasion for his melodramatic treatment of a case, rather than a straight-forward reporting of his purely logical and scientific methodology.

Too, Watson was a man of certain professional reticence. A physician, he recognized the value of discretion and tact, deliberately obfuscating many details of Holmes' career in the published narratives in order to prevent the possibility of public scandal.

Just as information remains elusive in the case of many other famous historical characters, from William Shakespeare to Cagliostro to Howard Hughes, some biographical tidbits remain obscure in the following profile of the world's greatest crimefighter. It is a rough outline—nothing more.

Sherlock Holmes was born on January 6, 1854, at the modest family holding of Mycroft, in the North Riding of Yorkshire, England. His parents were Siger Holmes, a somewhat eccentric gentleman farmer, and Violet, the daughter of Sir Edward Sherrinford, the naturalist and explorer.

On his mother's side, Sherlock was descended from the well-known Vernet family of French painters, a point in which Holmes took some pride. "Art in the blood is liable to take the strangest forms," he once observed, and regarded himself as an artist in his profession.

Sherlock was the younger of the two sons known to have been born to Siger and Violet Holmes, Mycroft being seven years older. (There is some speculation that there were three sons, the oldest of whom was named Sherrinford, but both Holmes and Watson are reticent about him, if indeed he existed.)

Little is known of Sherlock's early years. Siger Holmes was a man of parts who had lived in India until illness and injuries forced him home to England. The most concrete remark that may be made of these youthful years is that Sherlock's artistic training began then, most notably in the field of music. In time, he came to be a noted amateur music historian and author of a "Monograph on the Polyphonic Motets of Lassus," as well as a first-rate performer on the violin, one of the few forms of relaxation he allowed himself in later years.

There is no mention of formal schooling until his late teens, and the probability is that his father arranged private tutoring for the obviously gifted young Mycroft and Sherlock. Which university Holmes attended is a subject of some debate, but it is believed that he studied at either Oxford or Cambridge, and possibly both.

Holmes once remarked upon his eccentric course of studies, which may have been a reaction against the pursuit of some unattractive career which his father had selected for him. Indications point to his having left the university without a degree.

While attending school, Holmes appears to have shown the streak of reserve and the asocial nature that was to dominate his relationships the rest of his life. By his own account, he held himself aloof from his fellow students and had few friends. In all likelihood, he was considered bookish, and something of a queer duck.

He engaged in, and excelled at, several sports, but they were individual, not team, sports—boxing and fencing, primarily. The strong, stubborn, individualistic streak first emerged during these college days, never again to disappear.

This is not to say that Holmes had no friends at all, however. One of the friends he made at this time proved important in his career—a turning point in his perception of himself and his future role in society. This fellow student was Victor Trevor, the young son of James Trevor, a Justice of the Peace in Donnithorpe, Norfolk.

Holmes had already begun to develop the system of observation and inference that later allowed him to revolutionize the field of criminal investigation, but had considered it merely a hobby. His revelation that it might have a practical use, and that his talents could lie in the area of criminal detection, was suggested by James Trevor, whose secret past as a convict was deduced by Holmes from certain details, causing him to faint dead away. These deductions were the prelude to a Trevor family tragedy, a decent man's life ending because of the past. The experience permanently altered Holmes' own life.

Gillette wrote the play Sherlock Holmes *and starred in it himself. This portrait is one of a series of theatrical celebrities (circa 1902).*

He left the university and came to London to pursue new studies for a profession which he intended to create: consulting detective. It seems probable that this decision caused a permanent break with his equally strong-minded father; little more is heard of his parents after his move to London.

Taking rooms in Montague Street, around the corner from the British Museum, he studied in earnest all the fields in which he believed he would require knowledge—criminal history, law and sensational literature at the museum; anatomy, biology and chemistry (at which he was soon expert) at the University of London and St. Bartholomew's Hospital; and crime and contemporary urban life in the streets of London, from the affluent opulence of the West End to the dark violence of the East End ghettoes.

The long, hard hours of study were rewarded with little financial success when he opened his practice in 1877. His first known case occurred

William Gillette, a leading dramatic actor on the American stage, played Holmes for thirty years.

that year when he assumed the guise of a Corporal Holmes of the 19th North Yorkshires regiment to uncover a cheating scandal in the British Rifle Association.

More significantly, two years later Holmes enjoyed his first major success when, at the end of 1879, another former classmate, the aristocratic Reginald Musgrave, consulted him professionally. Holmes was able to solve the disappearance and murder of a family retainer—a crime that ultimately led to the discovery of a national treasure. With this case, conducted in an affluent stratum of society, Holmes' name began to circulate as a proficient solver of mysteries.

But then, on the heels of his triumph, Holmes left England for a year, going to America in the autumn of 1879 as a member of the Abbott Touring Company, performing Shakespearean tragedy and comedy across much of the United States.

Why Holmes chose to leave the country just as he had begun to be noticed in his profession is still a mystery. Perhaps the long period of overworking with little reward had taken its toll, making a change necessary. Perhaps it was no more than his natural eccentricity. Whatever the reason, it cannot be said that the American experience was without value for him. It allowed him to perfect the vital makeup and acting skills that were of inestimable value to him later in his career, and he learned a great deal about detection techniques that differed from those in England. Also, he acquired a lifelong interest in and affection for people and things native to the United States.

When Holmes returned to London, his practice again cold, he filled his leisure time with further study, but now he was able to solve cases even more quickly, and with less difficulty, than ever before. A few Scotland Yarders began to take notice of the sharp-eyed young amateur sleuth.

Larger quarters were needed by the end of 1880 for his growing practice, but he could not yet afford them on his modest income. What the situation required was an amiable yet unobtrusive roommate with whom Holmes could share expenses.

On New Year's Day, 1881, Holmes is working in the pathology lab at Bart's, attempting to develop a reliable test for bloodstains, when a medical acquaintance named Stamford comes to see him. In tow is another young doctor—a convalescent veteran of the Second Afghan War and the Army Medical Department named John H. Watson.

Dr. Watson is living meagerly on a half-pay wound pension and is also in search of lodgings he can share with someone else. Young Stamford effects an introduction, and Holmes sets the tone for their future life together with his opening remark, telling the astonished Watson, "You have been in Afghanistan, I perceive."

Watson was the only surviving member of his family, an older brother having dissipated the family inheritance and died insolvent. Watson had received his medical degree in 1878 from the University of London at an early age (born in 1852, he was two years Holmes' senior) and then joined the army medical corps.

This decision came as somewhat of a surprise to those who knew him because Watson's medical career had had an unusually promising beginning. There is reason to conjecture that the basis of his startling decision had something to do with a scandal involving women.

Sent to India with the Fifth Northumberland Fusiliers, Watson was reassigned to the Berkshires and was with them when they entered enemy territory, and he was with them, too, at "the fatal battle of Maiwand" on July 27, 1880—one of the worst defeats in British military history. The Berkshires were badly routed, and Watson himself suffered grave injuries before being taken from the battlefield.

Before he had recovered from his wounds, enteric fever had set in and he came close to death before being invalided out of the army and sent home in extremely poor condition to live on his small pension. By the end of 1880, Watson found himself growing increasingly disgusted at what he considered to be a cheap, useless, idle life in London—a self-perception which led to his meeting with Sherlock Holmes and agreeing to share rooms at 221B Baker Street, eventually to be the most famous address in the world.

(Nearly a century later, the rooms in Baker Street have taken on a dreamlike quality to many who view them in retrospect as an imaginary but magical shrine. In fact, they were a fairly typical London flat, reasonably modern for their time, and well-situated in a fashionable district of West London near Hyde Park and the Strand.)

The house was owned by Martha Hudson, a domestically inclined widow in her thirties who must have been frequently irked by her eccentric and occasionally dangerous boarder. Holmes' personality had sufficient force, however, to win her over. In time, Mrs. Hudson came to be as much an assistant as a housekeeper, and the entire house became the preserve of the detective when he required it.

The rooms shared by Holmes and Watson were on the second floor, up a staircase of seventeen steps, and each had his own bedroom. They shared a large sitting room with a bow window fronting onto Baker Street. The central feature of the room was a coal-burning fireplace, the mantle of which was cluttered with relics of

More than 100 actors have portrayed Sherlock Holmes, but few have resembled the great sleuth more than John Barrymore, who opposes Moriarty (Gustav von Seyffertitz) in a 1922 silent.

Holmes' cases, dottles of the day's pipes set out to dry for the next morning's first smoke, and Holmes' unanswered correspondence affixed to the mantlepiece by a jacknife.

Both men's personalities were in evidence in the room, but Holmes' predominated, from the chemical apparatus in one corner to the stacks of unfiled documents in confusion in another. Of the clutter, Watson once complained that criminal relics were likely to turn up in the butter dish during breakfast.

If the room seemed eccentric, it was banality itself when compared with Holmes—a man who seemed more unaware of convention than in defiance of it. He kept his cigars in a coal scuttle and his pipe tobacco in a Persian slipper. His filing system, the life blood of his informational resources, was rarely kept up and material piled higher and higher in total disarray, yet Holmes refused to discard a single scrap.

Though fit to the point of athleticism, despite taking no exercise for its own sake, Holmes tended toward long periods of lethargy punctuated by fits of energy, during which times he rose early and retired late, ran in and out at all hours, skipped meals—behaving generally in ways that drove both his housekeeper and roommate to distraction.

Fearing for Holmes' health during these periods of frenetic energy, Watson came to learn that it was the periods of inactivity which presented greater danger to the man he once described as "the best and wisest man whom I have ever known."

Boredom was a powerful enemy, and to help combat it Holmes sought relief with cocaine. By the mid-1880s, Holmes was injecting a seven-percent solution of cocaine into his veins as often as three times a day.

"My mind is like a racing engine," he once remarked, "tearing itself to pieces because it is not connected up with the work for which it was built."

Although he is an excellent musician, the violin is no more than an occasional recreation for Holmes. It never absorbs his full attention. He once flustered the long-suffering Mrs. Hudson by taking indoor target practice, pocking the wall with bullet holes to form the initials "VR" (a patriotic tribute to the queen, Victoria Regina).

Women held little interest for him. Had he wished, he would quite likely have been successful with them. Physically, he would surely have been interesting and attractive enough. Over six feet tall, both slender and muscular, he has a thin, hawk-like nose and sharp, piercing eyes. His treatment of the women who came to him as clients was unfailingly civil and frequently charming and chivalrous, demonstrating an understanding of their nature and an ability to win their confidence and put them at ease.

Not a misogynist, Holmes nevertheless avoids the subject of tender emotions. "Love is an emotional thing," he told the womanizing and incredulous Watson early in their friendship, "and whatever is emotional is opposed to that cold, true reason which I place above all things. I should never marry myself, lest I bias my judgment."

Holmes never did marry, and late in his career he remarked that he had never loved. Whether or not this is true is highly suspect. He would however, have proven to be a difficult husband, as well as an improbable one.

Watson was quickly drawn to Holmes and a mutual friendship developed rapidly. When they met, and even when they agreed to share rooms, Watson did not know how Holmes earned a living, and he was hesitant to inquire lest he be regarded as an idle snoop.

The revelation comes one morning as Watson criticizes a magazine article on deductive reasoning, only to find that the remarkable claims it makes for the writer's powers were penned by none other than his roommate, Sherlock Holmes.

Before the morning is out, Watson finds himself accompanying Holmes to the scene of a murder. It is the first of many such experiences for him. His tastes in life often border upon the bohemian and bizarre, and the investigation of a crime provides a thrilling scene for Watson. And Holmes finds him a valuable companion. In addition to being staunch and brave, Watson has another virtue in the detective's eyes that makes his presence desirable.

"It may be that you are not yourself luminous," he tells Watson, "but you are a conductor of light. Some people without possessing genius have a remarkable power of stimulating it."

If Holmes himself has a professional genius, he feels it is an infinite capacity for taking pains. A pioneer in systematizing a myriad of diverse influences, specialized fields of knowledge, and investigative procedures into the new science of detection, Holmes concentrates upon small details, claiming that they are the keys that allow him to penetrate a mystery in its entirety. His method, he tells Watson, is founded upon the observance of trifles, and he has trained himself to notice what others overlook.

(Even today, with a hundred years of hindsight, his powers in the field of criminal detection seem uncanny. He once smelled out a crime by noting the depth to which a sprig of parsley had sunk into butter on a hot day. Observation without knowledge, without intelligence and without deduction is quite useless.)

In addition to his self-training in such conventional fields as chemistry and anatomy, Holmes interested himself in more esoteric subjects, including graphology and comparative psychology (commonplace today, but rare in Victorian England). Studies in typically criminological areas, such as the tracing of footprints, were supplemented with such minutiae as the differentiation of typewriters, bicycle tire impressions, perfumes, newspaper types and the ashes of various tobaccos.

(The monographs Holmes wrote on many of these abstruse subjects helped lay the foundations for the systems of classification later developed by Scotland Yard, the French Sûreté, and the American Federal Bureau of Investigation. To this day, Holmes' essays on the ashes of 143 different kinds of tobacco, the dog in detective work, the influence of trades on the human hand, and the analysis of 160 codes and ciphers are regarded as the cornerstone works in their fields.)

Armed with knowledge in the broadest imaginable spectrum of studies, an enormous capacity for the observation of detail, and virtually infinite patience, the beginning of a case for Holmes is invariably the accumulation of data.

"It is a capital mistake to theorize before one has data," he asserts, and it is only after he has gathered all available physical evidence that he begins to interpret and theorize. Although he is not reluctant to race to the scene of a crime to gather information, paying no attention to the time or the weather, he is often able to solve a case without leaving his armchair at Baker Street.

Of invaluable assistance to him is his vast knowledge of the history of crime; his hours of reading about it in the British Museum pay off again and again.

"As a rule," he remarks with satisfaction, "when I have heard some slight indication of the course of events, I am able to guide myself by the thousands of other similar cases which occur to my memory." As a result, few cases baffle

A scene from "The Musgrave Ritual" by Steele, the greatest American illustrator of Holmes.

him for long, and almost none permanently withstand his scrutiny and investigation. If all else fails, he even turns to the process of elimination.

"It is an old maxim of mine," he observes, "that when you have excluded the impossible, whatever remains, however improbable, must be the truth."

Having mastered his studies and developed his own methodology, Sherlock Holmes' career underwent tremendous growth in the 1880s. It seemed that the new lodgings, and his new friend and chronicler of his adventures, were the necessary lure for attracting a legion of clients to his door.

With his professional services increasingly in demand, more and more of his time was spent in the streets and alleys of London, where he became a familiar figure to Scotland Yard inspectors, foot patrolmen and London journalists. While Holmes appreciated and conformed to the rigid dress codes in Victorian society, he frequently indulged himself in an eccentric attire that made him conspicuous to police and criminals alike; the Inverness cloak and double-billed deerstalker cap (along with the calabash pipe and magnifying glass) have become the universally-recognized symbols of the world's greatest detective.

In retrospect, Holmes' willingness to make himself conspicuous may seem surprising at first glance, but it was undoubtedly carefully calculated. The familiar presence of Sherlock Holmes on the streets of London may have helped to inhibit some of the predatory members of the population. Holmes himself acknowledged his influence by admitting that he disliked leaving the country because it aroused an undesirable excitement in the criminal class.

Holmes had a predilection for the unusual and bizarre in his work. Not all his cases were remunerative, but he received substantial fees for some investigations, allowing him the economic freedom to pursue others more to his taste, even where no monetary reward could be expected.

With clients ranging from the humblest to the most aristocratic, coming from every part of England and often from other countries, the 1880s provided Holmes with many of his most celebrated cases: "The Speckled Band," in which Holmes is able to prevent the murder of a young lady by her stepfather, who employs the most horrible method for his attempt; "The Adventure of the Second Stain," Holmes' first of many excursions into the exciting, rarefied and dangerous world of espionage and British security; "The Red-Headed League," ostensibly one of the most *outré* cases in his experience; and many other strange, difficult, famous, perilous and successful investigations.

For Watson these were exciting years as well. Living in a world he had scarcely known existed, he was privileged to live with and assist one of the most fascinating personalities in England. He had no medical practice, the financial urgency having disappeared; he was increasingly drawn instead to literary pursuits.

Evidence indicates that Watson first tried his hand at writing while he was recuperating in the early 1880s. Evidence also indicates that he enjoyed little success at this time. His first efforts were adventure stories, sometimes based on his experiences in India and Afghanistan, but they had little luck with publishers.

He finally turned to his friend and roommate as a subject, producing an account of the first case in which they were associated, calling it **A Study in Scarlet**. Watson was able to prevail upon his friend Arthur Conan Doyle, another struggling young physician and writer, to help him place it, which he eventually did, and it appeared in the **Beeton's Christmas Annual** for 1887, rapidly plummeting into obscurity.

That year was perhaps the single most significant one in the careers of both Holmes and Watson, who was disappointed, but not disheartened, by the failure of his story to catch the imagination of the public. Never losing his ability to be surprised by his friend, Watson raised a figurative eyebrow when his apparently misogynic roommate was suddenly touched by a woman.

In May 1887, the King of Bohemia's former mistress, the beautiful American opera singer Irene Adler, threatens him with a scandal. Holmes is enlisted to extricate him. The scandal is averted, to the permanent gratitude of British royalty, but only by the forebearance of the remarkable Miss Adler, who succeeds with apparent ease in circumventing Holmes' maneuvers. At the conclusion of the case, she sends him a photograph of herself in lieu of the compromising documents—a half-sincere, half-mocking tribute to the great detective's attentions.

The experience with Irene Adler, whom he calls "the daintiest thing under a bonnet on this planet," makes a lasting impression on Holmes. From that case until today, she has been referred to by him as *The* Woman. It is altogether possible that this respect and admiration for Irene Adler have nothing to do with romance. Seldom bested, and never before by a woman, Holmes' regard for the lovely lady may be purely intellectual, but the debonair Watson was never able to believe this.

In that same year, Holmes makes a fateful discovery—one that is to haunt his every moment for years. Having worked among the criminal underworld of London for nearly a decade, he has built up a widespread and effective network of informants whose eyes and ears have become extensions of his own.

Piecing together rumors and murmurings, hints and innuendoes, half-seen truths and infinitesimal scraps of information, Holmes becomes convinced that much of the crime in London, and most of that which has remained undetected or unpunished, is the work of a single brain. Before the conclusion of that year, he has succeeded in identifying that fiendish mind—the Napoleon of Crime, Professor James Moriarty.

If Holmes was the most remarkable man of his era, Moriarty was hardly a hairsbreadth behind. In many ways, the two men, destined to be bitter adversaries, were extraordinarily similar.

Moriarty also came from an undistinguished family, and also had a quickly recognized intellect of exceptional degree. He had two brothers. The youngest became an obscure stationmaster in the west of England. The oldest served his country as a military officer and rose to the rank of colonel. Curiously, both were also named James.

The middle James pursued a formal education leading to a promising career in mathematics; his treatises on the binomial theorem and **The Dynamics of an Asteroid** were celebrated in their day. By virtue of his scholarly gifts, the young professor won a Chair in Mathematics at a small university.

It was at this point, at the birth of a future in mathematics that might have rivaled Rutherford and perhaps challenged Einstein, that a flaw in Professor Moriarty's character came to the surface.

A scandal in the university town began to develop, the nature of which is still something of a mystery. Before rumors could become certain disclosures, Moriarty resigned his Chair and left the town, moving to London.

Under the false guise of an army coach for prospective officer cadets, Moriarty set up as a criminal consultant, offering his acute mind for hire in the planning of criminal acts.

By the mid-1880s, he was no longer the consultant of the criminal classes, but their master, "the organizer of half that is evil and nearly all that is undetected in this great city," as Holmes later describes him. He was also, according to Holmes, "a genius, a philosopher, an abstract thinker," and he ruled with an iron hand and a total lack of mercy.

At his right hand was Sebastian Moran, "the second most dangerous man in London," a cold and cruelly capable former army colonel who served as Moriarty's chief of staff, seeing to it that his instructions were ruthlessly carried out.

Clearly, with Holmes and Moriarty each having risen so quickly to the apex of their professions, and each as infallible as it is possible for human beings to be, a collision was inevitable.

In January 1888, Holmes is engaged in one of his greatest cases, later chronicled by Watson as **The Valley of Fear**. In addition to being a virtuoso performance and a dazzling display of deductive powers, the case is the first in which Holmes and Moriarty cross swords directly and consciously.

Love enters Watson's life in September of that year when a young lady named Mary Morstan seeks Holmes' help in a case that has every element of a tale from the Arabian Nights—disappearance, bizarre murder, beautiful girl in distress, lost Indian treasure, secret society.

For Watson, the beautiful client is the prime consideration in the case. As it comes to a close, he proposes marriage to her and is accepted. They are married the following spring and he leaves Holmes, setting up a medical practice in Paddington.

Holmes feels somewhat disappointed at the turn of events. Although financial considerations no longer require him to have a roommate, he has become accustomed to working with and thinking aloud to Watson, and the separation comes as something of a blow to him. Still, all is not lost with the geographical split; Watson continues to accompany Holmes on investigations as often as his practice and his wife permit.

Watson plays an important role in the other major case of September 1888, later published as **The Hound of the Baskervilles**. The case involves an ancient curse on an old Devonshire family and the threat of its extinction with the death of its last scion, Sir Henry Baskerville. Only Holmes' brilliance and unswerving disbelief in the supernatural avert disaster at the hands of one of the most imaginative and insidious adversaries he was ever to encounter.

Before the end of the signal year of 1888, Holmes is involved in one more sensational case—the detection and apprehension of the infamous Jack the Ripper.

At least five horrible murders of prostitutes in the crime-ridden streets of London's Whitechapel district have shocked and terrorized the entire city to a degree unmatched before or since. The police seem helpless against the cunning of the fiendish, faceless killer whose presence in the midnight streets empties entire districts of the frightened metropolis night after night in the summer and autumn of 1888.

Apparently for reasons of discretion, Watson never chronicles this grisly case. It was whispered that scandal and repercussions would spread widely if the Harlot Killer's true identity were disclosed to the public. (The true facts in the case have not been revealed to this day, and the official police position is that the case remains unsolved. No one seems to know who the Ripper was.)

The culprit may have been Montague Druitt,

the deranged solicitor whose body was pulled from the Thames soon after the murders ceased. It may have been the secret behind the sudden and still unexplained disappearance of Scotland Yard Inspector Athelney Jones, who had been associated with Holmes earlier in 1888 on the case of **The Sign of Four**. Some have suggested it was the aberrant Duke of Clarence, the Prince of Wales' son and heir apparent to the throne.

Whatever the identity of Jack the Ripper, if Watson knew he made no public verification of the fact, and he quite likely took his secret to the grave with him.

Although other notable cases required his attention during the next two-and-a-half years, Holmes devoted most of his energy to the campaign against Moriarty.

The two great opponents constantly tested each other's strengths and weaknesses, probing for an advantage, however slight, that could be pursued and expanded. It is a tribute to Holmes' abilities that he was able to gain the upper hand after a time, though the process was protracted and arduous, and not without its setbacks.

As early as 1887, he has found a weak link in Moriarty's organization. A man known as Porlock, who fears the professor too much to quit his gang, cooperates with Holmes secretly to forestall the criminal mastermind's nefarious plans. Death would be inevitable were he discovered by Moriarty, and Holmes keeps his identity a tightly guarded secret (a secret that remains unpenetrated to this day).

Holmes' early campaign has its frustrations. He has little respect for many Scotland Yarders, but even those in whom he has some confidence refuse to believe that Moriarty is a criminal at all, much less the nineteenth-century British equivalent of the Godfather. They begin to feel that Holmes has developed a monomania on the subject which almost amounts to persecution of a seemingly harmless pedagogue.

But, as time passes, Holmes carefully assembles his bits of evidence until the mosaic is so well constructed that they have no alternative but to accept Moriarty's status, though the villain has so carefully concealed his tracks that the possibility of prosecution and conviction is nil.

Nonetheless, Scotland Yard now makes officers available to Holmes so that a wide net can be cast to capture hard evidence as well as the arch-villain's minions—not significant themselves, but incommoding to Moriarty's plans. It is remarkable to note that Holmes orchestrates these efforts without permitting the public to notice even the merest ripple.

The contest between Holmes and Moriarty enters its penultimate stage during the first months of 1891, and by April Holmes has pulled the noose so tightly around Moriarty's neck that the Napoleon of Crime finally confronts Holmes in person—the first, though not the last, time they meet. Moriarty acknowledges Holmes' success to that point.

"Now, at the close of April," he says, "I find myself placed in such a position through your continual persecution that I am in positive danger of losing my liberty. The situation is becoming an impossible one."

It is even more perilous than Moriarty imagines. Holmes' case against him is almost complete, and he has merely to step back and let the police swoop down on him and his organization, destroying it forever. Moriarty's sole hope lies in Holmes' death. The confrontation ends with a declaration of total war between the two.

Moriarty wastes little time in making several attempts against the life of the detective, who realizes the quality of his foe and leaves with Watson on a trip away from England and the gang of cutthroats. Holmes and Watson are in Strasbourg when a telegram arrives to tell them that the police dragnet has failed to ensnare Moriarty, that he has escaped, and that his whereabouts are unknown.

Holmes knows that the arch-criminal will be in pursuit, revenge in his heart, and he does not have long to wait. On May 4, the evil professor and Holmes again confront each other, this time at the edge of the great Reichenbach Falls in the mountains high above the village of Meiringen.

Watson has been cleverly lured away, and Moriarty is now also unaccompanied. Holmes writes a farewell note to his friend. Then the two intellectual giants, the titans who embody the essence of Good and Evil, engage in a physical, hand-to-hand, one-to-one struggle on the slippery and treacherous footpath above the waterfall's roaring chasm.

When Watson returns, neither detective nor criminal remains. The Swiss authorities drag the river, but neither body is found. The loyal doctor returns to London with a heavy heart, and he finds solace only in writing about more of the strange mysteries which his brilliant friend had solved. The pain of his great loss has only begun to

A contemplative Rathbone is the quintessential Sherlock Holmes. Formerly typecast as a villain, he was never able to shake the Holmes image.

diminish when a new one strikes him as cruelly; his lovely wife Mary dies.

To take his mind away from his grief, Watson continues to write prolifically, and to interest himself in bizarre murder cases. It is on April 5, 1894, nearly three years after the final battle between Holmes and Moriarty, that Watson visits the scene of an inexplicable murder. A minor accident with an old bookseller occurs—the preoccupied Watson knocks into him and he follows Watson to his nearby home, hoping to sell him a book.

The old bookseller gains access to Watson's room and draws his attention to a gap on a bookshelf. When the harried doctor turns around again, Sherlock Holmes stands before him. For the only time in his life, Watson faints.

When he finally comes around, the now-undisguised Holmes tells him a remarkable story. Incredibly, he had survived the fight with Moriarty, who had plummeted to his doom into the raging cauldron below their arena. There had been a witness to the struggle, however—Moriarty's formidable

Rathbone with Nigel Bruce, who played Dr. Watson in all fourteen films (two for Fox, twelve for Universal) that a recent study showed to be the most popular film series on television.

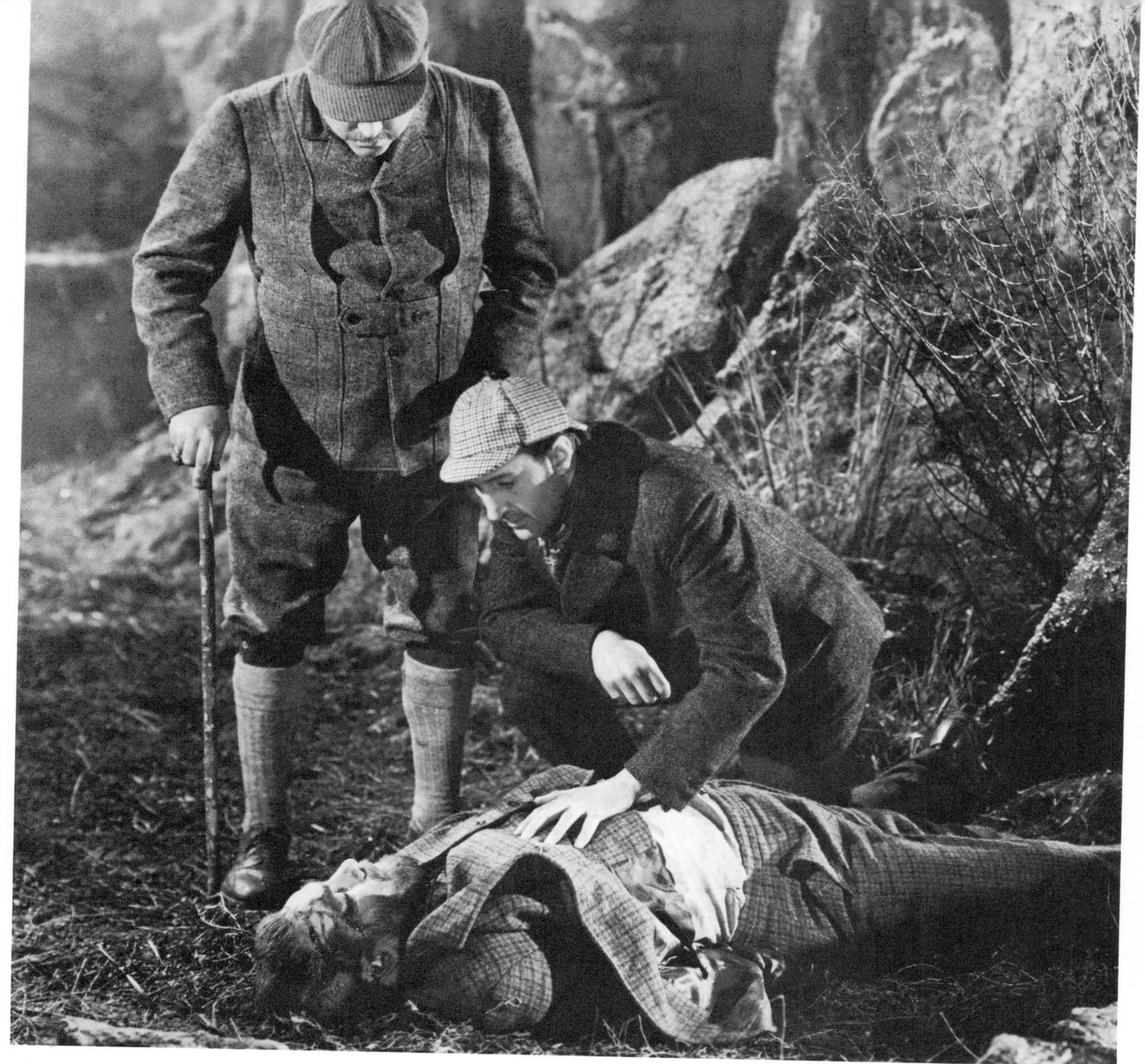

The first Rathbone/Bruce film, The Hound of the Baskervilles, *is the best of all Sherlock Holmes motion pictures and the first to have been properly set in Victorian costume and era.*

henchman, Colonel Sebastian Moran, who had ample reasons for wanting to see Holmes dead.

Holmes eluded him. A stubborn and implacable hunter, Moran had gained a considerable reputation as a fearless and deadly tracker of tigers in India, but Holmes managed to throw him off the trail within a week, escaping to Italy. Instead of returning to England to be among his friends and allies, Holmes disappeared.

Taking the name of a Norwegian explorer, Sigerson, Holmes began a long journey, spending two years in Tibet, meeting the head lama in Lhassa, and traveling to Persia, Arabia and the Sudan before settling for a while in Montpensier, France, where he engaged in chemical research for some weeks before returning to London. In all this time, only his brother Mycroft was aware that Sherlock Holmes still lived.

While it is possible that Holmes forsook his profession during these years, as he claims, it is more likely that he was, in fact, engaged in anonymous work for foreign policy interests in Whitehall; Holmes admits that he wrote a report on his trip to Khartoum (during the exceedingly dangerous period between Gordon's defeat and Kitchener's vengeance) for Whitehall. That single report may have been only the tip of the iceberg, but he tells nothing more to Watson.

Now, back in London, Holmes is not yet out of danger. Still at large, Moran knew of Holmes' return to London and Baker Street even before Watson did. While Moran is preparing his welcome, Holmes is laying a trap for the last vestige of the heinous Moriarty gang.

Taking watch in a dark and deserted house opposite Holmes' rooms, they wait while the faithful, long-suffering Mrs. Hudson crouches on the floor, once every quarter-hour turning slightly a bust of Holmes that throws his image upon the drawn windowshade.

The long vigil pays off when Moran creeps into the house and, using a powerful air rifle, fires a bullet through the bust's head. Within moments, the deceived ex-soldier is subdued by the police, who have lain in waiting for Holmes' signal.

Having disposed of his last threat, Holmes resumed practice and clients came unceasingly to the door of 221B. At the height of his powers, he had an almost unbroken string of successes with enough lucrative fees to banish forever the spare and insecure existence that marked the past.

Watson sold his medical practice and moved again into the rooms in Baker Street as conditions virtually duplicated their days together in the 1880s.

Though Holmes continued his endless battle against crime, he had lost some of his zest for the struggle with the passing of Moriarty; no mastermind engaged his, and no foe satisfactorily challenged his resources. Fortunately, a different realm presented itself, and Holmes became immersed in the increasingly complex world of espionage and counterintelligence work.

The 1890s had begun to see the change in international relations which ultimately led to World War I. As Great Britain began to respond to the challenge of the hostile ambitions of an industrial and militaristic Germany led by the aggressive Kaiser Wilhelm II, Mycroft Holmes assumed an importance in government unprecedented in British constitutional history. There were times, in fact, when he *was* the British government.

Mycroft had first come to Watson's attention in 1888 in a case he later chronicled as "The Adventure of the Greek Interpreter." Remarkably unlike his brother, Mycroft is obese and inactive, moving only when it is unavoidable, and then only in a set routine from his rooms in Pall Mall to his office in Whitehall to his club, The Diogenes. This eccentric club for eccentric men was created for the asocial—members are forbidden to notice other members, and speaking aloud can be punished by expulsion. Peculiar but brilliant, Mycroft is, according to Sherlock Holmes, his superior in intellectual powers and deductive reasoning, though so lethargic that he almost never troubles to bestir himself.

By virtue of an ability to absorb and integrate diverse chains of information, Mycroft had made himself indispensable; he was the focal point where different policies and problems could be brought together for a rational assessment. By the middle of the 1890s, he was the brain of the Foreign Office, the man who created policy and strategy for Her Majesty's Government, and marshaled the political, economic and military resources of the nation and empire to support them. He was also the motivating element of the buregoning British intelligence organization, more than one of whose attributes Mycroft had appropriated from Moriarty's own system of covert organization.

As espionage operations reached new heights in England, Mycroft was able to enlist the talents of one of the nation's most brilliant patriots—his brother Sherlock, who now divided his time between intelligence activities and crimefighting.

Although the 1890s were busy years for him, Sherlock Holmes was a changed man since his return from abroad. He had lost some of the zest for his detective work, his eccentricities were less pronounced, he was more introspective, and he had given up the occasional (and sometimes heavy) use of cocaine as a relief from boredom. He was financially secure, his reputation placed him above any other, and he was admired and respected by Scotland Yard, which was now happy to place its resources at his disposal when he required them. He was, in short, a total success, and the fact seemed to bore him. The British criminal, he told Watson, was a poor and uninspiring sort since Moriarty departed the scene.

As the turn of the century approached, Holmes began to find limits to his health and energy, though he was only nearing middle age. In 1897 he had worked himself close to the point of a breakdown and he required a long recuperation period on a vacation in Cornwall. It was clear that the partnership's active era was drawing to a close.

Watson, growing older, turned more domestic and decided to remarry in 1903, leaving his

Stewart Granger played an unconvincing Holmes in a 1972 television movie. The film's credibility was further damaged by a ferocious hound whose tail wagged persistently.

friend again to take rooms in Queen Anne Street and start a new medical practice in the fashionable Harley Street area with the abundant funds earned from his popular narratives.

The decision of his friend influenced Holmes to retire, though he was only forty-nine and still vigorous. After twenty-seven years in practice he longed to leave the smog-filled streets of London for the freshness of the English countryside, where he would be free to pursue other interests than crime.

He immersed himself more in music, both as an amateur performer and as a musicologist and historian, in philosophy (he has always been a pessimist, influenced by Winwood Reade and others of the school), and in beekeeping. By the end of 1903, Holmes had moved to a small farm in Sussex, near Eastbourne.

Holmes did not re-emerge until 1912. It had become obvious to Mycroft and others in the government that the most sensitive British military and foreign policy secrets were finding their way to Berlin and the Wilhelmstrasse. Despite the best efforts of the secret service, no inroads were made into the network of German agents operating in England.

Sherlock Holmes accepted the case and, at the beginning of August 1914, on the eve of World War I, he sprung the trap on the German mastermind, Freiherr Von Bork, and his agents, who spent the war years in a British prison.

Holmes devoted his entire energies to intelligence activities for the duration of the war, and Watson came out of retirement to serve as a doctor for the same period. Both survived the conflict.

Watson spent the years between the end of the war and his death in 1930 engaged in gardening and publishing further accounts of his friend's endlessly fascinating career.

Holmes returned to his small Sussex farm keeping bees and working on his *magnum opus,* **The Whole Art of Detection,** which seems at last to be nearing completion. Although he is well past one hundred years old (having learned secrets of long life while in the Tibetan monastery), it is not unreasonable to believe that Sherlock Holmes will continue to live—for a very long time.

SIR ARTHUR CONAN DOYLE (1859-1930) Born in Edinburgh, Scotland, he received his medical degree from the University of Edinburgh in 1885. He had already written several stories to help pay his way through school. He opened a medical practice, which was unsuccessful, and used his ample spare time to write prodigious quantities of fiction. Although largely remembered for his Sherlock Holmes stories today, he regarded his historical novels of chief importance, most notably **Micah Clarke** (1889) and **The White Company** (1891). Among his most popular science fiction are the tales about Professor Challenger, particularly **The Lost World** (1912) and **The Poison Belt** (1913). Knighted for his efforts to present Great Britain's cause to Europe with regard to the Boer War, he wrote the definitive study of that war and one of the best studies of World War I, a highly regarded multi-volume history. Other major accomplishments include the introduction of skiing to Switzerland, the successful attempts to free several unjustly convicted men from prison, the campaign to convince the British Army in World War I to use steel helmets and tanks, and the creation of the 200,000-member Volunteer Force. He devoted most of his later life to spiritualism, trying to convince the world to share his unshakable beliefs.

BIBLIOGRAPHY

1890 **A Study in Scarlet** (Lippincott; published in 1888 by Ward, Lock, London)
1891 **The Sign of the Four** (Collier; published in 1890 by Spencer Blacket, London)
1892 **The Adventures of Sherlock Holmes** (Harper)
1894 **The Memoirs of Sherlock Holmes** (Harper)
1902 **The Hound of the Baskervilles** (McClure, Phillips)
1905 **The Return of Sherlock Holmes** (McClure, Phillips)
1915 **The Valley of Fear** (Doran)
1917 **His Last Bow** (Doran)
1927 **The Case Book of Sherlock Holmes** (Doran)

FILMOGRAPHY

1929 **The Return of Sherlock Holmes** (Paramount) with Clive Brook (as Holmes), H. Reeves-Smith, Harry T. Morey; directed by Basil Dean.
1930 **Sherlock Holmes' Fatal Hour** (Twickenham; British title: **The Sleeping Cardinal**) with Arthur Wontner (as Holmes), Ian Fleming, Phillip Hewland, Leslie Perrins; directed by Leslie S. Hiscott.
1931 **The Speckled Band** (British and Dominions Studios) with Raymond Massey (as Holmes), Athole Stewart, Lyn Harding; directed by Jack Raymond.
1932 **The Hound of the Baskervilles** (Gainsborough) with Robert Rendel (as Holmes), Frederick Lloyd, Heather Angel; directed by V. Gareth Gundrey.
1932 **Sherlock Holmes** (Fox) with Clive Brook, Reginald Owen, Ernest Torrence, Miriam Jordan; directed by William K. Howard.
1932 **The Missing Rembrandt** (Twickenham) with Arthur Wontner, Ian Fleming, Francis L. Sullivan, Miles Mander; directed by Leslie S. Hiscott.
1932 **The Sign of Four** (World Wide) with Arthur Wontner, Ian Hunter, Isla Bevan, Ben Soutten; directed by Graham Cutts.
1933 **A Study in Scarlet** (World Wide) with Reginald Owen (as Holmes), Warburton Gamble, Alan Mowbray, Anna May Wong; directed by Edwin L. Marin.
1935 **The Triumph of Sherlock Holmes** (Real Art) with Arthur Wontner, Ian Fleming, Lyn Harding, Leslie Perrins, Jane Carr; directed by Leslie S. Hiscott.
1937 **Murder at the Baskervilles** (Twickenham; British title: **Silver Blaze**) with Arthur Wontner, Ian Fleming, Lyn Harding; directed by Thomas Bentley.

1939 **The Hound of the Baskervilles** (Twentieth Century-Fox) with Basil Rathbone (as Holmes), Richard Greene, Nigel Bruce, Wendy Barrie, Morton Lowry, Lionel Atwill, John Carradine; directed by Sidney Lanfield.

1939 **The Adventures of Sherlock Holmes** (Twentieth Century-Fox) with Basil Rathbone, Nigel Bruce, Ida Lupino, Alan Marshal, George Zucco, Terry Kilburn; directed by Alfred Werker.

1942 **Sherlock Holmes and the Voice of Terror** (Universal) with Basil Rathbone, Nigel Bruce, Evelyn Ankers, Thomas Gomez, Reginald Denny, Henry Daniell, Mary Gordon; directed by John Rawlins.

1942 **Sherlock Holmes and the Secret Weapon** (Universal) with Basil Rathbone, Nigel Bruce, Kaaren Verne, Lionel Atwill, Dennis Hoey; directed by Roy William Neill.

1943 **Sherlock Holmes in Washington** (Universal) with Basil Rathbone, Nigel Bruce, Henry Daniell, Marjorie Lord, George Zucco; directed by Roy William Neill.

1943 **Sherlock Holmes Faces Death** (Universal) with Basil Rathbone, Nigel Bruce, Hillary Brooke, Milburn Stone, Arthur Margetson, Halliwell Hobbes; directed by Roy William Neill.

1944 **Spider Woman** (Universal) with Basil Rathbone, Nigel Bruce, Gale Sondergaard; directed by Roy William Neill.

1944 **The Scarlet Claw** (Universal) with Basil Rathbone, Nigel Bruce, Kay Harding, Arthur Hohl, Gerard Hamer; directed by Roy William Neill.

1944 **The Pearl of Death** (Universal) with Basil Rathbone, Nigel Bruce, Evelyn Ankers, Miles Mander, Rondo Hatton; directed by Roy William Neill.

1945 **The House of Fear** (Universal) with Basil Rathbone, Nigel Bruce, Aubrey Mather, Gavin Muir, Paul Cavanagh, Holmes Herbert; directed by Roy William Neill.

1945 **The Woman in Green** (Universal) with Basil Rathbone, Nigel Bruce, Hillary Brooke, Henry Daniell, Paul Cavanagh, Matthew Boulton; directed by Roy William Neill.

1945 **Pursuit to Algiers** (Universal) with Basil Rathbone, Nigel Bruce, Marjorie Riordan, John Abbott, Martin Kosleck, Gerard Hamer; directed by Roy William Neill.

1946 **Terror by Night** (Universal) with Basil Rathbone, Nigel Bruce, Alan Mowbray, Renee Godfrey, Billy Bevan, Halliwell Hobbes; directed by Roy William Neill.

1946 **Dressed to Kill** (Universal) with Basil Rathbone, Nigel Bruce, Patricia Morison, Edmond Breon, Frederic Worlock, Harry Cording; directed by Roy William Neill.

1959 **The Hound of the Baskervilles** (Hammer Films—British) with Peter Cushing (as Holmes), André Morell, Christopher Lee, Ewen Solon, Marla Landi, Francis De Wolff, Miles Malleson, John Le Mesurier; directed by Terence Fisher.

1962 **Sherlock Holmes and the Deadly Necklace** (CCC-Criterion—German, original German title: **Sherlock Holmes und das Halsband des Todes**) with Christopher Lee (as Holmes), Thorley Walters, Senta Berger; directed by Terence Fisher.

1965 **A Study in Terror** (Columbia—British) with John Neville (as Holmes), Donald Houston, Robert Morley, Frank Finlay, Anthony Quayle, John Fraser, Barry Jones, Cecil Parker, Barbara Windsor; directed by James Hill.

1970 **The Private Life of Sherlock Holmes** (United Artists) with Robert Stephens (as Holmes), Colin Blakely, Christopher Lee, Irene Handl, Genevieve Page, Clive Revill, Tamara Toumanova, Stanley Holloway; directed by Billy Wilder.

1976 **The Seven-Per-Cent Solution** (Universal) with Nicol Williamson (as Holmes), Robert Duvall, Alan Arkin, Vanessa Redgrave, Laurence Olivier, Joel Grey, Samantha Eggar, Jeremy Kemp, Charles Gray, Georgia Brown, Régine; directed by Herbert Ross.

Jules Maigret

"There are no criminals."

Georges Simenon wrote that in 1960, about three-fourths of the way through a creative life of monumental proportions, most of it devoted to an exploration of that anarchic theme.

Virtually all of Simenon's novels, novelettes and short stories (more than 1,000) deal with crime and criminality and, in fact, with the ultimate crime—murder. Central figures in these novels, the characters who force the action, are criminals in every legal sense, yet they are very ordinary people. They are certainly not born as ready-made criminals, somehow identifiable because of physical or psychological deformities. They are merely victims of circumstance, irrevocably drawn to eliminating an offending segment of their personal universe with a bit of poison or a bullet.

Maigret, the detective hero of scores of books (all of which are made up of short novels or short stories—there is no full-length Maigret novel), devotes his life and considerable talents to discovering murderers, but he often is depressed by their capture.

Unlike most of the great detectives of literature, Maigret does not have immense powers of deduction. He cannot obtain a few clues, consider their ramifications, then swoop down like an avenging hawk of justice and triumphantly carry away a killer to stand trial.

Maigret's powers are intuitive. Like Father Brown, he attempts to slip into the skin of his quarry and think like him, act like him—indeed, become him as nearly as possible. When he has practically assumed his suspect's identity, he is sure of his man and is able to arrest him.

The danger of this method is demonstrated when Maigret accepts the killer's mind into his own body. Becoming more and more attuned to his way of thinking, the empathy often becomes so intense that he *understands* the lethal motives of the killer. When comprehension becomes that complete, it is difficult for Maigret to accept the need to arrest and imprison, or execute, the killer he is bound to bring to justice. He has, in an indefinable way, arrested an extension of

A younger, slimmer Maigret than one expects, on a paperback, The Short Cases of Inspector Maigret.

himself, necessarily causing some ambivalence, even sadness, at the conclusion of a case.

This sympathetic relationship with murderers is unusual in great detectives but it is quite real in Maigret as one of the manifestations of his exceptional compassion. It does not prevent him from being one of the most successful policemen in literature, but it does make it difficult for him to be light hearted and carefree.

Another major difference between Maigret and the other giants of detective fiction is his heritage. While most of the great crimefighters are British or American, Maigret follows in the footsteps of a scant few French detectives, primarily the legendary Vidocq, a real-life crook-cum-detective whose **Memoirs** so profoundly influenced Edgar Allan Poe and Lecoq, Emile Gaboriau's popular sleuth of the 1860s and 1870s.

Simenon's handling of Maigret's career parallels, in many ways, the adventures of another famous detective—Sherlock Holmes. In September 1929, Simenon wrote the first exploit of Maigret while aboard his yacht *Ostrogoth*, then quickly wrote numerous sequels, having conceived Maigret as a series detective at the outset.

Published in cheap paperback editions in France in 1931, they were instantly successful. By 1933 eighteen adventures were in print. Then, just as Arthur Conan Doyle tired of writing about Sherlock Holmes and tried to kill him off, Simenon decided he had had enough of Maigret and retired him. Forced to bring him back (in 1942) because of public pressure (just as Holmes had to be rescued from his plunge over the Reichenbach Falls), Simenon wrote an additional sixty-eight books about his detective up to 1972, when he retired him for good.

The books of Simenon are unique in that he was able to write one in three or four days, although he generally allowed himself the luxury of two weeks to complete a short Maigret novel. Other authors, such as John Creasey and Edgar Wallace, and such prolific pulp writers as Walter B. Gibson, were able to write at a similar pace, but none ever had the critical success enjoyed by Simenon. His books are rarities which simultaneously reach a large audience and still are reviewed as "literature," rather than hackwork, by serious critics.

Much of Simenon's life and attitudes is reflected in the person of Maigret, and the detective sometimes delivers the author's philosophy. Forced to write about Maigret more frequently than he wanted to, Simenon was greatly relieved to force him into retirement a few years ago.

Now, indulging himself by writing precisely what he wants to write, Simenon produces only a small, slow trickle of autobiographical essays which have, up to now, avoided analysis of one of the towering figures of mystery fiction—Jules Maigret.

In 1927 or 1928 (he isn't sure, he says, because he has no memory for dates), Jules Maigret met a young novelist named Georges Sim (alias Georges Simenon) who was to become the chronicler of his criminal investigations for nearly half a century. As a result of that fortuitous encounter, the detective's crimefighting career has been recorded in more books than any other significant Continental detective.

Maigret himself, however, narrated his personal reminiscences, published in 1950 as **Maigret's Memoirs**. While generally pleased with Simenon's efforts, he points out some of the oversimplifications, errors and other shortcomings in the published accounts of his adventures. Simenon has the admittedly difficult task of telling all the stories from Maigret's viewpoint, exactly as the detective sees the situations or as they are described to him. The books are not written in the first person, but neither are they told from an omniscient author's point of view.

Jules Amedée François Maigret was born in 1877 in central France, not far from Moulins, the only child of a farmer and his wife. When he was eight years old (and his father was thirty-two), Jules' mother became pregnant again, but died with her infant in childbirth.

Jules' father managed an estate of 7,500 acres, which included at least twenty small farms. His grandfather (who died when Jules was five) had been a tenant farmer there, and so had at least three generations of Maigrets before that, all of whom "had tilled the same soil."

Jules Maigret's father had come from a family of seven or eight children, most of whom had died of typhus, leaving only his father and his father's sister (who later married a baker and settled in Nantes). Jules' father went to high

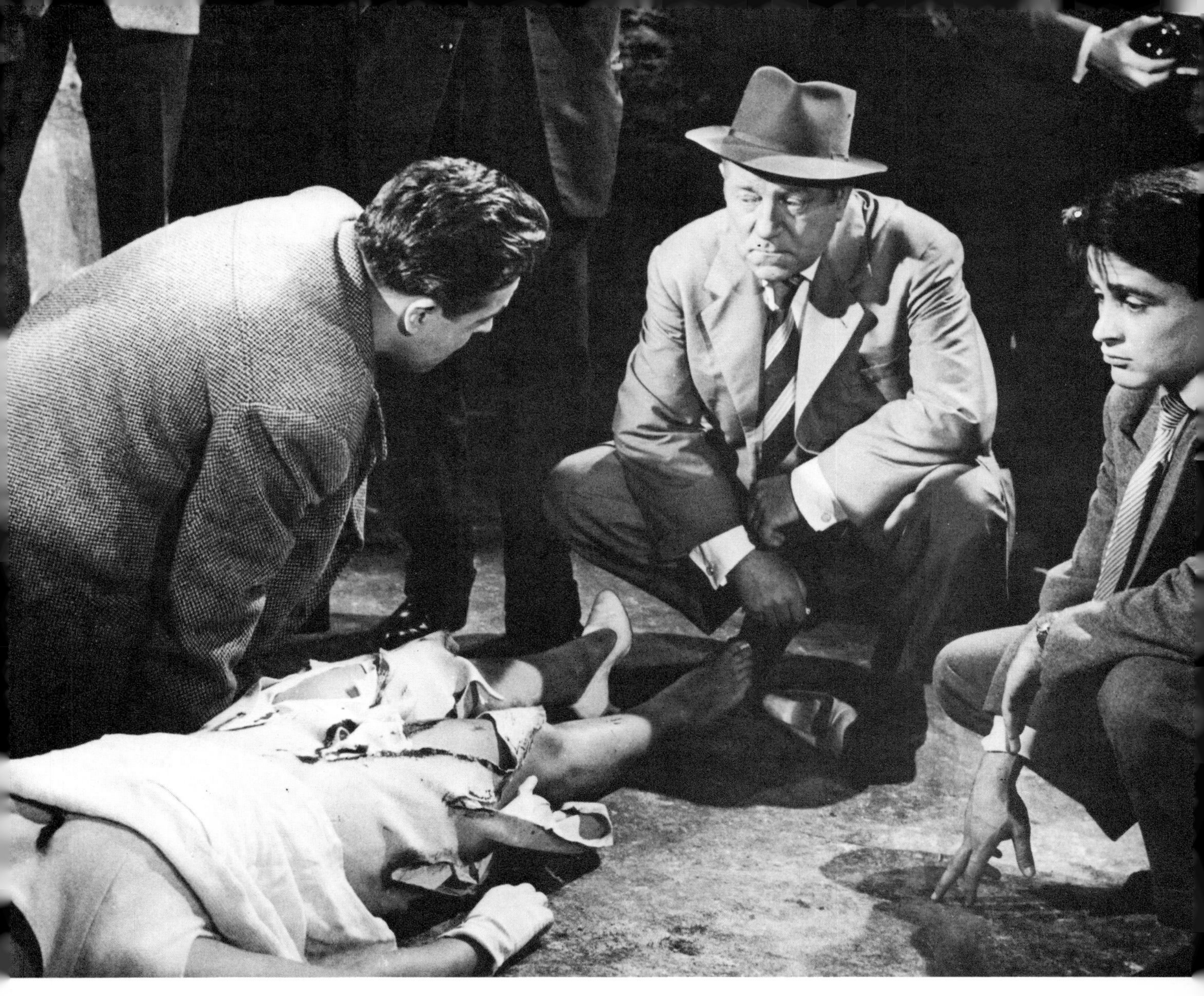

Jean Gabin captured perfectly the character of Inspector Maigret, *based on* Maigret Sets a Trap. *The deranged killer in this grim tale both eludes and taunts the frustrated detective.*

school at Moulins (which was unusual for a farmer's son), largely because of an interest taken in him by the village priest. After spending two years at an agricultural school, he returned home to join the staff of the chateau as assistant estate manager.

Jules describes his father as "very tall, very thin, his thinness emphasized by narrow trousers, bound in by leather gaiters to just below the knee. I always saw my father in leather gaiters. They were a sort of uniform for him. He wore no beard, but a long sandy moustache in which, when he came home in winter, I used to feel tiny ice-crystals when I kissed him."

His father seldom laughed, he further recalls, but when he did, "it was a surprise to discover how young, almost childish his laugh was, and to see how much simple pleasantries amused him."

The Maigrets lived in an attractive, one-story, rose-colored brick house in the courtyard of the chateau. After Jules' mother died, his father became morose, and a local girl was brought in to look after the house and the child. His father did not drink, "unlike most of the people I knew," Jules says, taking with his meals only half of a small decanter filled with light white wine made with grapes harvested on the estate.

After attending the village school, Jules was sent to board at the high school in Moulins because his father was unable to take him back and forth each night, picking him up only on Saturday nights. He stayed only a few months before moving to Nantes to stay with his aunt and her baker husband. His holidays were spent with his father.

"I won't go so far as to say we were strangers to one another," Jules recalls, "but I had my own private life, my ambitions, my problems. He was my father, whom I loved and respected, but whom I'd given up trying to understand. And it went on like that for years."

But not too many years. A broken man following his wife's death, Jules' father finally died of pleurisy at the age of forty-four, the same illness that was to kill his aunt ten years later.

With the death of his father, Jules Maigret abandoned his recently begun medical studies and left for Paris, taking residence in a little hotel on the Left Bank. As a medical student, he had found a satisfying challenge in attempting to predict the ultimate cause of death of the patients he encountered, just as he had tried to predict the future professions of his schoolmates when he had been a youngster.

Undecided about his own future, Maigret had decided to apply for a menial job when a chance meeting with an older acquaintance from the hotel interested him in a career as a policeman.

Maigret's friend, Jacquemain, a detective inspector at the Quai des Orfèvres, made his profession sound attractive enough to induce Maigret to join the police force.

Jacquemain, who has such an important influence on Maigret, is "rather short and squat, dark-haired, with a prematurely bald patch which he concealed by carefully combing his hair forward, and black moustaches with curled tips." He is accidentally killed by a stray bullet in a street brawl three years after introducing Maigret to the force.

When Maigret becomes a member of the department, he is given a uniform and, he recollects, "I wore it, not for long, for seven or eight months. As I had long legs and was very lean, very swift, strange as that may seem today, they gave me a bicycle and, in order that I might get to know Paris, where I was always losing my way, I was given the job of delivering notes to various police stations."

Better educated than most French policemen at this time, Maigret is given further advanced studies, largely as a result of his friendship with Detective Inspector Jacquemain, and is soon promoted to a plainclothes position as secretary to the station officer of the Saint Georges District, a job commonly known as "station officer's dog."

Taken under the wing of Xavier Guichard, a friend of Maigret's father and a high-ranking police official at the Quai des Orfèvres, Maigret's next post is with the public highways squad, where he is required to do a great deal of walking in very cheap hobnail-soled boots.

His salary is small, his room is squalid, and he is always hungry during these early years of his career. Then, he chances to bump into an old friend from medical school, Felix Jubert.

Jubert introduces Maigret to Mr. and Mrs. Leonard and their niece, Louise, described as a "rather plump young girl with a very fresh face and a sparkle in her eyes that was lacking in her friends." Not too long afterwards, Maigret asks her to marry him, and they move into a flat on the Boulevard Richard-Lenoir, where they remain throughout his career.

Georges Simenon, who is chronicling the career of Maigret, becomes a good friend of both the husband and wife, viewing her as "a good housewife, always busy cooking and polishing, always fussing over her great baby of a husband."

Warm and kindhearted, and extraordinarily understanding, she never complains about her husband's irregular hours when he is involved in a case, and takes care of him when he comes down with one of his innumerable colds. Normally in the background, separated from his professional life, she becomes involved in one case by noticing an inconsistency of costume in a young mother.

As a member of the public highways squad, Maigret learns even more about the streets of Paris than he did as a messenger. Of greater significance, he learns about the street habitués and the criminal types who "spend most of their nights at the police station."

Following these months of plainclothes work, during which he is not permitted to carry a gun, he is transferred to the vice squad (which is called the "social squad") for a few months, where he deals with pickpockets, shoplifters, prostitutes and other lowly lawbreakers, patrolling railway stations, large department stores and hotels.

When he is finally assigned to investigative detective work at the Quai des Orfèvres, he quickly rises in rank from detective to detective-sergeant to inspector to chief inspector and, finally, commissioner. He is most often (albeit frequently inaccurately, due to faulty translations from the French narratives to English) referred to as inspector in the published accounts of his adventures.

William Sharp accurately limned the pipe-smoking Inspector Jules Maigret for the dust jacket of the first American edition of Maigret in New York's Underworld, *partly set in the Bronx.*

At the age of thirty (1907), Maigret is transferred to the special squad, more familiarly known as the homicide squad, under Inspector Guillaume. Maigret is not blasé about his new assignment. "I could hear triumphant clarion calls ringing in my ears," he says. "The dream of my life was being realized." Running home to tell his wife the good news, he trips and falls at the door, picks himself up, and nearly faints.

On his first case in his new department, he is accompanied by his superior, Inspector Dufour. Wearing a disguise, Maigret is the first to arrive at an apartment house in the rue du Roi de Sicile, where he is to arrest a Czech for murder. As the tallest and heaviest man, he has the responsibility of making the actual physical arrest, grappling with the suspect until he is finally subdued (with the inspector's assistance) and the handcuffs slapped onto his wrists.

Maigret has clearly found his niche in the homicide division, where he works for many years. As the most respected member of the squad, he indulges himself in the luxury of reflecting and pontificating on his job:

"With all due deference to novelists," he says, "a detective is, above all, a professional. He is an *official.*

"He's not engaged in a guessing game, nor getting worked up over a relatively thrilling chase.

"When he spends a night in the rain, watching

Although clean-shaven during most of his life, artists seem to prefer Maigret with a moustache.

a door that doesn't open or a lighted window, when he patiently scans the pavement cafés on the boulevards for a familiar face, or prepares to spend hours questioning a pale, terrified individual, he is doing his daily job.

"He is earning his living, trying to earn as honestly as possible the money that the government gives him at the end of every month in remuneration for his services."

Maigret also provides some insight into his methods:

"Some investigations take months," he says, "and certain criminals are eventually arrested only after long years, and then sometimes by pure chance.

"In practically every case the process is the same.

"You have to *know*.

"To know the milieu in which a crime has been committed, to know the way of life, the habits, morals, reactions of the people involved in it, whether victims, criminals or merely witnesses.

"To enter into their world without surprise, easily, and to speak its language naturally.

"That is why we aren't wasting our time when we spend years pacing the pavements, climbing stairs or spying on pilferers in big stores.

"Like the cobbler, like the pastry cook, we are serving our apprenticeship, with this difference, that it goes on for practically the whole of our lives, because the number of different circles is almost infinite."

Obviously, Maigret is a tireless worker, plodding his way through every case in an infinitely patient search for the key to its solution.

"I come and I go and I sniff around," he says modestly. "People say I'm waiting for inspiration. What I'm waiting for is the one significant event that never fails to happen. The whole thing is to be there when it does so that I can take advantage of it."

Although he dearly loves to eat, Maigret is so dedicated that he often has beer and sandwiches sent up to his office for lunch. Since his apartment is within walking distance of the office, and he walks to work in the morning (when he is young), he often tries to go home to share lunch with his wife, but he rarely manages to make it, some new emergency inevitably turning up to prevent it.

More likely, if he gets out at all, he will lunch with his colleagues in his favorite restaurant, the Brasserie Dauphine, across the square from his office; his special table is always reserved for him.

Despite the nice location of his office (it overlooks the Seine), it is old and quite shabby. Years after the Quai is equipped with central heating, Maigret keeps a black coal stove in his office for the more personal warmth it gives, as well as the fact that it helps reduce tension if he stokes it during particularly trying moments of an interrogation. It is too efficient, however, his office frequently being so overheated that he is forced to open his window.

It is necessary to enter Maigret's office by passing through the run-down lobby of the Quai des Orfévres side of the Palais de Justice. After crossing the dingy lobby, Maigret has to walk up two flights of stairs to get to the office. Usually, he stops to look into the "aquarium"—a glass cage in which witnesses and suspects sit on old green velvet chairs, waiting to be questioned by him.

When Maigret interrogates someone, he displays extraordinary patience, once questioning a suspect for twenty-six hours without a single break. He waits and watches a house for three days and two nights, expecting a man to emerge from it. He has no food, no drink, and it rains constantly, but he is affected only when his supply of matches is exhausted and he is unable to smoke his pipe. (He normally smokes incessantly and has a collection of fifteen pipes lined up on his office desk.)

Otherwise in robust health, his long, chilling, rain-filled surveillances give him more colds than most humans could endure. His only other physical difficulties are incurred in the line of duty: he is wounded on four separate occasions.

Maigret's patience is less the result of a special dedication than a compensation for other shortcomings. He asks interminable questions during interviews, many of which seem irrelevant, but they sometimes contribute toward the weakening of a suspect.

Although kind-hearted and compassionate toward the weaker members of the uneducated and lower classes, he is implacable in his pursuit of genuine villains. Maigret looks nothing like a policeman, and gives no appearance of having great intelligence, seeming to be always sleepy. Despite his apparent dearth of intellectual capabilities, he does have intuitive gifts and perceptive talents of unusual magnitude, enabling him to understand people of the most diverse backgrounds.

Maigret's methods are effective. When he determines who his most likely suspects are, he insinuates himself into their lives, watching them constantly. He is forever on the perimeter of their lives, seeing, hearing and learning everything about them. More often than not, he learns the identity of the guilty person intuitively, and he either waits for a mistake, when he can arrest him, or waits for his formidable omnipresence to drive the criminal to seek him out to confess.

During his tedious, time-consuming vigils, Maigret often drinks. He likes to find a café from which to keep a close scrutiny on his prey, and to order a glass of white wine, or two, before moving on to another café, where he sips a leisurely calvados. Or he will have his favorite drink, beer, or possibly marc, or pernod, or an apéritif, or a cocktail or, occasionally, a whiskey. Whatever his particular preference at a specific time, he drinks relentlessly.

A gentle-looking Maigret as drawn by Vlaminck. It is his quality of kindliness that makes witnesses so relaxed and willing to talk to him.

The seemingly endless number of drinks, combined with the hearty meals, combine to make Maigret rather stocky. He is five feet, eleven inches tall and weighs 200 pounds, with broad shoulders and the heavy features which reflect his bourgeois origin. His hands, which are almost compulsively kept clean and meticulously cared for, are usually shoved into his pockets. When he was young, he had a long, reddish-brown moustache which he later trimmed to a toothbrush moustache, until he finally eliminated it altogether, remaining clean-shaven.

He wears well-cut suits made of high-quality material, and in the winter has a heavy overcoat with a velvet collar, and a bowler hat.

When a case is in progress, Maigret stays active, generally leaving his office to become part of the environment of the crime. While he blends into the lives of those involved in the investigation, the necessary background research is handled by his subordinates, inspectors Lucas, Janvier, Lapointe and Torrence.

Inspector Lucas, Maigret's right-hand man, worships his chief. A head shorter and only half as broad as Maigret, he smokes a pipe much like his, which is far too large for his face and looks absurd. Janvier is also entirely devoted to Maigret (who calls him *mon petit*—my little one—although he is middle-aged).

Not a member of the force, but also helpful on several cases, is Dr. Pardon, Maigret's personal physician and friend. He dines with the Maigrets about once a month. When medical problems or questions arise in a case, Maigret seeks Dr. Pardon for advice, despite his own medical training.

The only member of the scientific staff in the police department who is useful to Maigret is the tall, weedy, nearsighted young lab technician named Moers. He alone understands Maigret's preoccupation with character and psychology as the real clues to a crime, and he is able to provide physical and scientific evidence which point to those clues. He specializes in graphology.

Maigret's cases have taken him to many locales in France besides Paris, and he has even traveled to Belgium, Germany, the Netherlands and the United States in his pursuit of evil-doers.

He is forced to leave his wife while on a case, but otherwise he is very close to her. Curiously, he calls her "Madame Maigret" and she calls him "Maigret," but that should not be considered as even the slightest evidence to indicate a lack of affection for either one toward the other. Their favorite pastime is going for a walk together after dinner, or attending the neighborhood cinema (his favorite films are comedies).

The Maigrets have no children, but his wife's nephew, Philippe Lauer, also on the police force, is close to them.

The chronicler of his adventures, Maigret's old friend Simenon, is forced to give up his writing career in 1973 because of ill health, and Maigret now also retires. His position as commissioner is taken, appropriately enough, by the dedicated Lucas, and Maigret and his wife lead a quiet retirement at their country house in Meung-sur-Loire, near Orléans.

GEORGES SIMENON (1903-   ) Born in Liège, Belgium, Georges Jaques Christian Simenon was forced to drop out of school at sixteen due to economic necessity. While still a teenager, he became a police reporter and newspaper columnist, and had his first novel (written in ten days) published at the age of seventeen; **Au Pont des Arches** remains untranslated. A phenomenally prolific writer, he moved to Paris and often wrote as many as eighty pages a day, having his hundreds of stories published under a variety of pseudonyms, the most famous being Georges Sim. The first Maigret novel was successful and he wrote one a month for the period beginning with September 1929, becoming bored with the character after eighteen novels. He turned to intense psychological suspense tales for the next decade, returning to Maigret as a break from the arduous works. Able to produce a full-length book in three or four days, he often took as long as a month for the more difficult ones. One of the most prolific of all major writers, he has had more than two hundred novels published under his own name.

BIBLIOGRAPHY

1932 **The Crime of Inspector Maigret** (Covici-Friede)
1932 **The Death of Monsieur Gallet** (Covici-Friede)
1933 **The Crossroad Murders** (Covici-Friede)
1933 **The Strange Case of Peter the Lett** (Covici-Friede)
1934 **The Shadow in the Courtyard and The Crime at Lock 14** (Covici-Friede)
1940 **The Patience of Maigret** (Harcourt; contains **A Battle of Nerves** and **A Face for a Clue)**
1940 **Maigret Abroad** (Harcourt; contains **A Crime in Holland** and **At the Gai-Moulin**)
1940 **Maigret Travels South** (Harcourt; contains **Liberty Bar** and **The Madam of Bergerac**)
1941 **Maigret to the Rescue** (Harcourt; contains **The Flemish Shop** and **Guinguette by the Seine**)
1941 **Maigret Keeps a Rendezvous** (Harcourt; contains **The Sailors' Rendezvous** and **The Saint-Fiacre Affair**)
1941 **Maigret Sits It Out** (Harcourt; contains **The Lock at Charenton** and **Maigret Returns**)
1942 **Maigret and M. Labbé** (Harcourt; contains **Death of a Harbour-master** and **The Man from Everywhere**, which is not about Maigret)
1953 **No Vacation for Maigret** (Doubleday)
1954 **Maigret and the Strangled Stripper** (Doubleday)
1954 **Inspector Maigret and the Killers** (Doubleday)

1955 **Maigret in New York's Underworld** (Doubleday)
1955 **Inspector Maigret and the Dead Girl** (Doubleday)
1956 **Inspector Maigret and the Burglar's Wife** (Doubleday)
1957 **The Methods of Maigret** (Doubleday)
1958 **None of Maigret's Business** (Doubleday)
1959 **Madame Maigret's Own Case** (Doubleday)
1959 **The Short Cases of Inspector Maigret** (Doubleday)
1960 **Versus Inspector Maigret** (Doubleday; contains **Maigret and the Reluctant Witnesses** and **Maigret Has Scruples**)
1961 **Maigret Rents a Room** (Doubleday)
1964 **Maigret's Dead Man** (Doubleday)
1964 **Five Times Maigret** (Harcourt; contains **Maigret's Mistake, Maigret Goes to School,** and three reprints)
1965 **Maigret Cinq** (Harcourt; contains **Maigret and the Old Lady, Maigret's First Case,** and three reprints)
1968 **Maigret's Pickpocket** (Harcourt)
1968 **Maigret and the Headless Corpse** (Harcourt)
1969 **Maigret and the Calame Report** (Harcourt)
1969 **Maigret in Vichy** (Harcourt)
1970 **Maigret Hesitates** (Harcourt)
1970 **Maigret's Boyhood Friend** (Harcourt)
1971 **Maigret and the Killer** (Harcourt)
1971 **Maigret and the Wine Merchant** (Harcourt)
1972 **Maigret Sets a Trap** (Harcourt)
1972 **Maigret and the Madwoman** (Harcourt)
1973 **Maigret and the Informer** (Harcourt)
1973 **A Maigret Trio** (Harcourt; contains **Maigret's Failure, Maigret in Society** and **Maigret and the Lazy Burglar**)
1974 **Maigret Loses His Temper** (Harcourt)
1974 **Maigret and the Millionaires** (Harcourt)
1974 **Maigret and the Bum** (Harcourt)
1975 **Maigret and the Loner** (Harcourt)
1975 **Maigret and the Man on the Bench** (Harcourt)
1976 **Maigret and the Apparition** (Harcourt)
1976 **Maigret and the Black Sheep** (Harcourt)
1977 **Maigret and the Spinster** (Harcourt)

FILMOGRAPHY

1949 **The Man on the Eiffel Tower** (RKO) with Charles Laughton (as Inspector Maigret), Franchot Tone, Burgess Meredith, Robert Hutton, Jean Wallace; directed by Burgess Meredith.

There have also been many French films about Maigret, as well as Italian and German films.

Philip Marlowe

The history and development of the literary American private eye can be encapsulated with a small fistful of names, with each of the authors representative of a definite time frame. Dashiell Hammett's various operatives dominated the 1930s, Raymond Chandler's Philip Marlowe the 1940s, Mickey Spillane's Mike Hammer the 1950s, and Ross Macdonald's Lew Archer the 1960s and 1970s.

Perhaps the most idealistic of a breed in which idealism abounds, Marlowe is portrayed by Chandler as a modern knight "in search of a hidden truth." In an often-quoted description of his idealized seeker of truth and purity, and the difficult journey on which that noble quest takes him, Chandler wrote:

"Down these mean streets a man must go who is not himself mean, who is neither tarnished nor afraid. The detective in this kind of story must be such a man. He is the hero, he is everything. He must be a complete man and a common man and yet an unusual man. He must be, to use a rather weathered phrase, a man of honor. He is a relatively poor man, or he would not be a detective at all. He is a common man or he could not go among common people. He has a sense of character, or he would not know his job. He will take no man's money dishonestly and no man's insolence without a due and dispassionate revenge. He is a lonely man and his pride is that you will treat him as a proud man or be very sorry you ever saw him. He talks as the man of his age talks, that is, with rude wit, a lively sense of the grotesque, a disgust for sham, and a contempt for pettiness."

More than any important detective of the twentieth century, Marlowe fulfills these ideals and remains consistent with this exalted image, staying emotionally aloof from the corrupt world in which he dwells while at the same time plunging deeply into it professionally.

The first detective stories written by Chandler feature protagonists named Carmady, Dalmas, Malvern, Mallory and an anonymous hero. Later, these tales were reprinted and the names

The best cinematic portrayal of Marlowe was by Dick Powell in Murder My Sweet, *the Edgar-winning film version of* Farewell, My Lovely.

of them all changed to Marlowe. Although they differed from each other in details, they have the essential seeds of a single man, the principal characteristics of Philip Marlowe.

More than most literary entities, Marlowe is an idealized version of his own creator, Chandler's personal dream fulfillment—a thoughtful, gentle, introspective, intelligent and compassionate man.

With his multi-sided personality, Marlowe is not a caricature of the "hard-boiled dick," and is therefore an imposing challenge for an actor wishing to portray him. A surprising number of fine screen impersonations have been achieved.

Dick Powell, the first to play the role in a film using the Marlowe name, was the best, helping **Murder My Sweet** to win the first Edgar awarded by the Mystery Writers of America for the best film of the year.

Humphrey Bogart played Marlowe in the next motion picture, **The Big Sleep,** and was also good, although his Marlowe was virtually indistinguishable from his Sam Spade. Robert Montgomery and George Montgomery followed admirably, being succeeded by a satisfactory James Garner, an abominable Elliott Gould, and Robert Mitchum in a return to the serious, moody character limned in Chandler's fiction.

Whatever Philip Marlowe's motives may be for being a private detective, and they are often vague and ambiguous, financial gain does not rank high. He has to like his job, and find satisfaction in the opportunity to help those who need it, because he will certainly never get rich.

"I get paid for what I do," he says. "Not much by your standards, but I make out. One customer at a time is a good rule."

His fee follows the realities of inflation, jumping from 25 to 40 dollars a day (plus expenses) in a decade.

Like most private detectives, Marlowe started out as a law enforcement agent—an investigator for Los Angeles District Attorney Taggart Wilde. He was fired for insubordination, or "talking back," as he phrases it.

Although a gentle man, Marlowe has a short fuse at times, and is extremely sensitive when his principles are questioned.

"Uh, huh. I'm a very smart guy," he says sarcastically. "I haven't a feeling or a scruple in the world. All I have the itch for is money. I am so money greedy that for twenty-five bucks a day and expenses, mostly gasoline and whiskey, I do my thinking myself, what there is of it; I risk my whole future, the hatred of the cops... I dodge bullets and eat saps, and say thank you very much, if you have any more trouble, I hope you'll think of me. I'll just leave one of my cards in case something comes up. I do all this for twenty-five bucks a day."

Marlowe's fees are compatible with his lifestyle. He doesn't have very much, and doesn't seem to need much more. His complete financial resources total $1,200 in the bank and a few thousand dollars in bonds. He drives a car, never new, and changing from year to year, beginning with a convertible, going on to a Chrysler and then to an Oldsmobile.

His apartment is less than palatial. The Hobart Arms, on Franklin, locks its doors at 10 P.M., but it provides the service of a phone girl. An automatic elevator is reached by crossing a square, barren lobby with potted palms for decoration. It smells almost musty. On his floor, a bleak light shines along his corridor, at the end of which a red fire door looms, with an open screen in front that lets in a "lazy trickle of air that never quite swept the cooking smell out."

Later, Marlowe moves to the Bristol, with its tacky green and ivory hallway, and then to a house on Yucca Avenue in the Laurel Canyon district. This small hillside house is on a dead end street, with a long flight of redwood steps to the front door, and a grove of eucalyptus trees across the way. He rents it, furnished, from a woman who has gone to Idaho for a while.

Marlowe's living quarters are practically elegant compared with his office. He has one-and-a-half rooms on the seventh floor of a building on Hollywood Boulevard. The half-room is the reception area, the door to which is open, and bears the name "Philip Marlowe"; the communicating door, however, is locked.

The reception area was not designed to impress potential clients. It contains a faded red settee, two old semi-easy chairs, a child's size library table with venerable magazines stacked on it.

If a visitor gets past the locked door and into Marlowe's private office, absolutely no change in the ambience will be noted. The furnishings consist mainly of a rust-red carpet, "not very young"; five green filing cabinets, "three filled with the California climate"; three walnut chairs; and a desk atop which sit a blotter, pen set, ashtray, and telephone, and behind which is a squeaky swivel armchair. On the wall is an advertising calendar showing "the Quints rolling around a sky blue floor in pink dresses, with seal brown hair and sharp black eyes as large as mammoth prunes." Through the open window wafts the odor of a coffee shop, "strong enough to build a garage on."

Two items of supreme importance are contained in the desk drawers: a Colt .38 automatic, and the office bottle with a couple of glasses.

The bottle plays an important role in Marlowe's life. In fact, many bottles do. He appears to be a tireless drinker of an unusually catholic taste. A quick tabulation of the drinks he consumes includes the following: brandy and soda, Bacardi, whiskey sour, rye, scotch, dry martini, gimlets, Swedish beer, champagne, Old Granddad—not counting numerous reruns.

Marlowe doesn't eat as much as he drinks, but he doesn't starve himself, either. Breakfast is a big deal. Two, three or four cups of coffee are standard, and he often cooks his own eggs and bacon, switching to Canadian bacon from time to time. He also consumes toast (sometimes with honey, usually with butter), orange juice, French toast and, to top it off, a toothpick.

Lunch and dinner are less elaborate and less regular, generally consisting of something gastronomically uninspiring, such as the 84¢ dinner special in Bay City, lunch in countless coffee shops, and a bite in the "corn-beef joint on Flower."

He generally concludes a meal with a smoke, varying the type according to no discernible pattern. Most of his tobacco is consumed in the form of cigarettes (Camels) or pipes, although he smokes a cigar in his first recorded case; a few years later he says, "I can't smoke cigars." Whatever the smoke, he uses a lighter infrequently, preferring matches, with which he plays a game. I "snicked a match on my thumbnail," he says, "and for once it lit the cigarette. Usually it's two tries on my thumbnail and then using my foot."

Marlowe has no genuine addictions, although tobacco is close to being one, as is alcohol. So is chess. In solitary times, when he needs to relax, or just to get his mind off a case, Marlowe sits at a chessboard and plays imaginary games.

Once, he played a French defense "against Steinitz. He beat me in forty-four moves, but I had him sweating a couple of times," Marlowe muses. Steinitz, of course, had been dead for

Herman Geisen's illustration appeared on an early paperback version of Trouble is My Business.

fifty years, and the game was taken out of a book.

Another time, he set out his chessboard and "played a championship tournament game between Gortchakoff and Meninkin, seventy-two moves to a draw, a prize specimen of the irresistible force meeting the immovable object, a battle without armor, a war without blood, and as elaborate a waste of human intelligence as you could find anywhere outside an advertising agency."

Pleasure and masochism seem to be dual motivations for Marlowe as he sets up his board. After arranging the pieces in a classic situation called "The Sphinx," he contemplates the game.

"The Sphinx is an eleven-mover," he broods, "and it justifies its name. Chess problems seldom run to more than four or five moves. Beyond that the difficulty of solving them rises in almost geometrical progression. An eleven-mover is sheer unadulterated torture. Once in a long while when I feel mean enough I set it out and look for a new way to solve it. It's a nice quiet way to go crazy. You don't even scream, but you come awfully close."

Marlowe's evident expertise with the complex challenges of chess is not the only intellectual accomplishment he has cultivated. He went to college and says he "can still speak English if there's any demand for it." He also speaks Spanish, which he finds useful in certain sections of Los Angeles. He quotes Robert Browning, Flaubert, and T. S. Eliot.

While he enjoys classical art, he detests abstract expressionistic painting and, similarly, derives great pleasure from classical music, but is repelled by atonal music.

He does not amplify his brief statement about college, but it is likely that Marlowe played football there. A septum operation left scar tissue inside his nose, caused by trying to block a punt with his face. He certainly had the size to play the game, his 190 pounds being well-distributed on his six-foot, one-half-inch frame.

It is not unusual for women to be attracted to Marlowe. In addition to a nice build, he has good dark brown hair, which starts to have "plenty of gray" by the time he reaches forty, brown eyes, and teeth that look better than they are—"some nice inlays and one very high class porcelain jacket crown."

At the time of his first recorded case, he is thirty-three years old, and he is forty-two when he meets Linda Loring in **The Long Goodbye**. He falls in love with her and eventually sheds the stereotypical image of the solitary private eye by marrying her.

Previously lonely, if not ascetic, Marlowe has many reasons to be drawn to the millionairess. Extremely attractive, with thick black hair and very large dark eyes, she also has "all the honesty and a large part of the guts" of her family, according to Marlowe.

She offers to set him up in business, or to simply give him a million dollars, but Marlowe refuses. "I'm a poor man married to a rich wife," he says. "I don't know how to behave. I'm only sure of one thing—shabby office or not, that's where I became what I am. That's where I will be what I will be. For me there isn't any other way."

His profession probably means more to Marlowe than anything else in the world—wife, wealth, health or life. He is willing to make enormous sacrifices for what he perceives as his responsibility as a hired detective.

"I'm not here [in jail] for you," he tells a client. "I'm in here for me. No complaints. It's part of the deal. I'm in a business where people come to me with troubles. Big troubles, little troubles, but always troubles they don't want to take to the cops. How long would they come if any bruiser with a police shield could hold me upside down and draw my guts?"

Also, "You don't know what I have to go

through or over or under to do your job for you," he says. "I do it my way. I do my best to protect you and I break a few rules, but I break them in your favor. The client comes first,

Humphrey Bogart portrays Marlowe in The Big Sleep, *with Lauren Bacall hindering him in a variety of ways. The excellent screenplay was written in part by William Faulkner.*

unless he's crooked. Even then all I do is hand the job back to him and keep my mouth shut."

Nothing would please Marlowe's wife more than having him retire and remain at their Palm Springs estate, but that's not for him. He likes being a private detective, and he likes working in Los Angeles, although his attitude towards the city becomes more negative through the years.

Born in Santa Rosa, he soon became familiar with the sprawling Los Angeles area and its widely divergent population. He is equally familiar with, and comfortable in, the moneyed mansions of Beverly Hills and the tough, hostile streets of Bunker Hill and Central Avenue. By 1949, however, the disenchantment is nearly complete.

"I used to like this town," he says. "A long time ago, Los Angeles was just a big dry sunny place with ugly homes and no style, but good hearted and peaceful. Now . . . we've got the big money, the sharpshooters, the percentage workers, the fast-dollar boys, the hoodlums out of New York and Chicago and Detroit. The riffraff of a big hardboiled city with no more personality than a paper cup."

Still, despite the beatings from corrupt policemen, the dishonest clients, the loneliness (until his wife, Marlowe had no one—both his parents are dead, and he has no brothers or sisters, few friends, no lasting relationships), and the frequent bouts of depression, Marlowe is content in Los Angeles, as much a part of the milieu as sunshine and smog, automobiles and plastic.

RAYMOND CHANDLER (1888-1959) Although he was born in Chicago, Raymond Chandler was taken to England at an early age and received a very British education, graduating from Dulwich College, London. After serving with the Gordon Highlanders (Canada) in France during World War I, he returned to the United States and briefly resumed his journalistic career before becoming a successful business executive in the oil industry. In 1924, he married Pearl Cecily Bowen, seventeen years older than he, and remained devoted to her for thirty years until her death after a long illness in 1954. The Great Depression cost him his job and he began writing pulp fiction in 1933, quickly becoming one of the stars of **Black Mask** magazine. Despite a modest-sized *opera*, he is regarded, along with Dashiell Hammett, as one of the most influential developers of the "hard-boiled" school of detective fiction. He received Academy Award nominations for **Double Indemnity** (1944), for which he co-authored the screenplay with Billy Wilder, and **The Blue Dahlia** (1946), which he wrote single-handedly.

BIBLIOGRAPHY

1939 **The Big Sleep** (Knopf)
1940 **Farewell, My Lovely** (Knopf)
1942 **The High Window** (Knopf)
1943 **The Lady in the Lake** (Knopf)
1949 **The Little Sister** (Houghton Mifflin)
1950 **The Simple Art of Murder** (Houghton Mifflin; short stories about various detectives, the names of all being changed to Marlowe for this collection)
1953 **The Long Goodbye** (Houghton Mifflin)
1958 **Playback** (Houghton Mifflin)
1965 **The Smell of Fear** (London: Hamish Hamilton; short stories, including "The Pencil," the only short fiction originally written about Philip Marlowe)

FILMOGRAPHY

1944 **Murder My Sweet** (RKO) with Dick Powell (as Philip Marlowe), Claire Trevor, Anne Shirley, Mike Mazurki, Miles Mander, Otto Kruger; directed by Edward Dmytryk.
1946 **The Big Sleep** (Warner Brothers) with Humphrey Bogart (as Philip Marlowe), Lauren Bacall, Elisha Cook, Jr., Martha Vickers, Louïs Jean Heydt; directed by Howard Hawks.
1946 **Lady in the Lake** (MGM) with Robert Montgomery (as Philip Marlowe), Audrey Totter, Leon Ames, Lloyd Nolan; directed by Robert Montgomery.
1947 **The Brasher Doubloon** (Twentieth Century-Fox) with George Montgomery (as Philip Marlowe), Nancy Guild, Florence Bates, Fritz Kortner; directed by John Brahm.
1969 **Marlowe** (MGM) with James Garner (as Philip Marlowe), Gayle Hunnicutt, Rita Moreno, Carroll O'Connor; directed by Paul Bogart.
1973 **The Long Goodbye** (United Artists) with Elliott Gould (as Philip Marlowe), Nina van Pallandt, Sterling Hayden, Mark Rydell; directed by Robert Altman.
1975 **Farewell, My Lovely** (Avco Embassy) with Robert Mitchum (as Philip Marlowe), Charlotte Rampling; directed by Dick Richards.

Miss Jane Marple

It would be a simple matter for the uninformed reader to jump to the erroneous assumption that Miss Jane Marple, the most famous spinster sleuth in literature, and Agatha Christie, her creator, were one and the same. It would be a terrible mistake to do this today, and it would have been an even more terrible mistake to have done it in the presence of Mrs. Christie, who hotly denied the comparison whenever the subject came up, as it frequently did.

Miss Marple is elderly and has gray-white hair. In her later years, Dame Agatha, too, had gray-white hair. The resemblance ended there.

Margaret Rutherford was also elderly with gray-white hair when she memorably portrayed Miss Marple in four popular films. She also bore little resemblance to the amateur detective, however; if she has to be compared with someone, she was closer in physical appearance to the author.

Romping aggressively through her highly active adventures, the ample Miss Rutherford won the affection of audiences with her boisterous humor and tireless pursuit of clues and criminals. This was not Miss Marple's style, and Agatha Christie did not at all approve of the broad depiction of her sleuthing gentlewoman.

The author made no secret of her disaffection for the comedienne's portrayal of her beloved literary creation, although she was personally quite fond of Miss Rutherford, dedicating **The Mirror Crack'd** to her. While amusing, the films are slight, grade B efforts and do no justice to Miss Marple.

To find a prototype for Miss Marple, Agatha Christie had turned to her own grandmother, although she described the affinity as "faint."

Her grandmother, she said, "also a pink and white old lady who, although having led the most sheltered and Victorian of lives, nevertheless always appeared to be intimately acquainted with the depths of human depravity. One could be made to feel incredibly naive and credulous by her reproachful remark: 'But did you believe what they said to you? I never do!' "

Miss Marple was Agatha Christie's favorite character. As the author grew older, she began to use her detective as a medium for transmitting her personal philosophy in a subtle, inoffensive manner. Although overall she wrote many more books about Hercule Poirot, in later years Miss Marple novels appeared more often.

The first appearance of a story in which Miss Marple is involved occurred in 1928, and the last to be written about her, **Nemesis**, was published in 1971. During this time span she aged approximately twenty years. **Sleeping Murder**, conceived as the last Miss Marple book when it was written in the early 1940s, remained unpublished until 1976.

Perhaps reflecting the author's own feelings about her, Miss Marple becomes more and more likable as the series progresses. Rather a nasty village busybody and gossip when she first appears, she later mellows into a benign, tolerant and kindly eccentric, looking after the well-being of friends and neighbors, particularly young ones.

As she wrote the stories which were later collected as **The Tuesday Club Murders** (she always thought Miss Marple at her best in solving short problems), Agatha Christie admitted that she had conceived a great affection for "my fluffy old lady" and hoped she would be a success.

It is sometimes difficult to measure something as elusive as "success" but **Murder at the Vicarage**, the first Miss Marple novel, had an initial printing of 5,500 copies. **Sleeping Murder**, the last of the series, had an initial printing of 60,000—and that is a mere droplet in the Atlantic in relation to the number of copies that will ultimately be sold in book club editions, translations and paperbacks.

That is, without qualification, success.

If a single word is capable of defining the complex process of detection, the word that describes virtually the entire methodology of Miss Jane Marple, amateur sleuth, is "analogy."

Virtually every occurrence seems to have a precedent in the bloodstained history of St. Mary Mead, the quiet English village of which Miss Marple is the unofficial historian. No eccentricity of character, no inexplicable sequence of events, no curiosity of behavior, can take place without Miss Marple's recalling a similar set of circumstances in the past, from which she is invariably able to draw an analogy.

What makes this method dependable, she is convinced, is that human nature does not change. While it may seem pessimistic and cynical, her frequent encounters with crime and murder indicate that she may, in fact, be correct when she expects the worst of people. "There's a lot of wickedness in the world," she says.

She is mildly contemptuous of those who do not share her view. "The truth is, you see," she explains, "that most people, and I don't exclude policemen, are far too trusting for this wicked world."

Certainly no one can accuse her of being too trusting. She is suspicious of everyone—and everything. She accepts little at face value. "Any coincidence," she maintains, "is always worth noticing. You can throw it away later if it is only a coincidence."

In the first book in which she appears, **Murder at the Vicarage**, she is less than lovable—a long step from the grandmotherly lady that she becomes as she grows older. Although the local vicar likes her, noting that "she has, at least, a sense of humor," his wife loathes Miss Marple, calling her "the worst cat in the village. And she always knows every single thing that happens—and draws the worst inferences from it."

Miss Marple patronizingly tells the vicar's young wife, "You are very young. The young have such innocent minds." She proceeds to ignore the girl's indignant protest, patting her affectionately on the arm and saying, "Naturally, you think the best of everyone."

The vicar bemusedly scolds Miss Marple for gossiping, saying, "Charity thinketh no evil, you know. Inestimable harm may be done by the foolish wagging of tongues in ill-natured gossip." Miss Marple, totally unabashed, replies, "Dear vicar, you are so unworldly. I'm afraid that, observing human nature for as long as I have done, one gets not to expect very much from it. I daresay idle tittle-tattle is very wrong and unkind, but it is often true, isn't it?"

It is, perhaps, surprising to find such a pessimistic (or realistic) view of life in a quiet, genteel lady who has spent her entire life in a small village. Born in St. Mary Mead, Jane Marple is past eighty when she travels from it for the first time. To her, that village is a microcosm of the world, and whatever is to be found on the planet, in the way of human nature, is to be found there. Whatever existed or occurred in that village for three-quarters of a century, no matter how surreptitious or trivial, the likelihood is that it was observed by

All four films about Miss Marple starred Margaret Rutherford as the spinster sleuth. It is no secret that Agatha Christie, although an admirer of Miss Rutherford, disliked the films.

Miss Marple.

It is not that she merely stumbles upon her information. No, she leaves nothing as important as that to chance. She seeks it out, often aided by a pair of field glasses, which she half-heartedly claims to be using in pursuit of her avowed hobby of bird-watching. No one believes her for a moment, nor does she expect them to. She has little explaining to do, however, because she is seldom caught in the act of spying.

"In the art of seeing without being seen," the vicar says, "Miss Marple had no rival."

Almost nothing is known of her early years, and she is not introduced until she is seventy-four years old, which leaves unchronicled a great deal of her life. Still, one has the suspicion that most of that time was spent not dissimilarly to her present days.

She enjoys gardening, knitting (everyone in

the village and their distant relatives must own several of the white fleecy things that she knits at a pace that would have been the envy of Madame Defarge), and snooping and gossiping—not necessarily in that order.

Newspapers are a prime source of pleasure (and information) for her. "In the afternoon it was the custom of Miss Jane Marple to unfold her second newspaper (the **Daily Newsgiver**). Two newspapers were delivered at her house every morning. The first one (**The Times**) Miss Marple read while sipping her early morning tea. That is, if it was delivered in time."

Not surprisingly, she is interested in the news stories, not the features or columns of opinion. She has her own opinions, thank you, and doesn't feel a compelling necessity to know those of others. She begins with the front page news stories, and then reads all the notices of births, marriages and deaths.

Even at her age, she has a remarkable memory, able to retain every scrap of news and gossip that she is able to uncover, whether from a front page or through a keyhole. That miraculous retentive ability makes her a valuable witness in criminal cases.

"I think she is quite dependable," the vicar cautiously tells the chief constable of the village. "That is, in so far as she is talking of what she has actually seen. Beyond that, of course, when you get on to what she thinks—well, that is another matter. She has a powerful imagination, and systematically thinks the worst of everyone."

"The typical elderly spinster, in fact," jokes the chief constable.

As far as appearances are concerned, he is quite right. An attractive old lady, she is tall and thin, with great masses of white hair (which is occasionally described as gray), "a pink crinkled face," and a gentle, appealing—if slightly fussy—manner. Despite having the village-wide reputation of a cobra, her faded china-blue eyes are benign, soft, kindly and innocent, frequently with a youthful twinkle in them.

Generally dressed in fleecy wool clothes, she is also quite at ease in more formal attire, such as a black brocade dress, pinched in at the waist, with mechlin lace arranged in a cascade down the front of her bodice, black lace mittens and a black lace cap. Often, a shetland shawl is thrown over her head and shoulders.

Her appearance and manner are a source of smug amusement to her nephew, novelist Raymond West. Even her house pleases him because it seems to him to be the right setting for her personality.

It is a fine old house, small, with lots (perhaps a bit too much) of good furniture and decorations crowded into it. The drawing room is small and feminine, and the ceiling has broad black beams across it.

A small lane runs across the bottom of her special joy—the well-groomed rock garden. She used to tend it herself, but now requires a gardener (Edwards, later replaced by Laycock) to work it three days a week, because her doctor insists that she take it easy. "Active gardening has been forbidden for some time now," she realizes. "No stooping, no digging, no planting—at most a little light pruning." She is pleased neither with the restraint on her activity nor the quality of the work performed by the gardener.

The garden, the house, the village—all are tolerated with some condescension by West. "You'll adore my aunt Jane," he tells a female friend. "She's what I should describe as a perfect period piece. Victorian to the core. All her dressing tables have their legs swathed in chintz. She lives in a village. The kind of village where nothing ever happens, exactly like a stagnant pool."

Miss Marple is aware of his attitude, and allows him to retain it. She is quite fond of him, and has much reason to be grateful to him. He is generous with her, for one, paying for her holidays and augmenting her meager fixed income, and he also introduces her to the delights of detection.

The vicar, a long-time admirer of Miss Marple, has his own views of the self-consciously debonair West. "His poems have no capital letters in them, which is, I believe, the essence of modernity. His books are about unpleasant people leading lives of surpassing dullness. He has a tolerant affection for 'Aunt Jane,' whom he alludes to in her presence as a 'survival.' She listens to his talk with a flattering interest, and if there is sometimes an amused twinkle in her eye, I am sure he never notices it."

West lives in London with his wife Joan, arising scandalously late each day, and alternates smoking a pipe and cigarettes. His handsome income derives from his novels, but he also writes poetry. Miss Marple describes his books as "very clever."

Although he claims to have no interest in real-life murders because they are "crude," he forms a group which meets once a week to discuss unsolved mysteries. Called "The Tuesday Night Club," its membership includes Miss Marple; Joyce Lempriere, an artist with close-cropped black hair; Sir Henry Clithering, an ex-commissioner of

Scotland Yard and man of the world; Dr. Pender, and elderly clergyman of the parish; and Mr. Pitherick, a dried-up little solicitor.

When crimes are offered for examination, everyone has theories for their solution, but it is inevitably Miss Marple, armed with her abundant repertoire of analogies, who arrives at a satisfactory conclusion. Later, she is acknowledged to be unusually gifted in these intellectual exercises, and other members defer to her. They simply provide the incomplete puzzles and Miss Marple adds the missing ingredients, tying up the loose ends of even the most complicated problems.

Having discovered the fun of solving crimes, she soon finds herself in the position of helping the local police whenever a murder occurs—without having to wait for a Tuesday night meeting to indulge her talents.

In addition to giving his aunt the opportunity to display her evident gifts as an amateur detective, West opens another world for her—that portion of the world's geography that exists beyond the borders of St. Mary Mead. The wealthy nephew is pleased to give Miss Marple the chance to travel and broaden her experience. She is properly grateful:

"Yes," she allows, "the dear boy has been so successful with his clever books—he prides himself upon never writing about anything pleasant. The dear boy insisted on paying all my expenses. And his dear wife is making a name for herself, too, as an artist. Mostly jugs of dying flowers and broken combs on windowsills."

On the whole, she decides, he is fond of her. "He always had been—in a slightly exasperated and contemptuous way! Always trying to bring her up to date. Sending her books to read. Modern novels. So difficult—all about such unpleasant people, doing such very odd things and not, apparently, even enjoying them. 'Sex' as a word had not been much mentioned in Miss Marple's young days, but there had been plenty of it—not talked about so much—but enjoyed far more than nowadays, or so it seemed to her. Though usually labelled Sin, she couldn't help feeling that that was preferable to what it seemed nowadays—a kind of duty."

Miss Marple cannot deny that she preferred the more gracious and refined days of the past to the frenzied pace of the present day. "One had to face the fact," she acknowledges, "St. Mary Mead was not the place it had been. In a sense, of course, nothing was what it had been. You could blame the war (both the wars), or the younger generation, or women going out to work, or the atom bomb, or just the government—but what one really meant was the simple fact that one was growing old. Miss Marple, who was a very sensible old lady, knew that quite well. It was just that, in a queer way, she felt it more in St. Mary Mead, because it had been her home for so long."

The recent paperback series by Pocket Books features this portrait of a genteel Miss Marple.

As the years pass, Miss Marple comes to care less and less for the increasing modernization of society. She sees no changes for the better, no improvement in the quality of life, only the continued erosion of the values and standards of her own generation. Although she tries to keep up with the times, she thinks nostalgically of better years, when she was younger.

She has slowed down more than she is prepared to accept with equanimity. In addition to being denied the pleasure of pottering about her garden in her older age, she is unable to walk long distances and is forced to rely on other people to bring information to her, acting as her legmen.

While she inexorably ages, she grows more frail, but her mind never loses its sharpness. Her broad range of knowledge proves invaluable during investigations, although she dismisses her education as "plain and homegrown, just the product of life in a country village."

Others may know as much as she does, but Miss Marple has the unique ability to use her knowledge of human nature to solve murder mysteries more effectively and consistently than any other widely known female detective.

To discover the essential point of a case early in her career, she uses her eyesight (mainly through bird-watching glasses). In later years, she arrives at the same successful destination by using her insight.

In her quiet, modest little way, she achieves the same level of infallibility reached by the most flamboyant and arrogant of her contemporaries—equal, even, to a certain Belgian who is so pompous about his "little grey cells."

AGATHA CHRISTIE (1890-1976) Born Agatha Mary Clarissa Miller in Torquay, Devon, England, Dame Agatha (she was made a Commander Order of the British Empire [C.B.E.] in 1956 and Dame Commander Order of the British Empire [D.B.E.] in 1971) is the most widely read author of detective fiction who ever lived. She divorced her first husband, Colonel Archibald Christie, in 1928 (two years after her brief but much-publicized disappearance) and two years later met and married archeologist Max Mallowan. Her books have been translated into more than one hundred languages and have had sales in excess of 400 million. In addition to creating Miss Marple and Hercule Poirot, she has written about the mysterious Harley Quin, the sprightly Tommy and Tuppence Beresford, the philanthropic Parker Pyne, and others. Of her many mystery plays, **Witness for the Prosecution** is a masterpiece and **The Mousetrap** a phenomenon; still running after about a quarter-century, it is the longest-running play in the history of the London stage.

FILMOGRAPHY

1962 **Murder She Said** (MGM) with Margaret Rutherford (as Miss Marple), Arthur Kennedy, Muriel Pavlow, James Robertson Justice, Ronald Howard; directed by George Pollock.
1963 **Murder at the Gallop** (MGM with Margaret Rutherford, Robert Morley, Flora Robson, Charles Tingwell; directed by George Pollock.
1964 **Murder Most Foul** (MGM) with Margaret Rutherford, Ron Moody, Charles Tingwell, Megs Jenkins; directed by George Pollock.
1964 **Murder Ahoy!** (MGM) with Margaret Rutherford, Lionel Jeffries, Charles Tingwell, Francis Mathews; directed by George Pollock.
1966 **The Alphabet Murders** (MGM) with Tony Randall, Anita Ekberg, Robert Morley, Maurice Denham and Margaret Rutherford (as Miss Marple, making a very brief appearance in a Hercule Poirot film); directed by Frank Tashlin.

BIBLIOGRAPHY

1930 **Murder at the Vicarage** (Dodd, Mead)
1933 **The Tuesday Club Murders** (Dodd, Mead; published as **The Thirteen Problems** in 1932 by Collins, London)
1939 **The Regatta Mystery and Other Stories** (Dodd Mead; one of the nine stories is about Miss Marple)
1942 **The Body in the Library** (Dodd, Mead)
1942 **The Moving Finger** (Dodd, Mead)
1950 **Three Blind Mice and Other Stories** (Dodd, Mead; four of the nine stories are about Miss Marple)
1950 **A Murder Is Announced** (Dodd, Mead)
1952 **Murder with Mirrors** (Dodd, Mead; British title: **They Do It with Mirrors,** Collins, London)
1954 **A Pocket Full of Rye** (Dodd, Mead; published 1953 by Collins, London)
1957 **What Mrs. McGillicuddy Saw!** (Dodd, Mead; British title: **4:50 from Paddington**, Collins, London)
1960 **The Adventure of the Christmas Pudding and Other Stories** (London: Collins; not published in the U.S.; one of the six stories is about Miss Marple)
1961 **Double Sin and Other Stories** (Dodd, Mead; two of the eight stories are about Miss Marple)
1963 **The Mirror Crack'd** (Dodd, Mead; published as **The Mirror Crack'd from Side to Side** in 1962 by Collins, London)
1965 **A Caribbean Mystery** (Dodd, Mead; published in 1964 by Collins, London)
1966 **At Bertram's Hotel** (Dodd, Mead; published in 1965 by Collins, London)
1971 **Nemesis** (Dodd, Mead)
1976 **Sleeping Murder** (Dodd, Mead)

Perry Mason

The characteristic that most distinguishes Perry Mason from the other great detectives of fiction is that he is not primarily a detective. He is a lawyer, and when he requires detective work he hires someone else, Paul Drake, to do it. Mason does have many of the attributes shared by the most successful detectives—a love of justice, a deep-rooted belief in truth, and a mind acute enough to discover them from a jumble of lies, genuine information, half-truths, red herrings and apparent dead ends.

Although he is the most famous lawyer in fiction, Mason's earliest cases are straightforward, action-filled thrillers which have little to do with jurisprudence. In the first book about Mason, **The Case of the Velvet Claws**, he neither gives legal advice nor appears in court, acting pretty much like a private detective.

Unlike the later cases, and the popular television series starring Raymond Burr (which ran for ten years, starting in 1957), the early adventures are hard-boiled, two-fisted and noncerebral. A considerable disdain for the law is in evidence (as in most books about private detectives, particularly in the 1930s, when Mason's recorded career began), and results are more often obtained with a punch to the mouth or a blasting revolver than by a clever deduction.

Admittedly, there are certain elements of unreality about the Mason stories which have been perpetuated by the successful television program. Defying all odds, Mason never loses a case, and almost never goes to trial. In the overwhelming majority of the cases which have appeared in print, Mason uses an enviable legal strategy—getting an acquittal for his client in the courtroom at the preliminary hearing.

Erle Stanley Gardner, the author of the long series (more than eighty) of Perry Mason books, used crisp dialogue and a great deal of physical action in his narratives, preferring it to lengthy descriptive passages. A logical extension of this stylistic preference culminated in the Mason novels, in which most of the events and motivations are revealed during courtroom cross-examinations.

Most of Mason's clients have something to hide and therefore give the appearance of guilt, even though they are invariably innocent of the charges against them. Fortunately for them,

Mason is intelligent and resourceful enough to trap unsuspecting villains into giving themselves away, or forcing them into corners, resulting in an unusual number of confessions.

The infallibility of the Los Angeles-based attorney has had a deep and long-enduring appeal. The books recording his adventures have outsold the narratives of every other American crimefighter. It is impossible to keep accurate records of sales for the Perry Mason books because they are both mammoth and unending, but it has been estimated that Gardner titles have sold in excess of 200 million copies, of which the majority are about the lawyer whose name has become synonymous with legal justice. After the author's death in 1970, his already written but unpublished books continued to appear for several years, and new editions in paper covers and many foreign languages are still being reissued in an immeasurable, unstoppable wave.

Gardner, also a lawyer, served loosely as the prototype for Perry Mason. The name was acquired from another famous fictional lawyer, although of a diametrically opposite breed. Randolph Mason, the central figure in three books by Melville Davisson Post (the creator of Uncle Abner), was a successful, albeit unscrupulous, lawyer whose cases were published between 1896 and 1908. Totally amoral, if not downright scurrilous, Randolph Mason once advised his client to extricate himself from an apparently hopeless situation by committing murder.

Being introduced to Perry Mason could make a potential client, or just about anyone else, a trifle nervous. He has the appearance and manner more of a bounty hunter than a lawyer in 1933, the year of his first published case.

"Perry Mason sat at the big desk. There was about him the attitude of one who is waiting. His face in repose was like the face of a chess player who is studying the board. That face seldom changed expression. Only the eyes changed expression. He gave the impression of being a thinker and a fighter, a man who could work with infinite patience to jockey an adversary into just the right position, and then finish him with one terrific punch."

That description, in **The Case of the Velvet Claws**, is not misleading. Mason, particularly in his younger days, is exceptionally powerful and athletic, and very tough. His physicality helps give the impression of bigness, "not the bigness of fat, but of strength." He has long arms and legs, strong hands and fingers, broad shoulders, narrow hips, walks as if he is "reasonably young" and looks as if "he keeps himself in good condition." When he stands, he is well-balanced, with his feet flat on the floor and evenly spaced, "like a man getting ready to slug someone." And he probably is.

In **The Case of the Golddigger's Purse**, a suspect takes an ill-advised swing at Mason, who ducks under it and then knocks him out with a right to the stomach followed by a powerful right uppercut. In another urgent situation, an assailant chokes Mason's secretary, Della Street, almost killing her. The infuriated lawyer punches him, breaking his nose.

Among other athletic escapades, Mason impersonates a window washer, jumping from one sill to another at a dizzying height; he is chased by ferocious Doberman pinschers, just managing to climb a barbed-wire-and-broken-glass-topped wall; and, in a supreme moment of confidence, he stands his ground and stares down a gorilla which has just attacked him.

With that accomplishment as evidence, it is not unreasonable to suggest that Mason's most remarkable feature is his eyes. They are always steady and patient, changing expression quickly and frequently, though his face never does. His granite-hard face constantly maintains an expression of rugged patience and, although it remains unlined as late as 1965, the eyes squint at the corners when he is irritated.

Nothing irritates him more profoundly than blackmail, one of the most heinous of crimes. There are, he says, only four ways to deal with a blackmailer: (1) pay; (2) go to the police; (3) find a way to put the blackmailer on the defensive; (4) kill the blackmailer. Mason prefers methods (2) or (3). To prevent a blackmailer from getting a list of adopted children, to be used to blackmail the real parents, Mason is unhesitatingly willing to risk his reputation and his liberty.

That is not the only time he puts his career on

Perpetually identified with Mason, Raymond Burr starred in the television series for a decade. Here, Ruta Lee is accused of an ice-pick murder.

the line. He sees nothing extraordinary about risking everything, including his life, for a cause. His philosophy of life almost requires it, in fact.

"I play a no-limit game," he says in **The Case of the Caretaker's Cat**. "When I back my judgment I back it with everything I have. What the hell can a man lose? He can't lose his life because he doesn't own that anyway. He only has a lease on life. He can lose money, and money doesn't mean one damn thing as compared with character. All that really matters is man's ability to live life, to get the most out of it as he goes through it, and he gets the most kick out of it by playing a no-limit game."

It is rare for Mason to get through a case without taking the risk of arrest, disbarment, financial ruin or even death. Although he is familiar with the law, he does not flinch at breaking it in more than two dozen recorded instances, committing crimes ranging from assault and battery, breaking and entering, and reckless driving (his most common crimes) to bribery, destroying, concealing or withholding evidence, fleeing a warrant, trespassing, possession of stolen property, sending a false alarm, illegal wiretapping, illegal gambling and being an accessory after the fact.

Seldom arrested for the crimes he commits, he is sometimes arrested for those of which he is innocent, including suspicion of murder. In **The Case of the Half-Wakened Wife,** Mason is the co-defendant (with Paul Drake) in a $250,000 defamation of character suit. A few years later, he is hauled before the grievance committee of the California State Bar Association. In 1954, he is sentenced for contempt of court, fined $10,000 and given three months in jail, but the judge relents after Mason exposes a murderer.

He is unafraid to take these risks, supported by his judgment, because he invariably has the truth on his side. He relies on the truth, he says, because it is "the only weapon powerful enough; a lawyer doing the things I have done and relying on anything less powerful would be disbarred in a month."

Frequently, those who work for Mason are subject to similar legal difficulties. Della Street is arrested in **The Case of the Lame Canary** but is released almost immediately on a writ of habeas corpus; the following year (1938), she is arrested as an accessory after the fact after fleeing a subpoena to appear as a material witness. Altogether, she finds herself in the slammer on five separate occasions.

Della shares more than a criminal record with her employer. Not many secretaries can truthfully say they have been poisoned with their bosses, but she can. In **The Case of the Drowsy Mosquito**, both she and Perry swallow arsenic, but they quickly recover.

It is impossible for Mason to handle a case in a safe, conventional manner. "The trouble with me," he says late in his career, "is that I am a born grandstander. My friends call it a flair for the dramatic. My enemies call it four-flushing. That, coupled with a curiosity about people and an interest in anything that looks like a mystery, is always getting me into trouble."

Similarly, he makes no apologies for his sometimes bizarre behavior. "I have been able to order my life along unconventional patterns and no longer refrain from doing what I want to do simply because it is odd, unusual, distinctive, or unconventional."

Among the less ordinary features of his life and career is the matter of his fee. His office suite in downtown Los Angeles (Broadway and Seventh Street) is handsome and costly, and Mason complains of the upkeep on more than one occasion. Yet he sometimes turns down extremely lucrative fees, because of various principles, and has taken as little as five cents—from a neighbor he wanted to help.

There is, however, no fear of Mason's starving as long as he continues to practice. Although he turns down an offer of $100,000 from a millionaire for a dishonest job, he later receives an unasked-for $150,000 for completing an honest one. Early in his career, he takes a case on consignment, hoping to net $200,000-$300,000 for it.

Possibly because he has enough of it, money does not overly concern Mason, and he shows his generosity frequently. He has one client's wealthy father write a check for $150,000 to a children's hospital and once bought a pack of cigarettes with a $20 bill, thereby providing aid for the young daughter of the widowed cigar counter girl in his office building lobby.

Many of his clients are poor. As a court-appointed attorney, he actually loses money on some cases because of unreimbursed expenses. When a client asks him if he would defend a poor person against a millionaire, Mason replies, "I'd fight for a client against the devil himself."

Mason's financial position can only be regarded as extremely comfortable, though he makes no fuss about it. In his first recorded case, he lives in an apartment, but within a couple of years he has moved to a luxury apartment hotel because of the greater convenience. He is a member of an unspecified lodge, belongs to a private club at which he sometimes stops for a drink on the way home

Perry Mason, portrayed by Donald Woods in The Case of the Stuttering Bishop *(1937), in a typical courtroom scene. Inevitably, the guilty party (never his client) will confess.*

from work, and is a member of the Remuda Golf Club.

He is initially seen driving a Buick coupe, but in two years is behind the wheel of a convertible. Paul Drake says that Mason "drives like Hell on wet roads." While the exigencies of a case sometimes continue to cause him to drive recklessly, by the mid-1950s Mason drives a fairly late model, conservatively dark, medium-sized sedan, which he has pledged to drive carefully, much to Della's relief.

"The automobile has become a deadly weapon," he says. "Too many people with too many automobiles are going places at the same time. When I'm going to drive a car I never take more than one drink, and I have that very light."

That careful attention to moderation in his consumption of alcohol develops late in his life. In 1933, when he is forty-two years old (although it is not specifically stated in any of the stories, evidence indicates that Perry Mason was born in 1891), he keeps a bottle of rye whiskey in his desk. Throughout the scores of ensuing cases, he demonstrates one of the most catholic tastes in liquor of any crimefighter in literature, drinking steadily (though never to excess) and variously.

Compared with his dining habits, however, he is a virtual teetotaler. Only Nero Wolfe spends more time at the table than Mason, and it can be regarded as a small miracle that he is able to keep his trim physique. By the 1960s, however, he has to watch his calories and often skips lunch since he is unable to get enough outdoor exercise.

Mason not only loves to eat, he loves to eat well, and knows how to do it. When he takes Della to dinner, they feast on cream of tomato

A physically active Mason appeared in the early novels and in comic books such as The Case of the Shoplifter's Shoe, *published in 1947.*

soup, avocado and grapefruit salad, filet mignon (medium rare), artichokes, shoestring potatoes, plum pudding with brandy sauce, demitasse and old-fashioneds. But he is no snob about food, regarding as a wonderful treat some hot French bread and red wine, and breakfasting simply on a three-minute egg with salt and pepper and crisp buttered toast. When he goes on stag hunting trips, he is an enthusiastic amateur cook.

The hunting and fishing trips, on which he sometimes prefers to be alone, are a manifestation of his love of the outdoors. On vacation at a ski resort in Bear Valley, California, he skis, hikes and goes horseback riding. He has an interest in unusual cacti and rocks in the desert, and displays an immense knowledge of astronomy. Mason also acknowledges that he "knows a good deal about guns."

In much of his spare time he reads—the latest discoveries in psychology being his favorite topic in the 1930s, moving on to **Advance Decisions** (a periodical issued by a legal publishing company) in the 1940s and 1950s, and to mystery stories in the 1970s. In between (1960), he complains, "I don't have time to read . . . I keep too damn busy."

Often, he is simply too nervous to read for relaxation. He has a habit of drumming his fingers at such times, and frequently paces with his thumbs tucked in the armholes of his vest. He generally smokes (Raleighs) at an ordinary rate, but when he is under stress he becomes an uncontrollable chain smoker. After a day of hard physical exercise, deliberately self-imposed to make him weary and ready to sleep at night, he anxiously awakes after a few hours, bright-eyed, thinking of legal problems. Experience has shown him that he doesn't require a lot of sleep, a shave and a Turkish bath refreshing him adequately. On one particularly trying case, Mason finds himself unable to eat much at the lunchtime recess because of nerves.

In this 1960 case, Mason is forced to put his client, the defendant, on the stand—something he has only done twice before. He does not enjoy going to trial because of the unpredictability of jurors, but is even more reluctant to subject a client to the rigors of cross-examination. While he always does his best for clients, he does not always know whether or not they are guilty.

He has mixed feelings about defending a guilty client. Once, in **The Case of the Perjured Parrot**, he says, "I never take a case unless I am convinced my client was incapable of committing the crime charged."

Yet, in **The Case of the Counterfeit Eye**, he claims that the matter of guilt is without importance.

"I don't ask a client if he's guilty or innocent," he says. "Either way he's entitled to a day in court. If I should find one of my clients was really guilty of murder and wasn't morally or legally justified, I'd make the client plead guilty and throw himself on the mercy of the court."

That is probably the only instance in which Mason would fail to carry on a fight, no matter how hopeless it might seem. Intensely loyal to his clients, he claims to expect no reciprocity.

"I can't expect my clients to be loyal to me," he says. "My clients aren't blameless . . . probably a lot of them are guilty. That's not for me to determine. That's for the jury."

While professing not to expect loyalty from his clients, he is nonetheless furious at one who settles an accident case without first informing Mason. "You sold me out," he rages.

He has confidence himself, and is firmly convinced that he can swing any jury if the situation requires it. He does not believe in challenging jurors during the selection process, preferring to save his fights for the trial.

"I'm a trial lawyer," he tells Paul Drake. "I go into court on anything where there's a contest. I've specialized in criminal cases. I've done some personal injury work. I've tried a will contest now and then. Wherever there's a fight, I'm apt to be in the middle of it."

As tough, aggressive, intelligent and competent as he is, Mason knows that he cannot accomplish his goals by himself. "A lawyer can't afford to get too big," he says. "He always has to remember he's part of the machinery by which justice is dispensed. When it comes to a matter of justice or injustice, there isn't such a thing as big or little. Injustice is a social malignancy."

Several people help Mason in his quest for justice. Of primary importance is Della Street, the most famous secretary in fiction. Early in their respective careers, their relationship is purely (literally) employer and employee, but that inevitably changes, to the surprise of no one.

Mason is handsome, with a deep, well-modulated voice, thick curly hair, and a winning masculine charm which attracts many women. Della is unusually attractive, slim, about five feet, three inches tall, a firm, athletic, 112 pounds, with "perfect" legs. Unwaveringly loyal to Perry, risking her life and liberty for him on numerous occasions, she is frankly in love with him, yet refuses his five separate marriage proposals.

Mason has made it clear that he would not permit his wife to work, and she has said, "I wouldn't want to live unless I could work for a living." They are, then, at an impasse, and thereafter make the best of their situation, sharing many years of intimacy, traveling together, and remaining devoted to each other.

"You're not the marrying kind," she once tells him. "I don't think you need a wife, but I know damn well you need a secretary who's willing to go to jail occasionally to back your play."

Della is about fifteen years younger than Mason, but he manages to keep up with her. Like her employer, she is an excellent horseback rider—one of the many activities they enjoy sharing. Her family once had a great deal of money and subsequently lost it, presumably during the Great Depression, though she rarely talks about them.

When she does talk, Della has her moments of earthiness. Mason once tries to stifle a strong urge to swear, but she tells him not to hold back. "I've heard all the words before, and this is once I'd like to hear 'em again."

Equally prominent in Mason's professional life, if not his personal one, is Paul Drake, the private investigator whose firm owes 75 per cent of its business to Mason. His agency, conveniently located in the same office building as Mason's, is open twenty-four hours a day, as it has to be because of the eccentric hours he keeps when Mason involves him in a case. Those irregular hours wreak havoc on Drake's digestive system, forcing him to grab quick hamburgers on the run instead of quiet, relaxing meals. He frequently complains of stomach pains, taking more bicarbonate of soda and other stomach medicines than any human being might have been thought capable of ingesting. When things slow down a bit, *and* when he is on an expense account, he enjoys sumptuous dinners.

Tall and droop-shouldered, Drake prefers to sit sideways in the big high-backed leather chair in Mason's office, his long legs crossed over the

LT.

right-hand arm of the chair, the small of his back against the other arm. Usually hanging from his lower lip is a cigarette which he has rolled himself (with nicotine-stained fingers as evidence). His head thrusts forward on a long, skinny neck, and his large, glassy eyes protrude in an expression of perpetual droll humor.

Myrtle Lamar, the elevator operator in the office building, regards Mason as "inaccessible" but likes Drake, also a bachelor, and calls him "available." She is, however, wrong. Jilted when he was young, Drake has never really gotten over it and, in all likelihood, still carries a torch, though he does not discuss it. Aside from a few perfunctory passes at the lovely Della, he seems to have no interest in women. Whether or not there is a connection with his romantic life (or, more accurately, lack of it) would be difficult to ascertain, but Drake is exceptionally pessimistic and superstitious.

Several members of Mason's office staff have had recurring roles in his recorded exploits. In two early cases, a young clerk, Frank Everly, had vocal doubts about Mason's tactics; he was never heard from again. Jackson, another law clerk, worked for the firm from 1938 to 1944. Ponderously dignified, tall and thin, with a sharp face and long nose, Mason felt he was not a good fighter, that he was too ready to follow an opponent's lead.

Finding a good receptionist was difficult until Mason hired Gertie (Gertrude Lade) in 1939. Loyal and resourceful, she immediately settled comfortably into Mason's office. When she arrived she was "tall, thin as a rail, figure angular, face plain, spectacles." By the following year, she is described as a "big, good-natured blonde . . . ample figure." Since then, she has always had a weight problem, dieting constantly (or trying to, anyway).

Not everyone involved with Mason on a regular basis is friendly to him, as usual with people who have powerful personalities. Early in the recorded cases, Hamilton Burger and Mason seem to have no particular malice toward each other, though Burger considered Mason a better detective than attorney.

Burger has just been elected District Attorney in 1935 and Mason says of him: "I think he's inclined to be a square shooter. He wants to get convictions when he's certain he's prosecuting guilty people, but he doesn't want to convict innocent ones."

William Hopper played Paul Drake in the successful television series which starred Burr. Mason must clear the detective of a murder charge.

By the 1950s, there is open antagonism between the two. In **The Case of the Fugitive Nurse**, Burger throws a punch at Mason, who ducks under it and warns, "Don't do that again, Burger, unless you want your jaw smashed." Three years later, Burger becomes so irate when Mason thwarts him that a judge is forced to tell him, "Control yourself and either present this case or dismiss it." Another time, he is "so choked with anger he could hardly talk" and, still later, Mason delightedly rubs salt into Burger's wound by telling him "From the color of your face I think you'd better take off about 30 pounds."

A bachelor, Burger is muscular and broad-shouldered, suggestive of a huge bear. "Once he started to act, he threw himself into that action with a concentrated force that eliminated any possibility of re-examining the situation."

It is, perhaps, not difficult to understand Burger's violent hostility to Mason. Although regarded as a good D.A, his office never successfully prosecutes a case against a Mason client. Once, in **The Case of the Terrified Typist**, a jury finds Mason's client guilty, but before the narrative ends Mason has had the decision reversed.

Most of Mason's clients need a lawyer because they have been arrested by Lt. Arthur Tragg, one of the most astute members of the Los Angeles Police Department. A slender, sophisticated bachelor, he makes his first appearance in 1940, and by 1948 is promoted to head of the Homicide Bureau, though still at the rank of lieutenant, at which level he remains throughout the series. This stagnation of rank might rankle him more than he lets on, because he is almost unreasonably impatient. Before a flight to New Orleans, for example, he admits, "I'm one of those nervous travelers. I can't sit down and wait until someone calls the plane, but I have to pace the floor and look at the clock as though my eyes could push the minute hand around faster."

Although a constant foe of Mason, Tragg remains friendly toward him for more than thirty years, and Mason reciprocates that high regard, calling him "a live wire" and "a clever, fast thinker." Tragg returns the compliment, saying that Mason has "done more to solve murders than any man on the force."

Of himself, Tragg says, "I'm a servant of the people. I'm a cog in a big system. I play the game to get results. I'm dealing with criminals, and I have a job to do."

Mason has a job to do, too, and he does it

Raymond Burr was the model for Mason, selected as one of the twelve greatest detectives of literature for a series of Interpol stamps.

impeccably. "I get my business because I fight for it and because I fight for my clients," he says.

Tolerant of human frailties, and convinced that anyone who isn't a stuffed shirt has chapters in his life which are best left closed, he draws the line at condoning murder, which he describes as "the supreme culmination of hatred, just as marriage is the supreme culmination of love."

As a defender of justice, he has no illusions about his job, or about the people who hire him. "People don't pay a lawyer to think of what's probably going to happen," he says. "They expect him to think of and anticipate everything that could possibly happen."

One thing is certain to happen. Perry Mason will be forever remembered and honored as the ultimate lawyer-detective in literature.

ERLE STANLEY GARDNER (1889-1970) Born in Malden, Mass., Gardner and his family traveled extensively when he was young, and he spent many years on the West coast. His background included numerous part- and full-time jobs, including professional boxing, promoting fights, tire salesman and typist for a law firm. He became a lawyer in 1911, handling cases for the poor. In addition to full case loads and extensive research for his cases, he wrote at least 4,000 words a day during the 1920s, selling his first mystery story to a pulp magazine in 1923. Then the deluge. During the next decade, he wrote millions of words, sold hundreds of stories under a variety of names, and became successful enough to abandon his law practice in order to devote full time to his writing. The first Perry Mason novel appeared in 1933 and was a success—the beginning of the most successful series ever produced about a lawyer. He still ranks as the best-selling American author of all time, with sales in excess of 200 million.

BIBLIOGRAPHY

1933 **The Case of the Velvet Claws** (Morrow)
1933 **The Case of the Sulky Girl** (Morrow)
1934 **The Case of the Lucky Legs** (Morrow)
1934 **The Case of the Howling Dog** (Morrow)
1934 **The Case of the Curious Bride** (Morrow)
1935 **The Case of the Counterfeit Eye** (Morrow)
1935 **The Case of the Caretaker's Cat** (Morrow)
1936 **The Case of the Sleepwalker's Niece** (Morrow)
1936 **The Case of the Stuttering Bishop** (Morrow)
1937 **The Case of the Dangerous Dowager** (Morrow)
1937 **The Case of the Lame Canary** (Morrow)
1938 **The Case of the Substitute Face** (Morrow)
1938 **The Case of the Shoplifter's Shoe** (Morrow)
1939 **The Case of the Perjured Parrot** (Morrow)
1939 **The Case of the Rolling Bones** (Morrow)
1940 **The Case of the Baited Hook** (Morrow)
1940 **The Case of the Silent Partner** (Morrow)
1941 **The Case of the Haunted Husband** (Morrow)

1941 **The Case of the Empty Tin** (Morrow)
1942 **The Case of the Drowning Duck** (Morrow)
1942 **The Case of the Careless Kitten** (Morrow)
1943 **The Case of the Buried Clock** (Morrow)
1943 **The Case of the Drowsy Mosquito** (Morrow)
1944 **The Case of the Crooked Candle** (Morrow)
1944 **The Case of the Black-Eyed Blonde** (Morrow)
1945 **The Case of the Golddigger's Purse** (Morrow)
1945 **The Case of the Half-Wakened Wife** (Morrow)
1946 **The Case of the Borrowed Brunette** (Morrow)
1947 **The Case of the Fan-Dancer's Horse** (Morrow)
1947 **The Case of the Lazy Lover** (Morrow)
1948 **The Case of the Lonely Heiress** (Morrow)
1948 **The Case of the Vagabond Virgin** (Morrow)
1949 **The Case of the Dubious Bridegroom** (Morrow)
1949 **The Case of the Cautious Coquette** (Morrow)
1950 **The Case of the Negligent Nymph** (Morrow)
1950 **The Case of the One-Eyed Witness** (Morrow)
1951 **The Case of the Fiery Fingers** (Morrow)
1951 **The Case of the Angry Mourner** (Morrow)
1952 **The Case of the Moth-Eaten Mink** (Morrow)
1952 **The Case of the Grinning Gorilla** (Morrow)
1953 **The Case of the Hesitant Hostess** (Morrow)
1953 **The Case of the Green-Eyed Sister** (Morrow)
1954 **The Case of the Fugitive Nurse** (Morrow)
1954 **The Case of the Runaway Corpse** (Morrow)
1954 **The Case of the Restless Redhead** (Morrow)
1955 **The Case of the Glamorous Ghost** (Morrow)
1955 **The Case of the Sunbather's Diary** (Morrow)
1955 **The Case of the Nervous Accomplice** (Morrow)
1956 **The Case of the Terrified Typist** (Morrow)
1956 **The Case of the Demure Defendant** (Morrow)
1956 **The Case of the Gilded Lily** (Morrow)
1957 **The Case of the Lucky Loser** (Morrow)
1957 **The Case of the Screaming Woman** (Morrow)
1957 **The Case of the Daring Decoy** (Morrow)
1958 **The Case of the Long-Legged Models** (Morrow)
1958 **The Case of the Footloose Doll** (Morrow)
1958 **The Case of the Calendar Girl** (Morrow)
1959 **The Case of the Deadly Toy** (Morrow)
1959 **The Case of the Mythical Monkeys** (Morrow)
1959 **The Case of the Singing Skirt** (Morrow)
1959 **The Case of the Waylaid Wolf** (Morrow)
1960 **The Case of the Duplicate Daughter** (Morrow)
1960 **The Case of the Shapely Shadow** (Morrow)
1961 **The Case of the Spurious Spinster** (Morrow)
1961 **The Case of the Bigamous Spouse** (Morrow)
1962 **The Case of the Reluctant Model** (Morrow)
1962 **The Case of the Blonde Bonanza** (Morrow)
1962 **The Case of the Ice-Cold Hands** (Morrow)
1963 **The Case of the Mischievous Doll** (Morrow)
1963 **The Case of the Step-Daughter's Secret** (Morrow)
1963 **The Case of the Amorous Aunt** (Morrow)
1964 **The Case of the Daring Divorcee** (Morrow)
1964 **The Case of the Phantom Fortune** (Morrow)
1964 **The Case of the Horrified Heirs** (Morrow)
1965 **The Case of the Troubled Trustee** (Morrow)
1965 **The Case of the Beautiful Beggar** (Morrow)
1966 **The Case of the Worried Waitress** (Morrow)
1967 **The Case of the Queenly Contestant** (Morrow)
1968 **The Case of the Careless Cupid** (Morrow)
1969 **The Case of the Fabulous Fake** (Morrow)
1970 **The Case of the Crimson Kiss** (Morrow; one of the five stories is about Perry Mason)
1971 **The Case of the Crying Swallow** (Morrow; one of the four stories is about Perry Mason)
1972 **The Case of the Irate Witness** (Morrow; one of the four stories is about Perry Mason)
1972 **The Case of the Fenced-In Woman** (Morrow)
1973 **The Case of the Postponed Murder** (Morrow)

FILMOGRAPHY

1934 **The Case of the Howling Dog** (Warner Brothers) with Warren William (as Perry Mason), Mary Astor, Gordon Wescott, Helen Trenholme; directed by Alan Crosland.
1935 **The Case of the Curious Bride** (Warner Brothers) with Warren William, Margaret Lindsay, Allen Jenkins, Donald Woods; Claire Dodd; directed by Michael Curtiz.
1935 **The Case of the Lucky Legs** (Warner Brothers) with Warren William, Genevieve Tobin, Patricia Ellis, Lyle G. Talbot; directed by Archie L. Mayo.
1936 **The Case of the Velvet Claws** (Warner Brothers) with Warren William, Winifred Shaw, Gordon Elliott, Claire Dodd; directed by William Clemens.
1936 **The Case of the Black Cat** (Warner Brothers) with Ricardo Cortez (as Perry Mason), Gary Owen, June Travis; directed by William McGann.
1937 **The Case of the Stuttering Bishop** (Warner Brothers) with Donald Woods (as Perry Mason), Ann Dvorak, Robert McWade, Anne Nagel; directed by William Clemens.

Mr. Moto

John P. Marquand's Mr. Moto is a figure of mystery and eccentricity—the very model of Oriental inscrutability. He is unique in that, while he is divorced from Western ideas and values (unlike Charlie Chan, who is, after all, an American), he is a likable protagonist and a good guy (unlike virtually every other Asian to appear in mystery fiction until Moto's entrance; the insidious Dr. Fu Manchu was merely one of a horde of sinister Orientals).

Basically little more than a supporting character in the books in which he plays a role, Mr. Moto moves into the lives of disillusioned or disaffected Westerners and serves as a catalyst for their renewed interest in life. The apparent philanthropy is incidental to Moto, who is not especially concerned with them.

He is the number one agent of the imperial Japanese government and has his own problems, his own missions and his own secrets—it is even doubtful that his name is really "Moto." As a character in one of the later books about him points out, "-moto" is not a name at all, but a suffix to other Japanese names, such as Yamamoto, Kashimoto, etc.

In a strict sense, Mr. Moto is not a detective. The books in which he appears are espionage thrillers, leavened with large quantities of the local color and social observation which were later to win Marquand the Pulitzer Prize for fiction when he turned his attention homeward in his straight novel, **The Late George Apley**.

Mr. Moto appeared in five novels, beginning with **No Hero**, during the late 1930s, and a final adventure, **Stopover, Tokyo**, in 1957, which featured Moto and an American joining forces to fight an attempted Communist takeover of post-war Japan.

Without the use of makeup (except for thick eyeglasses and some brilliantine in his hair), Hungarian actor Peter Lorre effectively portrayed Moto in a successful series of films in the late 1930s. World War II, understandably, abruptly terminated the popularity of the Japanese hero, both in films and in books, with American audiences.

Mr. I.A. Moto is described by one of the people involved in his first recorded adventure as "a most accomplished gentleman." This is an

The Hungarian-born Peter Lorre played the subservient Japanese agent perfectly in eight films in the late 1930s. He used virtually no makeup beyond thick glasses and flattened hair.

understatement.

Even the obsequious Japanese himself, forever apologizing and saying "So sorry," "Excuse please" and "I am so stupid," is constrained to admit that he has talents and abilities.

"I can do many, many things," he says. "I can mix drinks and wait on tables and I am a very good valet. I can navigate and manage small boats. I have studied at two foreign universities. I also know carpentry and surveying and five Chinese dialects. So very many things come in useful."

This catalogue modestly omits some of Moto's most frequently used or essential areas of expertise, such as a thorough knowledge of judo, a comfortable familiarity with wiretapping and a dazzling gift for accurately throwing knives.

A "suave scion of Japanese nobility," Mr. Moto is diminutive, weighing less than a hundred pounds. He affects Western dress and is dapper to the point of foppishness, wearing pearl shirt studs and carrying a silk handkerchief with which he dusts his fingers.

Occasionally his outfits degenerate to downright outlandishness. He owns a black-and-white-check suit with a blatantly large pattern, regarding it as the height of Western fashion. He also owns a pair of yellow shoes.

Despite the freaks of costume in which he appears from time to time, Moto is not considered an object of humor or derision. Too much of his serious and intelligent personality slips to the surface for anyone to dismiss him as a comical caricature.

One of Moto's acquaintances is impressed with the seriousness and intensity of the Japanese. "I remember exactly the way the light struck Mr. Moto's face," he recalls, "bringing out the eager, watchful lines around his narrow eyes, and making his blunt nose cast a sideward shadow on his coffee-colored skin. I remember that he was smiling, with the curious reflex action of his race that makes the lips turn up at unconventional moments into a parody of mirth."

Moto does, indeed, grin and smile often. He also laughs politely at other people's jokes, showing his gold-filled front teeth. His features are "finely chiseled. His hands . . . slender and graceful." He has "opaque brown eyes" and eyebrows that are described as "reliable." His hair, which he wears in a "shoebrush" cut, turns from shiny black to graying in his last recorded case.

Born in the first decade of the twentieth century, Moto is a member of a noble and ancient Japanese family (he has a cousin who is a baron). Because his father was attached to the Japanese consulate, Moto spent much of his childhood in New York City, which no doubt accounts for the excellence of his English.

His command of the language is so complete, in fact, that he has great difficulty faking the semi-illiterate Japanese-English pidgin which he sometimes finds it advantageous to affect; he simply forgets to say "prease." He does have some trouble with American slang, though, and needs to have explained to him such phrases as "on the ball," "left me flat" and "made a pass."

During his stay in America, Moto attended college, proudly stating that "I have had the honor to study in the United States," and served as valet to several wealthy gentlemen. Whether he puts himself into service for money or because he was on an assignment remains obscure.

Moto enters the Japanese Secret Service in the late 1920s, traveling the world in the interests of his emperor. In addition to returning to the United States on missions in New York, Washington and Honolulu at least once a year, he often visits Paris, London and other European capitals.

But Moto's primary area of operation, the one in which he is most comfortable and effective, is the Far East, especially China. During the 1930s, it is said that Moto is certain to turn up wherever and whenever there is trouble in China—and always before the trouble has begun.

"Arranging things" is his job, he says, and he goes to considerable lengths to arrange them in the best interests of his country. He is not above surreptitious entry, enabling him to read a person's private correspondence, and he has no second thoughts about having his henchmen liquidate troublesome enemies. He is, however, a loyal ally, and to his friends his word is inviolate.

Despite his long stay in the United States and his familiarity with its customs, he is entirely Japanese, meticulously observing all the nuances of Oriental courtesy. He bows and smiles so naturally when meeting someone or when he enters a room that he does not have to think about it; it is a reflex action.

It is his habit to efface himself for the dual purpose of observing Eastern courtesy and, perhaps more vitally, assuring that his enemies will underestimate him. He carefully calculates its effects before proclaiming, "You are so clever and I am so very stupid."

When he leans close to someone to speak or whisper, he holds his hand in front of his mouth to avoid contaminating the listener with his breath. He frequently punctuates his sentences with a sharp intake of breath between his teeth, causing a sibilant hissing sound.

Mr. Moto is intensely patriotic, just as James Bond, Bulldog Drummond and other espionage agents of literature need to be. His ideology is somewhere to the right of the center of Japanese political thought. When he is captured during one of his missions, he says, "If they do not kill me, at any rate, having failed, I shall have to kill myself."

An apologist for Japanese imperialism, he compares it with American and British colonial expansion. There are limits, however. In one of his adventures, his adversary is the fanatical Mr. Tanaka, whose views are so single-mindedly imperialistic that Moto must stop him.

Before World War II, Mr. Moto has warm personal feelings for the United States and believes in amity between America and Japan—as long as that friendly relationship does not "interfere with what he and his own political faction conceive to be his nation's divine mission to establish hegemony in the East."

With the outbreak of the Second World War, his acquaintances in the West lost track of Moto, but it is reasonable to assume that he held an important position in the intelligence department of the Japanese military, contributing his energies to the war effort.

After the conclusion of hostilities between Japan and the United States, a middle-aged Moto works with representatives of the American military presence to prevent a Communist takeover of Japan. He describes his own policies at this time as "fascist, perhaps, but pro-Emperor, anti-Communist."

The war has left its scars, however, and he is not free of bitterness towards the United States. "Ha-ha," he says, "Americans are so sentimental when they are not using flame throwers and napalm."

To Westerners, even those who knew him for extended periods of time, Mr. I.A. Moto has always been shrouded in mystery, an enigmatic figure moving silently, deferentially and virtually unnoticed through the nether world of international espionage. It is not difficult to imagine that he is active still, a small, smiling, elderly man, busily "arranging things" in the service of his country.

JOHN P. MARQUAND (1893-1960) Born in Wilmington, Del., John P. Marquand graduated from Harvard University in 1915, worked briefly as a reporter for the **Boston Transcript** before serving as an officer in World War I. After returning to civilian life, he took a position with the **New York Tribune** before moving to an advertising agency as a copywriter. He began to write fiction and sold stories to **The Saturday Evening Post**, which later serialized the Mr. Moto novels. His reputation rests equally upon his mystery fiction, notably the series about the Japanese sleuth, and his bitterly ironic social commentary. He won the Pulitzer Prize for **The Late George Apley** (1937), the first of several equally successful social satires on upper-class life.

BIBLIOGRAPHY

1935 **No Hero** (Little, Brown)
1936 **Thank You, Mr. Moto** (Little, Brown)
1937 **Think Fast, Mr. Moto** (Little, Brown)
1938 **Mr. Moto Is So Sorry** (Little, Brown)
1942 **Last Laugh, Mr. Moto** (Little, Brown)
1957 **Stopover: Tokyo** (Little, Brown)

FILMOGRAPHY

1937 **Think Fast, Mr. Moto** (Twentieth Century-Fox) with Peter Lorre (as Mr. Moto), Virginia Field, Thomas Beck, Lotus Long; directed by Norman Foster.

1937 **Thank You, Mr. Moto** (Twentieth Century-Fox) with Peter Lorre, Thomas Beck, Pauline Frederick, Jayne Regan, Sidney Blackmer; directed by Norman Foster.

1938 **Mr. Moto's Gamble** (Twentieth Century-Fox) with Peter Lorre, Keye Luke, Lynn Bari, Harold Huber; directed by James Tinling.

1938 **Mr. Moto Takes a Chance** (Twentieth Century-Fox) with Peter Lorre, Rochelle Hudson, Robert Kent, J. Edward Bromberg; directed by Norman Foster.

1938 **Mysterious Mr. Moto** (Twentieth Century-Fox) with Peter Lorre, Henry Wilcoxon, Mary Maguire, Erik Rhodes, Leon Ames; directed by Norman Foster.

1939 **Mr. Moto's Last Warning** (Twentieth Century-Fox) with Peter Lorre, Ricardo Cortez, Virginia Field, John Carradine, George Sanders, Robert Coote; directed by Norman Foster.

1939 **Mr. Moto in Danger Island** (Twentieth Century-Fox) with Peter Lorre, Jean Hersholt, Amanda Duff, Warren Hymer; directed by Herman I. Leeds.

1939 **Mr. Moto Takes a Vacation** (Twentieth Century-Fox) with Peter Lorre, Joseph Schildkraut, Lionel Atwill, Virginia Field, John King; directed by Norman Foster.

1965 **The Return of Mr. Moto** (Twentieth Century-Fox) with Henry Silva (as Mr. Moto), Suzanne Lloyd, Terrence Longdon; directed by Ernest Morris.

Hercule Poirot

If the most remarkable characteristic of the eccentric little Belgian detective is not his peculiar appearance, it surely is his unmitigated arrogance. Or, possibly, it is his bizarre mannerisms of speech and behavior. Or, then again, it might be his extraordinary popularity with readers; Poirot's adventures outsell the complete works of Hemingway, Fitzgerald, Faulkner, Steinbeck, Hawthorne, Melville, Hardy and Conrad combined.

On the other hand, Poirot's greatest distinction could be his longevity. As the hero of books by a single author, no significant detective approaches the durability of Poirot's career, which spans fifty-five years, from the publication of the first book about him, **The Mysterious Affair at Styles**, in 1920, to the last, **Curtain**, in 1975.

Of some note, too, is his age. While Sherlock Holmes (born in 1854) spent two years in Tibet learning the secrets of long life, and still lives as a retired recluse today, Poirot seems unchallenged as the oldest active detective ever to tackle (if that is not too robust a word) a case.

Although Poirot's age is never specifically divulged, either by himself (he was rather sensitive about it) or by the chroniclers of his adventures, it is known that he retired (with honors, needless to say) from the Belgian Police in 1904; it is likely that he was sixty-five years old at the time. His last adventure took place one year before its publication, or in 1974, so a combination of simple deduction and arithmetic points to Poirot's having passed away at the age of 135. It is not surprising, then, to notice his frailty and feeble health in that last escapade.

Their elephantine ages are not the only traits shared by Holmes and Poirot. Like Dupin, the first detective, they each also had a faithful, if less than dazzlingly endowed intellectually, friend, roommate and chronicler. As Dupin enjoyed the companionship of his anonymous associate, and as Holmes had Watson, Poirot, in many cases, was followed about by Captain

This famous painting of Poirot by W. Smithson Broadhead appeared in The Weekly Sketch, *which published his first adventures in the 1920s.*

Arthur Hastings, who brought the little detective's investigations to the public.

When Hastings does not accompany Poirot on his adventures, Miss Ariadne Oliver often does. A mystery writer, she has wandered into many of Poirot's cases. Miss Oliver also bears a striking resemblance to Agatha Christie. Although she appears pseudonymously, the author appearing as a character in her own books is not unprecedented: S. S. Van Dine narrates the Philo Vance cases, and Ellery Queen carries the device to its extreme, giving the hero the same name as the author.

Also not without precedent, Agatha Christie tired of her detective. Although she did not risk the vengeance of a wrathful public by trying to kill him (as Conan Doyle did Holmes) or retire him (as Simenon did Maigret), she did write Poirot's "final" adventure, **Curtain**, early in the 1940s, then placed the manuscript in a bank vault with the intention of having it published posthumously.

Because of the gratifying success of the film **Murder on the Orient Express**, Dame Agatha allowed the publication of **Curtain** in 1975, which turned out to be the year before her own death. **Curtain** was a dramatic swan song for the diminutive Belgian, who had fallen out of favor with his creator; she much preferred Miss Marple, her other great series detective, in her later years. Poirot had a smaller and smaller role in his own adventures as the years passed, and had appeared in only three novels in the 1960s, compared with fourteen books in the 1930s.

Of Poirot's myriad arabesque locutions, perhaps the best-known is his reference to his brain as "the little grey cells." As an amusing term, it has become part of the English language, its derivation familiar to most listeners.

Curiously, however, according to English mystery writer and erudite scholar H. R. F. Keating, the colorful phrase has been adopted—as a literal and straight-faced usage, meaning "the brain" — by an entire African tribe, which read about Poirot in one of the 103 languages into which Agatha Christie's books have been translated.

Just as the world will always be grateful to young Stamford for introducing Sherlock Holmes and Dr. Watson, it can always take pleasure in a certain happy accident—the chance meeting of Captain Hastings and Hercule Poirot on the warm afternoon of July 16, 1916.

Literally bumping into each other at the entrance of a post office, the less-than-alert Hastings steps back to apologize but, to his astonishment, the little man into whom he has "cannoned" clasps him with both arms, utters a loud exclamation, and kisses him warmly.

Hastings, like Watson, has been invalided home from the front and has been agonizing through a long, depressing convalescence. Having returned to England, he is delighted to stumble across his old friend Poirot, whom he has not seen in several years. The first description of Poirot comes from the pen of the slow-witted but perceptive Hastings, who narrates the detective's first case.

"Poirot was an extraordinary looking little man," he writes. "He was hardly more than 5 feet, 4 inches, but carried himself with great dignity. His head was exactly the shape of an egg, and he always perched it a little on one side. His moustache was very stiff and military. The neatness of his attire was almost incredible. I believe a speck of dust would have caused him more pain than a bullet wound. Yet this quaint dandified little man who, I was sorry to see, limped badly, had been in his time one of the most celebrated members of the Belgian Police. As a detective, his *flair* had been extraordinary, and he had achieved triumphs by unravelling some of the most baffling cases of the day."

Later, Hastings continues to describe the bizarre Poirot: "For neatness of any kind he had an absolute passion. To see an ornament set crooked, or a speck of dust, or a slight disarray in one's attire was torture to the little man until he could ease his feelings by remedying the matter. 'Order' and 'Method' were his gods. He had a certain disdain for tangible evidence, such as footprints and cigarette ash, and would maintain that, taken by themselves, they would never enable a detective to solve a problem. Then he would tap his egg-shaped head with absurd complacency, and remark with great satisfaction, 'the true work, it is done from *within. The little grey cells*—remember always the little grey cells, *mon ami!*' "

It is the "little grey cells" which enable Poirot to enjoy an unfailing sequence of successes, along with his meticulous attention to trivia—he files away every scrap of data for future interpretation.

His method of investigation is established in

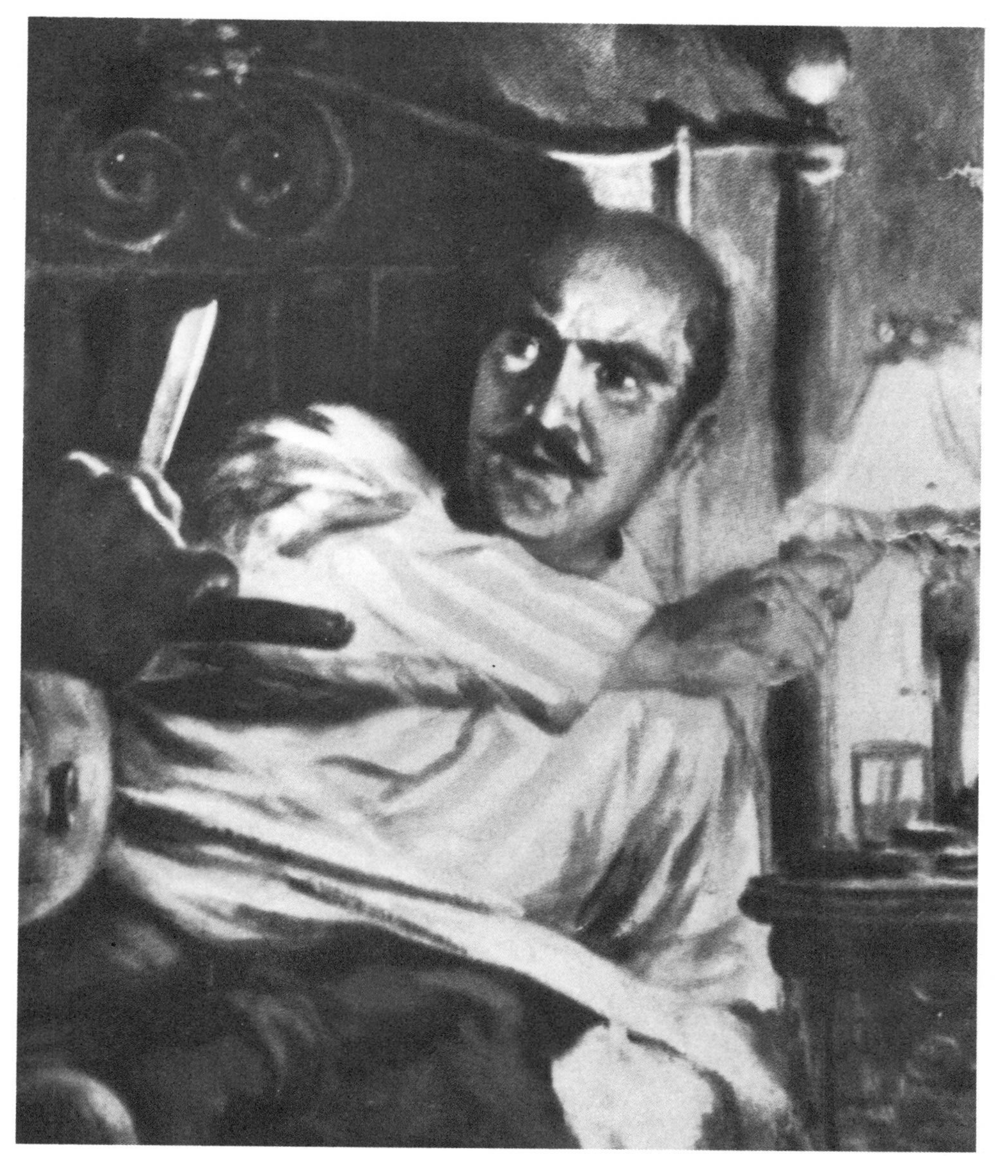

Robert Stanley depicted this imperiled Poirot for the cover of a 1947 Dell paperback, The Labors of Hercules, *a collection of twelve tales.*

his first recorded case, when the blathering Hastings rushes to Leastways Cottage to plead for his friend's help. As Hastings excitedly tells him of the murder at Styles (the house of his friend's mother, where he is a guest), Poirot makes "a careful and deliberate toilet," arranging his moustache "with exquisite care."

Poirot patiently listens to Hastings' babbled account, then serenely asks, "The mind is confused? Is it not so? Take time, *mon ami*. You are agitated. You are excited—it is but natural. Presently, when we are calmer, we will arrange the facts, neatly, each in its proper place. We will examine—and reject. Those of importance we will put on one side; those of no importance, pouf!" Screwing up his face, he puffs comically, and says, "Blow them away!"

When Hastings suggests that the difficulty is in determining what is important and what is not, Poirot responds: "Not so. *Voyons!* One fact leads to another—so we continue. Does the next fit in with that? *A merveille!* Good! We can proceed. This next little fact—no! Ah, that is curious! There is something missing—a link in the chain that is not there. We examine. We search. And that little curious fact, that possibly paltry little detail that will not tally, we put it here!" Gesturing extravagantly, he adds, "It is significant! It is tremendous!"

Pausing to take a breath, and shaking his finger at Hastings to punctuate his point, he warns: "Beware! Peril to the detective who says:

'It is so small—it does not matter. It will not agree. I will forget it.' That way lies confusion! Everything matters."

The exaggerated speech mannerisms, the phrases that absolutely require exclamation marks, the frequent and liberal sprinkling of French expressions—all are part of the Poirot style. It is not purely chance idiosyncracy of personality; it is a technique, an integral part of his effective methodology as a detective.

Entirely aware of what he is doing, Poirot uses the cloak of buffoonery to take advantage of unsuspecting witnesses or hostile suspects. When he interrogates someone, for example, he adopts even more outrageous foreign mannerisms and locutions than he normally uses, tricking his prey into underestimating him, making him careless, allowing him to assume that, because he is a foreigner, he cannot be overly clever.

But he is, of course, quite clever. He knows he is clever, and makes no exhausting effort to deny it. While he admits to being intelligent, he also admits to being modest. Incredibly, he makes the claim with a straight face.

If the truth be known, Poirot has no equal in the world of detection, possibly even in the world of politics, for possessing a mammoth ego. It is of such enormity that he can almost make Holmes (who once says that he does not number humility among the virtues) seem retiring. Not untypical of Poirot is his statement of self-assessment: "I have the habit of always being right—but I do not boast of it."

Discussing his methods with self-effacing restraint, Poirot says, "The trained observer, the expert, without doubt he is useful! But the others, the Hercule Poirots, they are above the experts! To them the experts bring the facts. Their business is the method of the crime, its logical deduction, the proper sequence and order of the facts; above all, the true psychology of the case."

As with most of the great private and amateur detectives, as well as some members of the official law enforcement agencies, it is insight and psychology which eventually result in the solution of a mystery, not the minutiae of evidence required by the principals in a story of police procedure.

"I do not run to and fro making journeys, and agitating myself," Poirot says. "My work is done from within—*here*," he affirms, tapping his forehead significantly.

Poirot has an advantage over most of the famous crimefighters in that he has functioned in three different modes of investigation. After an illustrious career with the Belgian Police, where he presumably gathered physical clues by the bushelful, or had others do it, and made conclusive inferences from them, he engages himself in several cases as an interested amateur, including the first and last of his recorded adventures. In between, he works as a private eye.

Taking rooms at 14, Farraway Street in London, with Hastings as a roommate following their successful handling of the mysterious affair at Styles, Poirot establishes a private practice and does "extraordinarily well" until coming into an inheritance and moving to the village of King's Abbot, in a house called The Larches, where he grows vegetable marrows.

Hastings by this time has married and gone to live in Argentina. Although Poirot has retired, he encounters murder, and confesses to missing his old friend and associate. He also misses his profession, and reminisces to a neighbor.

"My work was interesting work. The most interesting work there is in the world . . . the study of human nature.

"Also I had a friend," Poirot continues, "a friend who for many years never left my side. Occasionally of an imbecility to make one afraid, nevertheless he was very dear to me. Figure to yourself that I miss even his stupidity. His *naïveté*, his honest outlook, the pleasure of delighting and surprising him by my superior gifts—all these I miss more than I can tell you."

Poirot has been a bit hard on poor Hastings, who is not really quite as stupid as the conceited little detective would have it. Nor is he, to be brutally honest, too intelligent. When Poirot, with his annoying habit of keeping his deductions to himself, refuses to allow Hastings to share his insights, the stolid Englishman attempts to do some detective work on his own, with less than spectacular results.

Born around 1890, Hastings was an impecunious gentleman, forced to earn a living by working for Lloyds before World War I, during which he was wounded on the Somme. He has also worked as a recruiter for the army, but his great ambition is to be a detective.

"Well, I've always had a secret hankering to be a detective," he confides to a friend, who asks, "The real thing—Scotland Yard? Or Sherlock Holmes?"

"Oh, Sherlock Holmes by all means," he replies. "But really, seriously, I am awfully drawn to it. I came across a man in Belgium once, a very famous detective, and he quite inflamed me. He was a marvelous little fellow. He used to say that all good detective work was a mere matter of method. My system is based on his—though of course I have progressed rather further."

Whether he has progressed further than Poirot or not is best left undiscussed, but there is incontrovertible evidence that he is invariably astounded at Poirot's deductions.

He never becomes the detective he dreams of being. He is employed as a private secretary to a member of Parliament, and later is a rancher in Argentina, where he prospers.

Until his marriage and removal to South America, Hastings is an incurable romantic, falling for pretty women on almost every case in which he is involved. One he calls "Cinderella." By the time of the last case he shares with Poirot, Hastings is an aging widower, with fully grown children.

Many of the cases between the early recorded adventures and the last are observed by Ariadne Oliver, in Hastings' absence.

A large, agreeable widow, she starts to write mysteries about Sven Hjerson in the 1920s, when she is thirty-five years old. A prolific author, she had completed thirty-two novels by 1936, but Poirot doesn't think much of them, regarding them as highly improbable and stretching coincidence too far.

Miss Oliver is an ardent feminist, anxious to publicize herself, her work and her opinions. Handsome in an untidy fashion, with rebellious gray hair, she has the profile of an eagle.

Perhaps her greatest problem occurs as she ages. An inveterate eater of apples (once consuming five pounds of them at a single sitting while writing), she is forced to get false teeth in her late years. The other concession to her years is that she stops typing at her kitchen

The familiar waxed moustache, the arrogant arch of the eyebrow, the foppish habiliments—they have become as recognizably associated with Poirot as Sherlock Holmes' deerstalker.

Poirot searches for a clue in this illustration for a Pan paperback cover of The Mysterious Affair at Styles. *The first Poirot novel, it had six rejections before it was published.*

table, instead dictating her books to a secretary. Always a volunteer assistant to Poirot (although she is the detective herself in **The Pale Horse**), she acts as his legman late in their careers, as he is considerably older than she and is forced to assume the limitations of the armchair detective.

The longest continuing relationship that Poirot shares is with Georges, his valet, who had been previously employed by Lord Edward Frampton. He is not overly bright, and Poirot rarely discusses his cases with him, but he is an extremely efficient servant. Tall, cadaverous, wooden-faced and unemotional, he is intensely English and totally without imagination.

Equally devoid of imagination is Miss Lemon, Poirot's long-time secretary. What she lacks in humor and *élan* she makes up for with efficiency. She directs Poirot's life with a smoothness of precision that is a model. Incapable of making mistakes, she is always on time, energetic, healthy. and unemotional. She cannot be flustered.

A bit on the chilly side, she reads improving books, is truly ugly, and wears pince-nez. The ideal assistant for Poirot, "she had an instinct. Anything she mentioned as worth consideration usually was worth consideration. She was a born secretary." She had served in that capacity to another remarkable detective—Parker Pyne.

The only other person who has a recurring role in Poirot's life is Detective-Inspector Japp (later promoted to Chief Inspector), a little, "erect, soldierly figure," as stout as Poirot, with a dark, ferret-like face. "His highest talent," says Hastings about Japp, "lay in the gentle art of seeking favors under the guise of conferring them."

Hastings has no affection for James Japp. "He always was an offensive kind of devil," he says. "And no sense of humor. The kind of man who laughs when a chair is pulled away just as a man is about to sit down."

As far back as 1904, Japp worked with Poirot on the Abercrombie forgery case, in which the criminal who had eluded half the police in Europe was run down by Poirot in Belgium. Japp was impressed with the performance—"There's no man's judgment I'd sooner take than his," he says—and thereafter treats him deferentially, calling him "Mister" or "Monsieur" (which he pronounces "Moosier") Poirot.

Poirot does not return the respect. "I am disappointed in Japp," he says. "He has no method."

Method is of overwhelming importance to Poirot. Referring to someone as "a man of method" is his highest praise. No matter how furiously the maelstrom swirls around him, Poirot remains serene and methodical. His calm assurance in the midst of a tumultuous, nerve-jangling murder investigation comforts those involved, and he takes full advantage of his dominant position. By putting witnesses at ease while he questions them, by being courteous and attentive to everyone, even the servants, he learns much and gains their trust—despite his comical appearance and mannerisms.

And, make no mistake, Poirot is comical. When he errs, he calls himself an imbecile, or "a triple imbecile," and once admitted to being a 46-times imbecile. His flamboyance is rivaled only by his vanity.

Taking infinite pains with his moustache, he waxes it until the ends are stiffly pointed and curled to the point of caricature. He applies to it scents, waxes and pomades, and even carries a small comb and mirror in case a wind robs it of its glory. In spite of his advanced years, his hair remains suspiciously black; though he denies coloring it, he does admit to using a "tonic," Revivit.

Add to this fanatic attention to his moustache and hair the fact that he wears pointed black patent leather shoes, sometimes smokes ostentatious little Russian cigarettes, and carries a walking stick embossed with a gold band (initially required by a war injury, but later carried as an affectation) and you have, as he was once described by a participant in a murder case, a "music hall parody of a Frenchman."

It challenges the imagination to conceive of any other person resembling Poirot, but there is one who has more than a superficial similarity. The detective has a twin brother, Achille, who lives in Belgium until he tries to help on the case described by Hercule Poirot as his biggest (**The Big Four**). Mistaken for his twin, Achille is killed by the master criminal who is eventually defeated by the desolate sleuth.

Poirot outlives his brother by nearly half a century, finally passing away in 1974. Crippled with arthritis and forced into a wheelchair, his last words (in the letter he leaves to explain the salient points of his final case) to Hastings are, "They have been good days."

They were filled with a vast variety of experiences: travel (to Egypt, Syria, Mesopotamia, much of Europe), good food (he becomes a gourmet late in his life), reading (he likes Shakespeare, the Bible, Dickens, the classics of detective fiction—which he sometimes cannot solve—though he finds the Sherlock Holmes saga over-rated; he has high regard for Watson, however, who reminds him of Hastings), writing (he publishes a book on detective fiction in 1966 which "knocked Poe and the hard-boiled school"), wealth (his legacy made him affluent enough to afford an expensive Messaro Gratz and a chauffeur to drive it), hobbies (jigsaw puzzles, building card houses, old films, card games, particularly bridge, at which he excelled, and arranging love matches—for others).

He has no interest in the fair sex, and they seem willing enough to let him alone. It is likely that women, and romance, would offend his excessive attention to neatness, order and method; it is equally likely that that obsession would drive any women in his life to the brink of madness.

Perhaps it is just as well that his interest in love is no more intense than his concern for religion (a Catholic, he does not attend church except for a rare morning prayer). With a woman to distract him, it is possible that Poirot's career would have been shorter—an unthinkable tragedy.

AGATHA CHRISTIE (See Miss Jane Marple)

BIBLIOGRAPHY

1920 **The Mysterious Affair at Styles** (John Lane)
1923 **Murder on the Links** (John Lane)
1925 **Poirot Investigates** (Dodd, Mead; published in 1924 by John Lane, London)
1926 **The Murder of Roger Ackroyd** (Dodd, Mead)
1927 **The Big Four** (Dodd, Mead)
1928 **The Mystery of the Blue Train** (Dodd, Mead)
1932 **Peril at End House** (Dodd, Mead)
1933 **Thirteen at Dinner** (Dodd, Mead; British title: **Lord Edgware Dies**, Collins, London)
1934 **Murder in the Calais Coach** (Dodd, Mead; British title: **Murder on the Orient Express**, Collins, London)
1934 **Murder in Three Acts** (Dodd, Mead; British title: **Three-Act Tragedy**, Collins, London, 1935)
1935 **Death in the Air** (Dodd, Mead; British title: **Death in the Clouds**, Collins, London)
1936 **The A.B.C. Murders** (Dodd, Mead)
1936 **Murder in Mesopotamia** (Dodd, Mead)
1937 **Cards on the Table** (Dodd, Mead; published in 1936 by Collins, London)
1937 **Poirot Loses a Client** (Dodd, Mead; British title: **Dumb Witness**, Collins, London)
1937 **Dead Man's Mirror** (Dodd, Mead; British title: **Murder in the Mews**, Collins, London)
1938 **Death on the Nile** (Dodd, Mead; published in 1937 by Collins, London)
1938 **Appointment with Death** (Dodd, Mead)
1938 **Murder for Christmas** (Dodd, Mead; British title: **Hercule Poirot's Christmas**, Collins, London)
1939 **The Regatta Mystery and Other Stories** (Dodd, Mead; five of the nine stories are about Hercule Poirot)
1940 **Sad Cypress** (Dodd, Mead)
1941 **The Patriotic Murders** (Dodd, Mead; published in 1940 as **One, Two, Buckle My Shoe** by Collins, London)
1941 **Evil Under the Sun** (Dodd, Mead)
1942 **Murder in Retrospect** (Dodd, Mead; British title: **Five Little Pigs**, Collins, London, 1943)
1946 **The Hollow** (Dodd, Mead)
1947 **The Labors of Hercules** (Dodd, Mead)
1948 **There Is a Tide** (Dodd, Mead; British title: **Taken at the Flood**, Collins, London)
1948 **Witness for the Prosecution and Other Stories** (Dodd, Mead; one of the nine stories is about Hercule Poirot)
1950 **Three Blind Mice and Other Stories** (Dodd, Mead; three of the eight stories are about Hercule Poirot)
1951 **The Under Dog and Other Stories** (Dodd, Mead)
1952 **Mrs. McGinty's Dead** (Dodd, Mead)
1953 **Funerals Are Fatal** (Dodd, Mead; British title: **After the Funeral**, Collins, London)
1955 **Hickory, Dickory, Death** (Dodd, Mead; British title: **Hickory, Dickory, Dock**, Collins, London)
1956 **Dead Man's Folly** (Dodd, Mead)
1960 **Cat Among the Pigeons** (Dodd, Mead; published in 1959 by Collins, London)
1960 **The Adventure of the Christmas Pudding and Other Stories** (London: Collins; not published in the U.S.; five of the six stories are about Hercule Poirot)
1961 **Double Sin and Other Stories** (Dodd, Mead; four of the eight stories are about Hercule Poirot)
1964 **The Clocks** (Dodd, Mead; published in 1963 by Collins, London)
1967 **Third Girl** (Dodd, Mead; published in 1966 by Collins, London)
1969 **Hallowe'en Party** (Dodd, Mead)
1972 **Elephants Can Remember** (Dodd, Mead)
1975 **Curtain** (Dodd, Mead)

FILMOGRAPHY

1931 **Alibi** (Twickenham) with Austin Trevor (as Hercule Poirot), Franklin Dyall, Elizabeth Allan; directed by Leslie Hiscott.
1931 **Black Coffee** (Twickenham) with Austin Trevor, Richard Cooper, Adrianne Allen, Elizabeth Allan, Melville Cooper; directed by Leslie Hiscott.
1934 **Lord Edgware Dies** (Real Art) with Austin Trevor, Jane Carr, Richard Cooper, John Turnbull; directed by Henry Edwards.
1966 **The Alphabet Murders** (MGM) with Tony Randall (as Hercule Poirot), Anita Ekberg, Robert Morley, Maurice Denham, Margaret Rutherford (in a brief appearance as Miss Marple); directed by Frank Tashlin.
1974 **Murder on the Orient Express** (EMI) with Albert Finney (as Hercule Poirot), Lauren Bacall, Martin Balsam, Ingrid Bergman, Jacqueline Bisset, Jean-Pierre Cassel, Sean Connery, John Gielgud, Wendy Hiller, Anthony Perkins, Vanessa Redgrave, Rachel Roberts, Richard Widmark, Michael York; directed by Sidney Lumet.

Ellery Queen

The history of Ellery Queen is one of the longest, most complicated and most significant in all detective fiction.

Even something as apparently straightforward as the detective's name is a tangle of confusion. Ellery Queen is the name of the author who writes about an amateur detective who is also named Ellery Queen. Not surprisingly, neither name is real.

Once a closely guarded secret, it is now well known that the creator of the most famous American detective in literature is actually two people—Frederic Dannay and the late Manfred B. Lee, Brooklyn-born cousins who collaborated on the Queen saga for more than forty years, creating a detective whose name is familiar in books, magazines, motion pictures, radio and television series, and an endless array of such secondary items as comic books, puzzles, juvenile novels and games.

In what must rank as one of the most brilliant and far-sighted promotional decisions ever made, they assumed an unforgettable pseudonym. Noting that many people remember the name of a favorite detective hero, but often forget the name of the author, they decided to give their detective the same name as the one they selected for their byline.

Well, it almost works that way. In point of fact, their detective has another name, which has never been revealed. He adopted the alias so that he could retain his privacy.

In the introduction to the first Ellery Queen novel, **The Roman Hat Mystery** (1929), J. J. McCue, a judge and stockbroker, and close friend of both Ellery and his policeman father, Richard Queen, reveals that his efforts have persuaded Ellery to allow the publication of **The Roman Hat Mystery**, a mystery novel written by the young Queen.

But, writes McCue in the introduction, "Ellery is a peculiar man. I was forced solemnly and by all I held dear to swear that the identities of my friends and of the important characters concerned in the story be veiled by pseudonyms; and that on pain of instant annihilation, their names be permanently withheld from the reading public. Consequently, 'Richard Queen' and 'Ellery Queen' are not the true names of those gentlemen. Ellery himself made the selections, and I might add at once that his choices were deliberately contrived to baffle the reader who might endeavor to ferret the truth from some apparent clue or anagram."

Whoever Ellery Queen actually is, he is a most complicated literary riddle. He defeats the possibility of definition, identification or description because he has several personalities, undergoing major alterations with each book.

When first introduced to the reading public, he is very much like Philo Vance, which is to say one would not mind reading about him, but one would also not particularly want to know him.

If that is harsh judgment, it is not unsupported. Manfred B. Lee once said of the early Ellery Queen: "He was probably the biggest prig that ever came down the pike."

Ostensibly a writer, Ellery is rarely seen at the typewriter in the early years, apparently devoting most of his time to his rare book collection and to patronizingly butting in on the official cases of his father (whom he calls "pater").

Arrogant, foppish, lazy and rude, Ellery's early talent lies purely in his mental and deductive abilities. He is a model of rational thought, solving perhaps the most complex, intricate and baffling mysteries ever conceived. Neither before nor after his first decade as a fictional sleuth were crimes of such apparent perfection and insolubility constructed.

As he grows older (as a fictional entity only; evidence indicates that he was born in 1905, which would have put him in his early twenties at the time of **The Roman Hat Mystery**, but he seems to be in his early thirties for his subsequent four-decade-long career) he matures nicely. He acquires a greater social conscience, becomes genuinely involved with the people on a case in personal terms, regarding their problems as vital elements in their lives and not merely abstract puzzles, treats his father with respect, and takes his literary career seriously, struggling to meet deadlines.

Becoming a more complex and complete character as the years passed, Ellery was rightly called "The Great Man" by his creators (in private, of course, as modesty would dictate) and "the logical successor to Sherlock Holmes" by the London **Times**.

One of the more interesting and unusual techniques employed by the authors to tweak the noses of their fans is a "challenge to the reader." At a point in the action, everything is stopped while the authors inform their audience that they now have all the clues necessary to solve the mystery; this daring challenge was also a popular feature of the long-running radio series and of the most recent of several television series.

Like another famous detective, Philo Vance (which is also a pseudonym), Ellery Queen retires to Italy, which is where J. J. McCue acquires the manuscript of the first Queen book, bringing the career of the gifted amateur detective to the attention of the public for the first time.

Inspector Richard Queen, one of the most heavily decorated officials of the New York City Police Department, freely admits that he owes much of his success to the assistance of his son Ellery, a mystery writer of some distinction.

Despite his seemingly changeable personality, Inspector Queen is reputed to have "a heart of gold" and sometimes appears to be out of his milieu as a policeman. "Inside he was harmless, and keen, and not a little hurt by the cruelties of the world," says J. J. McCue, an old family friend.

Small, almost withered, Inspector Queen nonetheless has abundant energy, which is frequently held in check as he attempts to maintain an air of deliberation. He walks stoop-shouldered with short, quick steps and is, in general, unimpressive physically. His distinction is a kindly, gentle, benevolent smile and manner that others find endearing.

He has thick gray hair and moustaches, which he bites when he is perplexed. Aside from snuff-taking, he is abstemious, all his time and energy being devoted to his son and crimefighting.

McCue says of Inspector Queen that "He knew his crime. He knew his criminals. He knew his law. [He] garnered a record of solved capital crimes which to this day is unique in the police history of New York City."

A master at unraveling mysteries, Queen spent thirty-two successful years on the force, matter-of-factly regarding his job as less difficult than others did. "Ordinary crime detection," he says, "is almost a mechanical matter. Most crimes are committed by 'criminals'—that is to say, by individuals habituated by environment and repetitious conduct to the pursuit of law-breaking. Such persons in 99 out of a hundred

William Gargan was a tougher, less intellectual Queen than Bellamy; Lindsay continued as Nikki.

cases have police records.

"The detective in these 99 cases has much to go on. Bertillon measurements, fingerprint records. Moreover, he has a little file of the criminal's idiosyncracies . . . these idiosyncracies of method are sometimes as definite clues to the identity of a criminal as his fingerprints. But most of all, we have come to depend upon the underworld's 'squealers,' 'stool pigeons' . . . for the solution of certain crimes. They are as essential to the big city's police as a knowledge of the proper source-book is to the lawyer. I firmly believe that every police department in the world would collapse in six months if the institution of underworld informing were to come to an end."

It is at this philosophical point that Ellery Queen comes into the picture. Not an official policeman, he does not approach crime and its solution in the same way as his father. He attacks a case from an intellectual position, convinced of its superiority in dealing with difficult cases.

"Where the police detective woefully falls down," he says, "is in the case of the crime whose perpetrator is *not* an habitual criminal, who has therefore left no fingerprints which will correspond with another set in your files, about whose idiosyncracies *nothing* is known for the ludicrously simple reason that he has never been a criminal before. Such a person, generally speaking, is not of the underworld, and you can

A portrait of Ellery Queen by Frank Godwin (left) for "The Spanish Cape Mystery," published in Redbook *magazine (April 1935). A very different portrayal on the right in a* Better Little Book, *"The Adventure of the Last Man Club" (1940), a fictionalized tale from the radio series.*

therefore pump your stool pigeon to your heart's delight without eliciting the slightest morsel of useful information."

Warming to the subject, Ellery explains why he finds crime such good sport. "You have nothing to go on," he is happy to say, "except the crime itself, and such clues and pertinences as that crime reveals upon observation and investigation. Obviously—and I say this with proper respect for my father's ancient profession—obviously to nab the criminal in such a case is the more difficult job by many headaches. Which explains two things—the hideously high percentage of unsolved crimes in this country, and my own absorbing avocation."

Between them, Ellery and Richard Queen form an unbeatable combination, "major cogs in the wheels of New York City's police machinery," says McCue, "particularly during the second and third decades of the century."

If it is difficult to describe accurately the relationship between Richard and Ellery, again it is best to turn to their closest mutual friend for the nearest explanation to approach the mark.

"The spiritual bonds between father and son," wrote J. J. McCue, "have until this time remained secret from all except a few favored intimates, among whom I was fortunate enough to be numbered. The old man, perhaps the most famous executive of the detective division in the last half-century, overshadowing in public renown, it is to be feared, even those gentlemen who sat briefly in the police commissioner's suite—the old man, let me repeat, owed a respectable portion of his reputation to his son's genius.

"In matters of pure tenacity, when possibilities lay frankly open on every hand, Richard Queen was a peerless investigator. He had a crystal-clear mind for detail; a retentive memory for complexities of motive and plot; a cool viewpoint when the obstacles seemed insuperable. Give him a hundred facts, bungled and torn, out of proportion and sequence, and he had them assembled in short order. He was like a bloodhound who follows the true scent in the clutter of a hopelessly tangled trail.

"But the intuitive sense, the gift of imagination, belonged to Ellery Queen the fiction writer. The two might have been twins possessing abnormally developed faculties of mind, impotent by themselves but vigorous when applied one to the other. Richard Queen, far from resenting the bond which made his success so spectacularly possible—as a less generous nature might have done—took pains to make it plain to his friends. The slender, gray old man whose name was anathema to contemporary lawbreakers, used to utter 'confession' as he called it, with a *naiveté* explicable only on the score of his proud fatherhood."

Ellery and Richard Queen share an uncommon closeness in more than their crimefighting adventures. They also live together in a small bachelor establishment on West 87th Street, the top floor of a three-family brownstone described as "a relic of late Victorian times." Passing through the huge oaken door marked "The Queens," a visitor would have no difficulty identifying the apartment as a male domicile.

A pipe-rack for Ellery's pipes hangs over the hearth, a solid oak beam serving as a mantel for the fireplace. Shining crossed sabres hang from the wall—"a gift from the old fencing master of Nuremburg" with whom Richard had lived in his younger days during his studies in Germany. Another wall is completely covered by a tapestry depicting the chase. Both Queens hate it, but it was given to Richard Queen by the Duke of ———, whose son was saved from a "noisome scandal" by the policeman. Beneath the tapestry is a heavy mission table with a parchment-shaded lamp and a pair of bronze book-ends enclosing a three-volume set of the **Arabian Nights' Entertainments**.

Past the small, narrow foyer, which is oppressive and gloomy, is the large, cheerful living room. Bookcases line three walls from floor to ceiling; lamps, comfortable chairs, and brightly colored leather cushions are everywhere. It is, in short, "the most comfortable room two intellectual gentlemen of luxurious tastes could devise for their living quarters."

After their move to Italy, the Queens turn their apartment into a small private museum to display the curios they had collected during their more productive years. Ellery's enormous collection of books on violence, possibly as complete as any in the world, does not remain on the premises. In all likelihood, it was dispersed into the collections of friends. The unpublished documents containing records of

Ralph Bellamy successfully played Ellery Queen in a series of four grade B films in the 1940s. Margaret Lindsay had the role of Nikki Porter, his secretary—a character created for radio.

Jim Hutton as Ellery and David Wayne as Inspector Richard Queen in the most recent revival on NBC.

Lee Bowman is one of several actors who have portrayed Queen in a number of television series.

cases solved by the Queens are stored away from prying eyes, in the city's police archives.

Living with the Queens during their New York crimefighting years, and accompanying them to Italy, is Djuna, the "man-of-all-work, general factotum, errand boy, valet, and mascot." An orphan as long as he can remember, Djuna (he has no discernible surname) was picked up to help by Richard Queen while Ellery was in college. "Slim and small, nervous and joyous, bubbling over with spirit yet quiet as a mouse when the occasion demanded," the boy worships Richard Queen and has a shy kinship with Ellery. The policeman says of Djuna that he "could hear a flea singing to its mate in the middle of the night."

Other helpmates appear with some regularity in the lives of the two Queens. Richard's right-hand man is Detective Sergeant Thomas Velie, the tall, iron-jawed policeman who is just a bit behind everyone else. Not overly intelligent, he is less antagonistic than most other cops who have to deal with amateur detectives, even going so far as to call Ellery "maestro."

Other policemen assigned to Inspector Queen's command are Doyle, Ritter, Hesse, Flint, Johnson, Piggott and Hagstrom. Dr. Samuel Prouty, the assistant to the Chief Medical Examiner, is often involved in cases (Inspector Queen always calls him "Doc"). Inspector John Rummell is on the Narcotics Squad; his son, Beau, begins a detective agency with Ellery (Ellery Queen, Inc., Confidential Investigations). Rummell soon marries, however; the private eye business is quickly abandoned, and Ellery returns to the typewriter to produce more mysteries.

A short time after his abortive business attempt, Ellery meets Nikki Porter and hires her to be his secretary. "A small, slim miss with nice red hair," the attractive Nikki soon becomes more than a business associate of the sophisticated young author. She is far from being the only romantic involvement of his life.

Not long before meeting Nikki, Ellery Queen is lured to Hollywood to write scripts for Magna Studios, drawing an inordinately high salary while doing practically nothing to earn it. He meets gossip columnist Paula Paris, a lovely recluse by whom he is absolutely dazzled. She smokes Russian cigarettes, has a musical voice, clear white skin, an interesting streak of gray in her black-lacquer hair, a shadowy dimple at the left side of her mouth, and an acute case of "homophobia"—an irrational fear of men. Ellery regards her as the most beautiful woman he has met in Hollywood, but their affair ends when he returns to New York.

To find the peace and quiet needed to write a novel, Ellery travels to the small village of Wrightsville. He does not find peace. Virtually every time he appears there, murders occur. He also meets Rima Anderson, who was named for the bird girl in W. H. Hudson's **Green Mansions**. A gentle flower child, she "had a special, unbelievable quality of *consistency* . . . like a miniature fruit at its ripest." Her innocent child-woman eyes and musical, lilting voice are instrumental in causing Ellery to fall in love with his client and, when the case is closed and he must return to New York, he hints that he will return for her. He never does, however, and she is not heard from again. He ultimately marries someone else, and has a son, Ellery, Jr.

While many of his mannerisms may be irritating to most people, women seem to find him attractive. He is quite tall, towering over his father by a full six inches. "There was a square cut to his shoulders and an agreeable swing to his body as he walked." He dresses well and "carries a light stick. On his nose perched what seemed an incongruous note in so athletic a man—a rimless pince-nez. But the brow above, the long delicate lines of the face, the bright eyes were those of a man of thought rather than action."

In his early years, the major actions in which Ellery engages are absentmindedly and interminably tapping his stick on the floor and wiping his pince-nez, as well as making a monumental project out of lighting a cigarette.

Happily, in his later years, Ellery abandons the pince-nez, the stick and virtually all of his most grating speech mannerisms and personality shortcomings.

In **Cat of Many Tails**, Ellery is seriously depressed by an early failure as a detective, which has resulted in tragedy. Although he determines to give up investigative work and stick to the creation of mystery fiction, his father convinces him to help stop a deranged killer, and Ellery becomes a special investigator (unpaid) for the mayor until the murderer is stopped.

At the end of his adventure, a famous Viennese psychiatrist tells him, "You have failed before, you will fail again. This is the nature and role of man. The work you have chosen to do is a sublimation, of great social value. You must continue."

In his early career, his ego would have impelled him to believe the psychiatrist. Since he has been active for twenty years at this point, the appeal is, instead, to his social conscience. Most significant, perhaps, is that he heeds the advice, and remains a brilliant amateur detective for over two decades more.

The cover of The Witch's Victim, *an* Ellery Queen *comic book adventure, bears this portrait.*

ELLERY QUEEN (pseudonym of Frederic Dannay, 1905- , and Manfred Bennington Lee, 1905-1971) Born Daniel Nathan in Brooklyn, N.Y., Dannay never attended college but has proven himself to be one of the finest editors of American fiction as the creator of **Ellery Queen's Mystery Magazine** (beginning in 1941), the most important magazine ever devoted to crime fiction. A noted scholar, he also formed the finest collection of detective short stories in the world. Lee was born Manford Lepofsky, also in Brooklyn, and wrote promotional material for a motion picture company until he and his cousin collaborated on **The Roman Hat Mystery** (1929) and other Ellery Queen fictions. They also wrote four novels as Barnaby Ross. In addition to forty books about Ellery Queen, Dannay and Lee wrote for the films of the mid-1930s, wrote the scripts for the Ellery Queen radio series for nine years, and edited more than a hundred anthologies. Dannay also produced three landmark reference books in the field of mystery and detection.

FILMOGRAPHY

1935 **The Spanish Cape Mystery** (Republic) with Donald Cook (as Ellery Queen), Helen Twelvetrees, Berton Churchill, Frank Sheridan; directed by Lewis D. Collins.
1937 **The Mandarin Mystery** (Republic) with Eddie Quillan (as Ellery Queen), Charlotte Henry, Rita Le Roy, Wade Boteler, Franklin Pangborn; directed by Ralph Staub.
1940 **Ellery Queen, Master Detective** (Columbia) with Ralph Bellamy (as Ellery Queen), Margaret Lindsay, Charley Grapewin, James Burke, Michael Whalen, Marsha Hunt; directed by Kurt Neumann.
1941 **Ellery Queen's Penthouse Mystery** (Columbia) with Ralph Bellamy, Margaret Lindsay, Anna May Wong, Eduardo Ciannelli, Frank Albertson; directed by James Hogan.
1941 **Ellery Queen and the Perfect Crime** (Columbia) with Ralph Bellamy, Margaret Lindsay, Spring Byington, H. B. Warner, Douglas Dumbrille; directed by James Hogan.
1941 **Ellery Queen and the Murder Ring** (Columbia) with Ralph Bellamy, Margaret Lindsay, Mona Barrie, Paul Hurst, George Zucco, Blanche Yurka; directed by James Hogan.
1942 **A Close Call for Ellery Queen** (Columbia) with William Gargan (as Ellery Queen), Margaret Lindsay, Ralph Morgan, Kay Linaker, Edward Norris, Micheline Cheirel; directed by James Hogan.
1942 **A Desperate Chance for Ellery Queen** (Columbia) with William Gargan, Margaret Lindsay, John Litel, Lillian Bond, Jack LaRue; directed by James Hogan.
1942 **Enemy Agents Meet Ellery Queen** (Columbia) with William Gargan, Margaret Lindsay, Gale Sondergaard, Gilbert Roland, Sig Rumann; directed by James Hogan.

BIBLIOGRAPHY

1929 **The Roman Hat Mystery** (Stokes)
1930 **The French Powder Mystery** (Stokes)
1931 **The Dutch Shoe Mystery** (Stokes)
1932 **The Greek Coffin Mystery** (Stokes)
1932 **The Egyptian Cross Mystery** (Stokes)
1933 **The American Gun Mystery** (Stokes)
1933 **The Siamese Twin Mystery** (Stokes)
1934 **The Adventures of Ellery Queen** (Stokes)
1934 **The Chinese Orange Mystery** (Stokes)
1935 **The Spanish Cape Mystery** (Stokes)
1936 **Halfway House** (Stokes)
1937 **The Door Between** (Stokes)
1938 **The Devil to Pay** (Stokes)
1938 **The Four of Hearts** (Stokes)
1939 **The Dragon's Teeth** (Stokes)
1940 **The New Adventures of Ellery Queen** (Stokes)
1942 **Calamity Town** (Little, Brown)
1943 **There Was an Old Woman** (Little, Brown)
1945 **The Case Book of Ellery Queen** (Bestseller)
1945 **The Murderer Is a Fox** (Little, Brown)
1948 **Ten Days' Wonder** (Little, Brown)
1949 **Cat of Many Tails** (Little, Brown)
1950 **Double, Double** (Little, Brown)
1951 **The Origin of Evil** (Little, Brown)
1952 **Calendar of Crime** (Little, Brown)
1952 **The King Is Dead** (Little, Brown)
1953 **The Scarlet Letters** (Little, Brown)
1955 **Q.B.I.: Queen's Bureau of Investigation** (Little, Brown)
1956 **Inspector Queen's Own Case** (Simon & Schuster)
1958 **The Finishing Stroke** (Simon & Schuster)
1963 **The Player on the Other Side** (Random House)
1964 **And On the Eighth Day** (Random House)
1965 **The Fourth Side of the Triangle** (Random House)
1965 **Queens Full** (Random House)
1966 **A Study in Terror** (Lancer)
1967 **Face to Face** (New American Library)
1968 **The House of Brass** (New American Library)
1968 **Q.E.D.: Queen's Experiments in Detection** (New American Library)
1970 **The Last Woman in His Life** (World)
1971 **A Fine and Private Place** (World)

The Shadow

The Shadow, appropriately difficult to view clearly and distinctly, has two slightly different forms, two backgrounds, two different methods of operation. One long and successful history of The Shadow is the version presented on radio; the other, equally popular, appeared in the pages of a magazine.

The Sunday night radio series about The Shadow was one of the most successful melodramas ever aired. The character made his debut in August 1930, serving as the eerie-voiced, anonymous narrator of strange tales on the "Detective Story" program. His instant grip on listeners soon resulted in the series named after him, which ran until Dec. 26, 1954. His role had been changed to the hero of the series, battling evil-doers for thirty exhausting minutes every week.

"Who knows what evil lurks in the hearts of men? The Shadow knows!" Those lines, opening the program, quickly became legendary and, even today, are recited by countless aficionados of mysteries. The show had an exceptional level of creativity and imagination, but it was at its best when the voice of the sinister Master of Darkness belonged to Orson Welles (1937-1938). After the opening lines and the appropriate music, The Shadow was introduced (somewhat superfluously, since everyone listening already knew who he was):

"The Shadow, Lamont Cranston, a man of wealth, a student of science and a master of other people's minds, devotes his life to righting wrongs, protecting the innocent and punishing the guilty. Using advanced methods that may ultimately become available to all law enforcement agencies, Cranston is known to the underworld as The Shadow—never seen, only heard, as haunting to superstitious minds as a ghost, as inevitable as a guilty conscience."

The "Detective Story" program was sponsored by Street & Smith, a magazine publisher, which gave the macabre-sounding host not only his own radio show, but his own magazine as well.

The Shadow magazine was launched in the spring of 1931 with the featured novel, **The Living Shadow**, written by Maxwell Grant, a "house name" created by Street & Smith. During the next eighteen years, 325 issues were published, each with a short novel recounting an adventure of The Shadow.

The reader was assured, in an official-sounding notice, that the tales had been adjudged "a true account of my activities at that time" by none other than The Shadow himself, and that Grant had been given the "exclusive privilege" to serve as the raconteur of his cases.

Several writers used the Grant pseudonym, but the author of the vast majority of the adventures (282, including all the early ones) is Walter B. Gibson.

Gibson wrote the staggering total of 15 million words about The Shadow. To meet that awesome demand, he sometimes typed as many as 15,000 words a day—about 60 pages of typescript. He often found himself "living, thinking, even dreaming the story in continued process," he said. "Ideas came faster and faster. At the finish of the story, I often had to take a few days off as my fingertips were too sore to begin work on the next book."

When the magazine was conceived, Gibson, then aged thirty-three, was asked to write the crucial first story. He was, at that time, he says, "specializing in factual articles on ghosts and witchcraft as well as crime. I had also written books for . . . Houdini, Thurston, and Blackstone, which gave me a further reputation in the realm of the mysterious." Street & Smith could not have chosen a better person to entrust with their new periodical. "Fortunately," continues Gibson, "I had already been thinking in terms of a mysterious . . . personage, who would materialize from darkness . . . aiding friends . . . and balking foemen . . . then merging back into the night."

A hero of the Great Depression, The Shadow has outlived his time. His adventures are frequently reprinted in paperback form today, the old radio programs are successfully revived in syndication, rare showings of the vintage motion pictures and serials are filled to overflowing, and nostalgia buffs covet the fragile comic books (which Gibson also wrote), magazines, toys, games, radio premiums and books that are so avidly collected today—at prices that numb the soul.

The Shadow has not lost his ability to cloud men's minds.

In the darkness, in the nighttime of which he is master, The Shadow is seldom seen. His entrance to the world as a crimefighter whose exploits are recorded is eerie and anonymous, as faceless and invisible as a human being can be. He is, in fact, a pair of powerful hands, reaching out of the midnight fog to prevent a young man named Harry Vincent from leaping off a bridge to his death below.

Quickly, Vincent's despair over the loss of a girl transforms to alarm, "For he could not have sworn he was looking at a human being. The stranger's face was entirely obscured by a broad-brimmed felt hat bent downward over his features; and the long black coat looked almost like part of the thickening fog."

Having saved Vincent's life, The Shadow then asks for it, telling him, "I shall improve it. I shall make it useful. But I shall risk it, too. Perhaps I shall lose it, for I have lost lives, just as I have saved them. This is my promise: life, with enjoyment, with danger, with excitement and—with money. Life, above all, with honor. But if I give it, I demand obedience . . . That must come always. I do not ask for cleverness, for strength or skill, although I want them, and will expect them to the best of your ability."

Without serious hesitation, Vincent accepts the offer, becoming one of The Shadow's top operatives. The Shadow must have made similar offers to quite a few people from disparate walks of life, because his agents are positively legion.

Among many others, his associates include the quiet Burbank, the indispensable "inside" man through whom The Shadow transmits and receives messages from other agents; Cliff Marsland and Hawkeye, who infiltrate the underworld; Clyde Burke, a reporter with the New York **Classic**; taxi driver Mo Shrevnitz, better known as "Shrevvy," whose cab The Shadow uses when he is in a hurry; Stanley, the chauffeur of his luxurious limousine, who never quite realizes what is going on; Jericho, the "giant African" of "tremendous strength"; investment broker Rutledge Mann, to whom he goes for advice on important financial matters; the beautiful Margo Lane, "his friend and constant companion" and the only person to know The Shadow's true identity (according to

Steranko's evocative artwork for the cover of The Black Master, *a Pyramid paperback novel.*

The menacing crimefighter on the cover of The Living Shadow, *his first adventure in book form.*

the narrations on the radio program, in which she plays a far greater role than in the magazines); and, most important, millionaire-socialite-explorer Lamont Cranston.

Although the radio series portrayed The Shadow as a disguised Lamont Cranston, he is, in fact, an entirely separate person, as documented in the pages of the magazine.

The Shadow merely poses as Cranston, a man of "deep understanding" who is pleased to give his permission and allows The Shadow to become his alter ego. The Shadow appears in many guises and disguises, often posing as Fritz, the janitor at police headquarters, or socialite George Clarendon.

With his talents at acting and disguise fully developed, The Shadow has little fear of being unmasked and gives Maxwell Grant permission to reveal his past identity in **The Shadow Unmasks**. He was once Kent Allard, but that identity no longer has any importance, being a concluded chapter in The Shadow's life.

An American air ace in World War I, Allard was known as the Dark Eagle. He pretended to be shot down over Germany and, "using disguises by day and black garb at night, he worked his way back to the allied lines, releasing many prisoners and guiding them along the route to safety."

After the war, Allard disappeared during a flight over the jungles of Guatemala, where he was worshipped as a "bird god" by the Xinca Indians. He emerged from the jungle with great wealth and a priceless girasol, or fire opal, a gift from the Xincas, who had plucked the stone from the eye of their great idol.

The fire opal became a ring, which The Shadow always wears, and the fortune was used to establish his giant crimefighting network. It gives him admittance to Manhattan's exclusive Cobalt Club, a retreat for the city's richest and most influential men. As Lamont Cranston, he is an habitué of the club, among whose members is Police Commissioner Ralph Weston. Cranston is frequently present, or at least within earshot, when the commissioner receives reports from Joe Cardona, who begins his career as a detective in the first recorded adventure of The Shadow but quickly works his way up to inspector. While Cardona is a good, hard-working cop, Weston is portrayed as an intelligent helpmate to Cranston, an "amateur criminologist," in the magazines, but on the radio program he is a stupid, vain man who hates Cranston and ignores his helpful advice, but eagerly accepts the credit and glory for solving a case which Cranston has brought to its successful conclusion.

Another difference between the radio and magazine portrayals of The Shadow's affairs is the matter of his invisibility. No matter how it is accomplished, the ability to disappear is a remarkable achievement. According to the radio adventures, he acquired the hypnotic power to "cloud men's minds so that they cannot see him" in the Orient, and can thus apparently vanish.

In the magazine, he does not actually disappear. At least, it is not certain whether he does or not. The Shadow merely wears a black slouch hat and black cloak and blends into the shadows of the nighttime. He appears in the same fashion, stepping out of a darkened

A revival of interest in the adventures of the pulp hero has produced a series of reprints by Pyramid with cover illustrations by Steranko, who captures the spirit of the originals.

doorway or a thick fog, with no clue as to how he got there, or where he goes when he steps back into invisibility.

Spectacular as that trick is, it is not the only one of The Shadow's many gifts. Often described as "the superman," he is all of that—and more. He can speak any language in his chilling, whispered, sibilant voice. He invents mysterious invisible inks and special secret codes. He can successfully defy gravity, scaling tall buildings with suction cups strapped to his hands and feet. He has such tremendous strength that he can, again and again, defeat giant villains or entire gangs single-handedly in hand-to-hand combat. No death trap can hold him, and he escapes from situations that are the envy of magicians everywhere (and several of his ploys did, in fact, find their ways into the acts of noted stage illusionists). Even if he is captured, or wounded, or hopelessly outmanned, he never wavers from the conviction that he will ultimately triumph, that his twin .45 automatics will spit hot death, and that "Cowardly murderers . . . snarling, bestial fiends" will fall with "dying curses on their evil lips."

The villains he engages in mortal combat comprise a veritable army of the worst criminals and madmen who ever lived. Among the arch-fiends who battle The Shadow (and, incidentally, give their names to the published accounts) are

The Crime Cult, Mox, The Silent Seven, Double Z, The Black Master, The Ghost Makers, Kings of Crime, The Five Chameleons and the sinister Oriental supervillain, Siwan Khan, an adversary on four occasions.

The Shadow also takes on foreign agents, battling The Red Menace in more than one instance. In a struggle that is less ideological, more an attempt to prevent the takeover of the world by The Red Envoy in one adventure, The Shadow is as successful in foreign territory as he is in New York.

Russia has played more than one role in The Shadow's life. His fabulous purple girasol was once in the collection of the czars. This large, strange gem "that shone with a deep crimson hue" which "seemed like a living coal reflecting the glow of its owner's hypnotic eyes" has a vague history. The Shadow has offered as authentic statements both that the fire opal came from the czars and that it came from the Xincan idol. It seems likely that there are two such gems (one for each eye) and that he owns them both, but he is never specific about the existence of the twin treasures.

Even less clear is the physical appearance of The Shadow. Aside from his hypnotic eyes, his hawk-like nose and long, white fingers, it would be impossible to guess at his looks. But it would be a simple matter to identify him by his trademark—the sinister, haunting, uniquely recognizable laugh.

The Shadow's laugh serves a multitude of purposes, and it can be used to inspire virtually any emotion. Sometimes mirthful, sometimes chilling, he uses it to inspire confidence in those he is helping, to announce his presence at the site of a battle, to pass the time while he lays plans, to show contempt. Most of all, his laugh is a mocking cry of triumph: ". . . from the swiftly moving sedan came a peal of taunting laughter; a long, loud laugh that echoed through the night and died away among the trees."

Once again, The Shadow has triumphed over the forces of Evil, and he has again proven the rightness of his philosophy:

"The weed of crime bears bitter fruit. Crime does not pay. The Shadow knows!"

MAXWELL GRANT Used as a "house name" by Street & Smith authors, Maxwell Grant is most closely identified with the long series of novels about The Shadow, the most famous pulp fiction character of all time. The author whose name became almost interchangeable with it is Walter B. Gibson (1897-   ), who was permitted to use the famous Maxwell Grant byline for a series about another detective fiction hero—Norgil the Magician. Gibson's first career was as a magician and writer about magic whose articles in the **Philadelphia Public Ledger** introduced him to Houdini and Thurston, for both of whom he ghost-wrote articles and books, and with whom he performed as a stage illusionist of considerable reputation. He continues to give occasional conjuring shows, and remains a prolific writer—although falling substantially short of the one-and-a-half million words he produced in his peak years.

BIBLIOGRAPHY

Under the Street & Smith "house name" of Maxwell Grant, The Shadow appeared in 325 short novels in the magazine which bore his name. Of those, 282 were written by Walter B. Gibson, who also wrote an original novel for paperback publication. Many of the 326 novels about The Shadow have been published in paperback, collected in omnibus volumes of two or more stories, and/or published in hardcover. Pyramid has successfully published a long series of reprints and plans to continue the series indefinitely.

FILMOGRAPHY

1937 **The Shadow Strikes** (Grand National) with Rod La Rocque (as The Shadow), Lynn Anders; directed by Lynn Shores.
1938 **International Crime** (Grand National) with Rod La Rocque; directed by Charles Lamont.
1940 **The Shadow** (Columbia serial) with Victor Jory (as The Shadow), Veda Ann Borg; directed by James Horne.
1946 **The Shadow Returns** (Monogram) with Kane Richmond (as The Shadow), Barbara Reed, Tom Dugan, Joseph Crehan; directed by Phil Rosen.
1946 **Behind the Mask** (Monogram) with Kane Richmond, Barbara Reed, Tom Dugan, Joseph Crehan; directed by Phil Karlson.
1946 **The Missing Lady** (Monogram) with Kane Richmond, Barbara Reed, Tom Dugan, Joseph Crehan; directed by Phil Karlson.
1958 **Bourbon Street Shadows** (Republic; also released as **Invisible Avenger**) with Richard Derr (as The Shadow), Mark Daniels, Helen Westcott; directed by James Wong Howe and John Sledge.

John Shaft

Historically, there have been few black detectives, an unalterable truth accurately reflected in mystery fiction. Rare exceptions in early American detective fiction include Florian Slappey, who served as a purely comic character in the 1920s and 1930s, and, more recently, Pharaoh Love, who reached a new extreme as a minority by being not only black, but a homosexual as well.

With new levels of social consciousness in the 1960s and 1970s, more blacks found their way onto police forces or began operating as private detectives. The crime literature of the time mirrors those real-life changes.

Virgil Tibbs of the Pasadena Police Department made the breakthrough in John Ball's acclaimed **In the Heat of the Night**, and Ernest Tidyman's John Shaft quickly attained heroic stature when he was portrayed by Richard Roundtree in motion pictures and a television series.

Shaft isn't exactly the type of detective who makes a good hero. He isn't super-smart, for one thing, ultimately cracking his cases with brute force and wanton violence. Where there is room during an investigation for strategy, wit, and out-thinking the bad guys, he doesn't use it. His gun serves as a substitute for his brains, and people invariably get killed in his adventures.

A private eye, Shaft's office is in New York, and that is where his cases (with two exceptions, which occur in Jamaica and London) take place. The city is his turf, he feels as if he owns the streets, and he is comfortable with the people of the streets—the people with whom he grew up.

The John Shaft whose adventures appear on the screen is more sophisticated than the tough guy of the books, who has many of the traits of the people he is hired to pursue. He is a thug, and he can be mean. But he is effective, and never fails to crack a case—though he generally gets beat up along the way.

As a black man in a black environment, Shaft's cases inevitably are about the things that happen to blacks. The ramifications of the black experience are vital to him, and he is openly, but not fanatically, proud of his heritage. He distrusts and dislikes whites, particularly Jews, and actively hates homosexuals. He likes women, but treats most of them like so much meat.

Perhaps the best assessment of Shaft appears in an early book: "If there's anything that will keep him going, it's probably the fact that he is alone, he is black and he does believe he is going to survive."

Quite likely, he is correct. Shaft will survive, not on the hard streets of Harlem but as a literary figure of unusual power.

Shaft is a product of Harlem. He was born there, and his parents probably died there. His mother died when he was two years old. She had worked two jobs—seamstress by day, charwoman by night. She popped uppers to keep going through the long hours; she got dizzy one day while washing the windows of their own fourth-floor walk-up apartment and splattered herself on the sidewalk below. He is less sure about the fate of his father, who split when he was born, but he has been told that he was a numbers runner and that someone slit his throat.

He became a foster child, one of whose guardians drank too much, and took to the streets, becoming a juvenile delinquent, petty thief and general nuisance to the cops, who arrested him several times on juvenile offenses. One of the incidents leading to an arrest resulted in a serious injury from a bicycle chain; the scar remains with him to this day. More accurately, it is two scars, one on his right hand and one on his forehead: as the chain swung down at him, he threw his hand up to shield his eye, resulting in the matching saddle-stitch scars.

Getting into a different kind of fight, he joined the Marines, where he was a light-heavyweight boxer. After training at Parris Island, he was sent to Vietnam, and won honors as a hero. He was wounded, but got a chest full of "fruit salad" for killing fourteen Vietnamese kids because "one didn't know who was going to shoot first."

When he returned to the United States, he went to C.C.N.Y. (although he may also have taken some courses at N.Y.U.) but did not get a degree. He has given serious thought to a professional career, probably law ("doctors cut up too many people"), but never actually done anything about it. He took a job with a well-known private detective agency, remaining with it for two years while he learned the business, then went out on his own, opening an office in Times Square.

Although he describes the office as temporary, filling it with seedy, used furniture, he keeps it throughout his recorded adventures and even allows it to be redecorated by a classy white chick with whom he is having an affair. He likes her a lot better than the new decor, which is mainly white plastic, with white file cabinets, his license in an aluminum frame on the walls, a pale blue telephone with a memo pad attached, and a day bed.

The office remains in its same location, however, and seems more than a trifle out of character for the third floor of an old Times Square building. The building suits him because he knows its layout and he uses it to elude people who are following him, ducking in and out of its various entrances. The neighborhood suits him because he knows all the local street people, such as the shoeshine boy who keeps a close watch on the comings and goings of foot traffic. Shaft likes, he says, the "attitude" of the area.

He doesn't like it enough to live there, however. He lives in an apartment on the corner of Jane and Hudson Streets in Greenwich Village. The two and a half rooms must rank among the sloppiest in the city. There are always dirty coffee cups, a multitude of empty glasses, and overflowing ashtrays which stick to table tops. Although he eventually gets a cleaning lady, whom he refers to as his "personal black," the chore of cleaning up the place usually falls onto the "little girls" who spend the night with him.

He has little difficulty getting girls to come home with him, and he is a tireless, if unimaginative, lover. His excellent body turns women on to him, and he knows it. He is about six feet tall and 190 pounds of muscle. He runs a lot on his cases, but mainly he keeps in shape by working out at the McBurney YMCA gymnasium.

In 1970, at the time of his first recorded case, he is twenty-eight and ages at the same rate as everyone else; by 1974, when he is 32, he has started to notice gray hairs. His fairly dark complexion is described as being similar to "French-roast coffee." A bland expression on his oval face is useful as a mask, both to hide his emotions and to make himself appear inconspicuous.

Scars abound on his body. In addition to those on his hand and forehead, acquired as a youth,

The Bantam paperback edition of Shaft's Carnival of Killers *features a cool Shaft, a black private eye with similarities to Mike Hammer and the earlier hard-boiled dicks of the 1930s.*

he has souvenirs of Vietnam on the left thigh and abdomen. Because he so frequently gets beat up, he acquires additional scars as his career progresses, but he doesn't mind because women notice them.

And he notices women. He has a special girlfriend, Ellie, of whom he speaks with deference, but they split up and he shows no remorse, taking up with an assortment of lovelies with whom he enjoys the delights of abundant sex and a clean apartment. To him, women are for bedding, and he seldom lets his emotions sweep him away, although he does admire certain qualities in a few women he's known. It is his opinion that sex is the universal panacea for women who are lonely, widowed, divorced, or otherwise unhappy, nervous, dissatisfied or upset.

One of his favorite places for picking up girls is the "No Name" bar on Hudson Street. He also likes the place because it is convenient, and from it he can watch the entrance to his apartment house if he thinks he is being followed.

The "No Name" is owned by Shaft's friend

Shaft, *published in paperback by Bantam, is a black private eye who towers over his environment.*

Rollie Nickerson, an actor who has trouble getting parts. His problem is that he is six feet, nine inches tall and there seem to be limited requirements for basketball players in contemporary drama.

Nickerson allows Shaft to play bartender. It is Shaft's theory that no one notices a bartender, much less a black bartender, and this "invisibility" allows him to keep an eye on hit men who have come looking for him. This method of making himself blend into his environment is one of Shaft's most successful techniques as a detective. He calls it playing "nigger." He takes jobs as a security man, or a janitor, or a uniformed messenger, in order to acquire information; regarded as no more significant than a piece of furniture, others talk freely around such nonentities. They are simply not noticed. While playing "nigger," he discovers "the black underground of cleanup men" who inconspicuously go about their work but actually know everything that is going on in the upper-class white world to which they provide their services.

Even when Shaft is not playing his stereotypical "nigger" routine, he uses blackness, and his familiarity with the black milieu, to gather information. He slaps hands, jives and raps with other blacks, picking up scraps of news and inside dope from chauffeurs, shoe-shine boys, and other members of the black community who are engaged in less legitimate forms of commerce.

It is evident that Shaft's blackness provides him with a context in which to operate, and he shares the attitudes of many others in his community. He is not exactly bitter, but he knows that most whites do not particularly like blacks, and he does not particularly like them back.

He is not, however, a member of either the black underworld or the black revolutionary movement. He considers the movement "a crock" and has only contempt for it, although one of his best friends is deeply involved with it.

Although Shaft claims to have grown up friendless, a childhood buddy with whom he is still on good terms is Ben Buford, a black revolutionary so strongly given to spouting rhetoric about the movement that Shaft is hard pressed not to bust him in the mouth.

Their friendship actually stems from Buford's mother—she had been kind to Shaft when he was young, and he is still very fond of her. Contacting her is the only way to reach Buford, who is constantly hiding out and surrounded by a phalanx of faithful brothers. Basically distrustful, Buford actually has Shaft blindfolded when he is brought to his hideout, but he still provides some vital, if grudging help on one of the private detective's most dangerous cases.

Shaft gets involved with the Mafia when he tries to help Knocks Persons, a local Harlem underworld figure. (Persons acquired the "Knocks" sobriquet for all the bruises he had received—and administered—through the years.) Knocks' daughter has been kidnapped by Mafia toughs who want to take over his business interests, which cover virtually everything above 110th Street that nets money illegally, and he asks Shaft to help get her back. Shaft persuades Buford to assist, and he makes his "army" available.

Few whites enter Shaft's sphere, but Marvin Green, his accountant, is one. Green's wife, who is black, is the closest Shaft has ever been, he says, to having a sister. When he earns a quick fortune, Shaft allows Green to invest it for him.

The other important white person with whom Shaft has contact is Lt. Victor Anderozzi, the head of a special investigative detail assigned to the 17th Precinct, who reports directly to the

Commissioner of Police. Just under six feet tall and thinner than Shaft, with a gray face and black hooded eyes, Anderozzi has a relationship with Shaft that is generally friendly, but occasionally comes perilously close to being openly hostile. They call each other ethnic epithets continually, and threaten each other good-naturedly whenever they have the opportunity.

Anderozzi allows Shaft the freedom to do things his own way because he figures (a) Shaft will do it that way anyway, and (b) that may be the only way in which the thing can be accomplished. Nonetheless, he often puts another cop on his tail in an attempt to offer him some protection. It generally doesn't work too effectively, and Shaft gets another beating before bringing the case to its conclusion.

Shaft becomes enmeshed in a wide variety of cases. The exploits that have been recorded in books are of major consequence and involve murder, organized crime, drugs, kidnapping, jewel robbery and the splashy type of criminal activity that makes front page news. But when he talks about his career, he says that he handles only divorce cases, runaway wives, runaway husbands, security situations and those humdrum, bread-and-butter jobs that are of no interest to anyone except those directly involved.

The evidence indicates that Shaft's cases run more often than he cares to admit to the more spectacular, because only they can pay for some of his more expensive tastes.

He wears a Tiffany watch (or rather wore it, until it was stolen from him), a present to himself for "survival"; has a dapper wardrobe custom-tailored for him in Chicago; drinks expensive liquor; and even buys expensive French roast coffee beans at McNulty's, an epicurean shop in the Village.

He has come a long way from his impoverished childhood, and he knows it and enjoys it, but he doesn't allow himself to get too carried away with a sense of being better, or cooler, than he really is. If he becomes overly impressed with John Shaft, he merely has to remind himself that, not long ago, he had to be enlightened by Nickerson about what to do in a *ménage à trois*.

A man of action, Shaft is quick to use his gun if he needs it, as evidenced by this jacket illustration for Shaft among the Jews.

Ernest Tidyman's vigorous fictional dectective is portrayed on the cover of the Bantam paperback edition of Shaft Has a Ball.

ERNEST TIDYMAN (1928-) Born in Cleveland, Ohio, Tidyman worked as a writer and editor at the **Cleveland News** until moving to New York for positions with the **New York Post** and **The New York Times.** His first book, **Shaft,**became an immensely popular film, starring Richard Roundtree, in 1971. Tidyman wrote the screenplay for it, as well as the screenplay of **The French Connection**, for which he won the Academy Award, Writers Guild Award, and the Edgar Allan Poe Award of the Mystery Writers of America. Among his other screenplays are **Shaft's Big Score** (1972) and **High Plains Drifter** (1973), produced the same year as his novel of the same name.

BIBLIOGRAPHY

1970 **Shaft** (Macmillan)
1972 **Shaft Among the Jews** (Dial Press)
1972 **Shaft's Big Score** (Bantam)
1973 **Shaft Has a Ball** (Bantam)
1973 **Good-bye, Mr. Shaft** (Dial Press)
1974 **Shaft's Carnival of Killers** (Bantam)
1977 **The Last Shaft** (Little Brown)

FILMOGRAPHY

1971 **Shaft** (MGM) with Richard Roundtree (as John Shaft), Moses Gunn; directed by Gordon Parks.
1972 **Shaft's Big Score** (MGM) with Richard Roundtree, Moses Gunn; directed by Gordon Parks.
1973 **Shaft in Africa** (MGM) with Richard Roundtree, Frank Finlay; directed by John Guillermin.

Sam Spade

A fortuitous and inspired example of motion picture casting brought Humphrey Bogart to the screen as Sam Spade in the perfect detective film, **The Maltese Falcon**. Already a well-regarded actor, the role established Bogart as a cinematic immortal, while cementing Sam Spade in the public consciousness as the ultimate "hard-boiled" private eye.

Black Mask magazine enjoyed—and fully merited—a reputation as the best and most famous of the thousands of pulp magazines that flooded newsstands during the years between the World Wars. Dashiell Hammett was one of its star writers, reaching his pinnacle with the five-part serialization of **The Maltese Falcon** in 1929. Published in book form in the following year, it was quickly accepted as a masterpiece of detective fiction—a status it holds just as firmly today, nearly half a century later.

For a character so familiar, it is astonishing to realize that Sam Spade is the detective hero of only one novel and three short stories, plus three versions of the same story on film. Not the first of the tough private eyes of his time, he became the model, the prototype, for all the "hard-boiled dicks" who followed. It is not unreasonable to suggest that Philip Marlowe and, by extension, Lew Archer, could not have come into existence without the precedence of Spade.

According to Hammett, Spade had no real-life counterpart. The detective was "idealized," wrote the author, "in the sense that he is what most of the private detectives I've worked with would like to have been."

Himself a private operative for the Pinkerton Detective Agency for almost a decade, Hammett spoke authoritatively when he noted that the typical private eye wants "to be a hard and shifty fellow, able to take care of himself in any situation, able to get the best of anybody he comes in contact with."

Most of the other characters in Spade's most famous adventure are based on real-life people encountered by Hammett during his years as a detective, and even the story of the priceless black bird has its roots in fact. A genuine bird of fabulous value exists, and it enjoys a long, blood-stained history. A gem-encrusted statue in a European museum is credited with being the original Maltese falcon, but mystery writer John Ball, the creator of Virgil Tibbs, claims that his exquisitely carved jade bird is the true prototype.

Spade's partner in their detective agency, Miles Archer, gave his last name to Ross Macdonald's lonely and compassionate private investigator, Lew Archer.

Sam Spade is a partner in the private detective agency of Spade & Archer, in San Francisco. Archer is in his forties, about ten years older than Spade, but he isn't as good a detective, or as smart, as his younger partner. He is killed almost immediately after the firm takes the case later published as **The Maltese Falcon**.

Spade didn't like his partner much, and had an active affair with his wife, Iva, a blonde with an exquisite figure. Iva briefly suspects that Spade killed Archer, so that he could marry her. The notion is absurd. He is not sentimental about his partner. Miles died, he tells his client, "with ten thousand insurance, no children, and a wife who didn't like him." Before a day had passed, he has told Effie Perrine, their secretary, to remove the old agency name from the door, replacing it with "Samuel Spade."

Quickly after the murder of her husband, Iva rushes to Spade for solace, which she gets, and a permanent liaison, which she does not. The detective already has his eye on his new client, the voluptuous redhead, Brigid O'Shaughnessy, the twenty-two-year-old described by Effie as a "knockout." Effie is somewhat jealous of both Iva and Brigid because she, too, is attracted to Spade.

Just over six feet tall, the "smooth thickness of his arms, legs, and body, the sag of his big round shoulders, made his body like a bear's. It was like a shaved bear's: his chest was hairless. His skin was childishly soft and pink."

If Spade's attraction to beautiful women is physical, it was doubtful if his physique inspired desire. With his slightly peculiar build, his clothes never fit him properly, either. Perhaps there is something about his face:

"Samuel Spade's jaw was long and bony, his chin a jutting v under the more flexible v of his mouth. His nostrils curved back to make another, smaller, v. His yellow-gray eyes were horizontal. The v *motif* was picked up again by thickish brows rising outward from twin creases above a hooked nose, and his pale brown hair grew down—from high flat temples—in a point on his forehead. He looked rather pleasantly like a blond satan."

Cool, always on guard, isolated and solitary, Spade operates somewhere in the shadowy area of the criminal world, not quite an officer of the law, nor a flouter of it. Always following his personal code of conduct and ethics, which he places above society's, he fluctuates from one end of the spectrum to the other. His policy gains him the hostility of criminals and law enforcement officials alike; it also gains their respect, because he never deviates from his own set of principles.

In San Francisco, which he calls "my burg," he is like a bounty hunter. He knows every hood in town and strides confidently among them, wise-cracking with them, bluffing them, laughing at their loaded guns (he never carries one himself because he doesn't like them), able to hold his own in any physical confrontation.

Totally self-disciplined, Spade varies his moral judgment to suit whatever danger or corruption he encounters, always working toward a better, healthier society. Cynical and idealistic, Spade keeps his defenses up against sentiment, enabling him to see people for what and who they really are.

Spade enjoys some freedoms unshared by most of his contemporaries, including the ability to turn his back on the temptations of money and sex (both of which, however, he values and enjoys). Freedom from conventional morality allows him to act as he feels like acting. Casper Gutman, the fat man who single-mindedly pursues the Maltese falcon, calls Spade "astonishing, amazing"; Brigid calls him "wild, unpredictable."

Much of Spade's behavior and personality may be explained by his reaction to a case he had handled in the 1920s, some years before he became involved in the quest for the priceless falcon (which he refers to unceremoniously as the "dingus"):

A man named Flitcraft disappeared suddenly (Spade tells Brigid O'Shaughnessy), leaving behind his business, family and friends. When

The most memorable American private eye in cinematic history is Sam Spade, portrayed by Humphrey Bogart in The Maltese Falcon *(1941).*

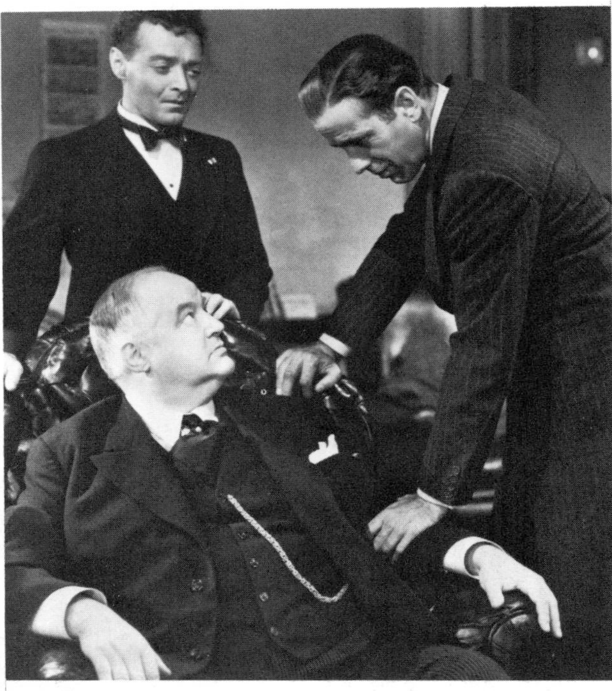

In the quintessential American private eye film, The Maltese Falcon, *Sydney Greenstreet and Peter Lorre seek help from Sam Spade.*

The classic scene from The Maltese Falcon: *Bogart, Peter Lorre, Mary Astor, Sydney Greenstreet.*

Spade found him, years after his disappearance, he had a new family and an entirely new life. Flitcraft explained to the detective that he had been nearly killed by a beam falling from a construction site, and it had made him suddenly aware of the randomness of life, the promiscuity of death. On the spot, he had determined to give up his well-ordered, carefully organized life, and search for something more fulfilling.

The incident made a deep impression on Spade, and he quickly came to realize that, at any moment, the beam might fall. Spade survives in his hard, tough environment because he expects falling beams, and spends time and energy watching for them.

Surrounded by violence, Spade uses his shrewdness and his judgment to keep others off balance. Though he does not carry any weapons, he has no fear of those who do. He has, in fact, few fears of any kind.

He certainly has no fear of the people scrambling after a sixteenth-century gold and jeweled statue of a falcon, about a foot high and of inestimable value. Hired by Gutman to retrieve the bird, Spade must deal with a vast

A Sam Spade who is younger than one expects decorates the cover of a 1944 Dell paperback, A Man Called Spade and Other Stories, *which contains the three short stories involving him.*

sideshow of peculiar characters, including the Levantine homosexual, Joel Cairo; the dangerous seaman, Floyd Thursby; the ineffectual assistant to Gutman, Wilmer; and the statuesque Brigid.

Refusing to be bought or compromised, Spade ultimately turns in to the official police everyone involved in the case who has committed a crime of whatever magnitude. Superficially a man whose character could bear little scrutiny, the toughest detective of his time showed his morality and sense of justice to be above question.

DASHIELL HAMMETT (See Nick and Nora Charles)

BIBLIOGRAPHY

1930 **The Maltese Falcon** (Knopf)
1944 **The Adventures of Sam Spade and Other Stories** (Mercury; Spade appears in three of the short stories)

FILMOGRAPHY

1931 **The Maltese Falcon** (Warner Brothers) with Ricardo Cortez (as Sam Spade), Bebe Daniels, Dudley Digges, Una Merkel, Thelma Todd; directed by Roy Del Ruth.
1936 **Satan Met a Lady** (Warner Brothers) with Warren William (as Sam Spade, renamed Ted Shayne for this film version of **The Maltese Falcon**), Bette Davis, Alison Skipworth, Arthur Treacher, Marie Wilson; directed by William Dieterle.
1941 **The Maltese Falcon** (Warner Brothers) with Humphrey Bogart (as Sam Spade), Mary Astor, Sydney Greenstreet, Peter Lorre, Elisha Cook, Jr.; directed by John Huston.

Dr. Thorndyke

When R. Austin Freeman read the textbooks of Professor Alfred Swaine Taylor (1806-1880) as a student, he was impressed by the man and the science of forensic medicine. Years later, when he created his famous medico-legal detective Dr. John Evelyn Thorndyke, the memory of **Principles and Practice of Medical Jurisprudence** (1865) and similar texts took on an importance never intended for them. Professor Taylor became the real-life prototype for Thorndyke, although Freeman denied it, claiming that his fictional crimefighter "was deliberately created to play a certain part."

One of the most important detective stories ever written was based on one of Professor Taylor's actual cases. "The Case of Oscar Brodski," the landmark story first published in **The Singing Bone** (1912), is the first inverted detective story—a tale in which the culprit and method of the crime are identified at the outset, and in which the main attention is then devoted to an explanation of how the crime was detected and the criminal identified.

Unlike many of the great crimefighters of fiction who rely on intuition or character analysis to solve mysteries, Dr. Thorndyke's procedure "consists in the interrogation of things rather than persons: of the ascertainment of physical facts which can be made visible to eyes other than his own."

Although his devotion to detail has gained him the title of the "Great Fathomer," Thorndyke is himself difficult to fathom. He is so unemotional, so much in control of himself at all times, that it is impossible to see into his mind, to get under the surface to his personality, if it exists, and discover if he is truly a man—or merely a textbook with legs.

But what a facade to penetrate! The handsomest of all detectives, Thorndyke was endowed with every possible advantage by Freeman. "His distinguished appearance," wrote the author of his creation, "is not merely a concession to my personal taste but also a protest against the monsters of ugliness whom some detective writers have evolved. These are quite opposed to natural truth. In real life, a first-class man of any kind usually tends to be a good-looking man."

Thorndyke has a long literary history, but ages slowly. When he is introduced in **The Red**

Thumb Mark in 1907, he is in his late thirties; by the time of his last adventure, **The Unconscious Witness**, published in 1942, he is only about fifty. Freeman explains that remarkable achievement by simply saying that he "put the brake on passing years."

Worth noting is that the saga of Dr. Thorndyke is that at least part of it has remained in print for seventy years, perennially in Great Britain and sporadically in the United States.

In a statement calculated to drive all men with ego straight to an asylum, Thorndyke is described as "quite normal. He has no gifts of intuition or other supernormal qualities . . . He is just a highly intellectual man of great and varied knowledge with exceptionally acute reasoning powers and endowed with . . . the capacity to perceive the essential nature of a problem before detailed evidence comes to light."

Although this may sound suspiciously like intuition, it cannot be, because Thorndyke is well known to lack this ability. It is, instead, "Scientific Imagination."

"Special knowledge," says Thorndyke, "is the stock in trade of the medical jurist." It is indeed, and Thorndyke, in contrast to the assertion that he is "quite normal," certainly has an intimidating stock of it.

That special knowledge is abundant, disparate and encyclopedic, covering virtually every area of scientific exploration, including profound familiarity with the oceans and tides, astronomy, footprints, fingerprints, anthropology, international commerce, zoology (with special emphasis on animal hair), ciphers, locks, metallurgy, botany (including an ability to identify the pond from which a certain weed was removed), chemistry, tattoos, marine biology, mineralogy, entomology, the history and geography of London, walking sticks, typewriters, medieval history, paper and its manufacture, ballistics, tobacco, textiles, precious stones, geology and hieroglyphics—to scratch the surface.

This catalogue of knowledge, together with his other bits of education, is used to interpret clues. He discovers and examines everything of a physical nature that can be found at the scene of the crime, and makes deductions from it. "Quick observation and rapid inference come by practice," Thorndyke says.

It is essential for Thorndyke to have an idea of the nature of a crime before he arrives at the scene. After his arrival, he works at a frenzied pace, taking precise measurements, sketching a diagram of the locale (which is published with the account of his adventure), and preserving every possible piece of evidence. Of those that are large enough, he makes plaster casts; of those that aren't, he makes microscope slides. He checks into everything and takes notes. "To be sketchy is to be vague," he says.

On a case, Thorndyke maintains, the investigator must be aware of "first, the danger of delay; the vital importance of instant action before that frail and fleeting thing that we call a clue has time to evaporate . . . second, the necessity of pursuing the most trivial clue to an absolute finish . . . third, the urgent need of a trained scientist to aid the police; and last [he concludes with what is, for him, humor], never [go out] without the invaluable green case."

Thorndyke's research case, covered in green canvas, is as indispensable to him as Sherlock Holmes' magnifying glass or Hercule Poirot's "little grey cells." Only one foot square and four inches deep, it carries a miniature microscope, test tubes, slides, tools, chemicals and anything else he might happen to require on a specific investigation.

While Thorndyke's interest in physical evidence is overwhelming, it is not exclusive. He recognizes the importance of human relationships, and emotions.

"We should be bad biologists and worse physicians," he says, "if we should underestimate the importance of that which is nature's chiefest care. The one salient biological truth is the importance of sex; and we are deaf and blind if we do not hear and see it in everything. . . . And as man is to the lower organisms, so is human love to their merely reflex manifestations of sex. The love of a serious and honorable man for a woman who is worthy of him is . . . the foundation of social life and its failure is a serious calamity, not only to those whose lives may be thereby spoilt, but to society at large."

Thorndyke's philosophy is one thing; the way he lives his life is another. He has no room in his life for the fair sex, although he is exceedingly attractive to them.

Tall, strong, athletic and slender (five feet, eleven inches tall and 13 stone, or 182 pounds),

Dr. Thorndyke, whose adventures have remained in print for seven decades, is one of the forgotten detectives of literature, perhaps because none of his cases has been filmed.

he is exceptionally handsome and has "an imposing presence, with a symmetrical face of the classical type and a Grecian nose." He is, furthermore, "free from eccentricities" and endowed with "the dignity of presence, appearance and manner appropriate to his high professional and social standing."

Thorndyke's high professional standing combines medicine and law: he is a forensic scientist and lawyer. He presumably achieved a high social standing largely because of his professional one—little is known of his family or personal background.

Aside from the fact that he was born on July 4, 1870, nothing is known of Thorndyke's early life. He attended St. Margaret's Hospital's Medical School, where he met Christopher Jervis, M.D., his friend and the chronicler of many of his exploits. Over the years, his connection with St. Margaret's becomes even stronger, as he takes on the positions of Medical Registrar, Pathologist, Museum Curator, and Professor of Medical Jurisprudence, in that order.

In 1896, Thorndyke is called to the bar and he tries his first case the following year, handling the defense in Regina *v.* Gummer. In later years, he is also attached to the staff of South London Hospital, where he conducts classes in toxicology, and serves as a director of the Griffin Life Assurance Company, for whom he investigates many cases.

Thorndyke's cases are his life. His home is a combination office, laboratory and living quarters, located one flight above street level at 5A, King's Bench Walk, Inner Temple, London. Behind a heavy door, known as "The Oak," is a wood-paneled living room with a fireplace, where policemen and prospective clients are entertained. On the same floor is a small office that doubles as a law library.

The next floor up houses the laboratory workshop, where he and his assistant, Nathaniel Polton, conduct experiments. Everything required in a well-stocked chemistry laboratory may be found here, as well as bizarre tools of no definable function or description, and a furnace that serves double duty for metallurgy work and cooking food (the apartment has no kitchen). The top floor contains bedrooms for Thorndyke and Polton and, for a while, Jervis.

Jervis did not see Thorndyke for some years after they left medical school at St. Margaret's. A chance encounter at the beginning of what was to become the first recorded adventure of the "Great Fathomer" turns out to be very important in Jervis' life. He meets Juliet Gibson, his future wife, and he joins Thorndyke as a junior partner.

In the tradition of many others who have willingly accepted a subservient role to a great detective—Jervis refers to himself as the "second violin in Thorndyke's orchestra"—he is frequently out of his intellectual depth, and is forced to bear the title of "Expert Misunderstander."

Although he seems more capable when Thorndyke is not around, Jervis readily admits his mystification at the detective's powers. "The ways of John Thorndyke," he says, "were, indeed, beyond all comprehension."

Thorndyke, rather mockingly, refers to Jervis as "my learned friend." On one occasion, the medico-legal expert makes a typically brilliant deduction from an examination of a test tube

A somewhat modern-looking Thorndyke illustrates the dust wrapper of the first edition of A Silent Witness *(1915).*

full of fleas and lice. The awed Jervis makes a stupid remark, and Thorndyke arrogantly tells him: "There were two very striking facts, one of which I fancy you did not observe. The fleas were not the common human flea; they were Asiatic rat fleas."

Straight-faced, Jervis admits: "You are quite right. I did not notice that."

The other important character in Thorndyke's professional life is Nathaniel Polton, his full-time assistant and jack-of-all-trades. Hired by Thorndyke in 1895 (a full year before the detective actually begins his career), Polton is totally devoted to him, once even allowing his eyelashes to be snipped off to help with a case. He is the cook and housekeeper in their bachelor establishment, serves as laboratory assistant and has invented such useful items for his boss as a periscope walking stick and glasses which enable the wearer to see behind himself without turning his head.

Orphaned at an early age and separated from his sister Margaret, Polton became apprenticed to a watchmaker (and still retains an interest in old clocks) and then constructed optical instruments. He was not successful; he found himself unemployed and starving when Thorndyke hired him, and he has remained grateful. His hardships have left their mark: although he is younger than Thorndyke, his "crinkly" face makes him appear much older, and Jervis describes him as "a small, elderly man" at their first meeting.

Polton does some of Thorndyke's legwork, and some is occasionally done by Mr. Snuper, a private enquiry agent, but the "Great Fathomer" does most of his own investigative work himself, apparently with boundless energy. "My practice is my recreation," he says.

Little time remains for nonprofessional endeavors, but some of Thorndyke's other interests include bicycle riding, a knowledge and appreciation of contemporary artists, smoking (pipes and Trichinopoly cigars), fishing (he is devoted to Walton's **The Compleat Angler**) and, since he is given to exclaiming "Yoicks!" and "Tally Ho!," probably riding to hounds, though he does not mention it specifically to Jervis.

Still, his primary avocations are closely related to his career, and he sees nothing extraordinary about using his spare time to study peculiar wills. At the outset of his career, merely for his personal edification and as an intellectual exercise, he planned the murders of high-ranking officials, then sought flaws in those plans. He kept the notes for future reference.

That particular form of mental gymnastics may be revealing in ways that Thorndyke may not have imagined. Although he is a lawyer, he is not above breaking the law, and if the taking of a life better serves the cause of justice than saving it, he approves of permitting God's mills to grind.

Because the law is incapable of protecting people from blackmailers, he does not disapprove of their killing their tormentors. In the case chronicled as **The Cat's Eye**, he allows criminals to die in their own death trap instead of making a rescue attempt.

No rancor, no grim satisfaction, no boiling revenge motivate Dr. John Evelyn Thorndyke to pursue such a course. Normally mild-mannered, even kindly and philanthropic, he merely remains unemotional and detached. The decision is, to him, purely the triumph of logic and reason.

Jervis holds a lamp while Thorndyke sweeps up evidence in this illustration by E.J. Prittie.

Freeman approved of this portrait of Thorndyke by H.M. Brock for Pearson's *magazine (1908).*

R. AUSTIN FREEMAN (1862-1943) Born in the Soho district of London, Richard Austin Freeman became a physician and spent seven years in Africa as assistant colonial surgeon. His ill health forced his return to England, where he wrote numerous crime and mystery books about Dr. Thorndyke and other detectives, as well as several rogues. In collaboration with John J. Pitcairn, under the Clifford Ashdown pseudonym, he wrote stories about Romney Pringle, a thief, and other fiction. Freeman's most notable contribution to the development of mystery fiction is his invention of the "inverted" detective story, in which the reader witnesses the crime, the suspense then resting on *how* the criminal is caught, not on who he is or if he will be brought to justice.

BIBLIOGRAPHY

1911 **The Red Thumb Mark** (Newton; published in 1907 by Collingwood, London)
1912 **The Vanishing Man** (Dodd, Mead; published as **The Eye of Osiris** in 1911 by Hodder & Stoughton, London)
1913 **The Mystery of 31, New Inn** (Winston; published in 1912 by Hodder & Stoughton, London)
1915 **A Silent Witness** (Winston; originally published in 1914 by Hodder & Stoughton, London)
1918 **The Great Portrait Mystery** (London: Hodder & Stoughton; two of the stories are about Dr. Thorndyke; not published in the United States)
1922 **Helen Vardon's Confession** (London: Hodder & Stoughton; not published in the United States)
1923 **The Singing Bone** (Dodd, Mead; published in 1912 by Hodder & Stoughton, London)
1924 **The Blue Scarab** (Dodd, Mead; originally published as **Dr. Thorndyke's Case Book** in 1923 by Hodder & Stoughton, London)
1925 **The Mystery of Angelina Frood** (Dodd, Mead; published in 1924 by Hodder & Stoughton, London)
1925 **The Shadow of the Wolf** (Dodd, Mead)
1926 **The Puzzle Lock** (Dodd, Mead; published in 1925 by Hodder & Stoughton, London)
1926 **The D'Arblay Mystery** (Dodd, Mead)
1927 **The Cat's Eye** (Dodd, Mead; originally published in 1923 by Hodder & Stoughton, London)
1927 **The Magic Casket** (Dodd, Mead)
1928 **A Certain Dr. Thorndyke** (Dodd, Mead; published in 1927 by Hodder & Stoughton, London)
1928 **As a Thief in the Night** (Dodd, Mead)
1930 **Mr. Pottermack's Oversight** (Dodd, Mead)
1931 **Dr. Thorndyke's Cases** (Dodd, Mead; published in 1909 as **John Thorndyke's Cases** by Chatto & Windus; London)
1931 **Pontifex, Son and Thorndyke** (Dodd, Mead)
1932 **Dr. Thorndyke's Discovery** (Dodd, Mead; published as **When Rogues Fall Out** by Hodder & Stoughton, London)
1933 **Dr. Thorndyke Intervenes** (Dodd, Mead)
1934 **For the Defense: Dr. Thorndyke** (Dodd, Mead; British title: **For the Defence: Dr. Thorndyke**)
1936 **The Penrose Mystery** (Dodd, Mead)
1937 **Death at the Inn** (Dodd, Mead; British title: **Felo de Se?**)
1939 **The Stoneware Monkey** (Dodd, Mead; published 1938 by Hodder & Stoughton, London)
1940 **Mr. Polton Explains** (Dodd, Mead)
1942 **The Unconscious Witness** (Dodd, Mead; British title: **The Jacob Street Mystery**)
1973 **The Best Dr. Thorndyke Detective Stories** (Dover; contains the first book publication of the novelette **31, New Inn**)

Philo Vance

Of all the strange phenomena of detective fiction, perhaps the oddest is the inexplicably meteoric rise and decline of the fortunes of Philo Vance. In the decade beginning with 1926, he was the most loved and read crimefighter whose exploits were recorded in book form (he was the first great detective to make standard best-seller lists).

Vance exploded on the literary scene in 1926 in **The Benson Murder Case**, the result of the literary efforts of S. S. Van Dine (the pseudonym of Willard Huntington Wright) and the editorial direction of Maxwell Perkins, the legendary genius who was responsible for making Thomas Wolfe readable, and who helped produce the masterpieces of F. Scott Fitzgerald and Ernest Hemingway.

A now-familiar biographical anecdote describes how Wright, an art and literary critic of modest means, pursued a work schedule so rigorous it produced a breakdown in health, confining him to bed for two years with a heart condition. Prohibited from scholarly tasks, his favorite diversion became reading mystery novels, and he was soon struck with the notion that he could conceive better fiction than he was reading.

As a scholar of some reputation (he wrote the article on Nietzsche for the **Encyclopaedia Britannica**), he was reluctant to use his own name on something as frivolous as detective books, so he assumed an old family name, Van Dyne, together with the "steamship" initials, for a pseudonym.

He wrote three outlines for novels, each 10,000 words long, and offered them to Perkins, who liked them immediately and extravagantly. Wright followed with second drafts, of 30,000 words each, then doubled the length for the final manuscript version, filling in dialogue and more complete characterization and description.

The books took off, William Powell and others portrayed him effectively on the screen, and Philo Vance was a name on the lips of all literate Americans. Then, as quickly as his star had ascended, it plummeted, and Vance virtually vanished overnight, achieving the obscurity which his detractors claim he so richly merited.

And, despite (or perhaps because of) his incredible popularity, Vance had his detractors. Of all the negative remarks uttered and written about the snobbish detective, none is more eloquent than the poem composed by Ogden Nash:

Philo Vance
Needs a kick in the pance.

In addition to serving as the author of the books in which Vance conducts investigations, S. S. Van Dine also has the function of narrator. When the detective is asked (in **The Garden Murder Case**) what he would be without Van Dine, Vance answers, "...an obscure, but free, spirit. And I'd never have unconsciously provided the inspiration for Ogden Nash's poetic masterpiece."

While it is likely that he would have had the good sense and taste to deny it, the inspiration for Vance appears to have been mainly Van Dine himself. Like his literary creation, Van Dine was a Harvard graduate, an aesthete, and a brilliant, undeviating and genial snob.

Vance also bears notable similarities to the early Ellery Queen, whom he preceded by three years, and Lord Peter Wimsey, whom he succeeded in print by three years.

Philo Vance, incidentally, is not the great detective's real name. It is an alias, adopted to protect his genuine identity. Whether the purpose was to protect him from the revenge of criminals or the vilification of those who had read his adventures, is not known.

Philo Vance has no aversion to providing to anyone within earshot the benefit of his enormous knowledge in almost every field of human endeavor. He is rather reticent about much of his private life, especially his early years and his affairs of the heart, however, even to his friend, adviser and chronicler, S. S. Van Dine.

Obtuse references and logical deductions therefrom indicate that Vance was born about 1886 of socially prominent ancestry. Both his mother and father died within a short time of each other when he was thirteen, and he was left under the guardianship of his paternal aunt, Agatha.

When she died, leaving him as her sole heir, he was free forever of the cares of economic necessity. His childhood was reasonably normal, although he admits to having written some bad poetry and musical compositions at the age of six.

During his undergraduate years at Harvard, he led an active social and athletic life, playing football, tennis, competing at pole-vaulting and sprinting, and serving as captain of the fencing team. But it was his studies which dominated his time and interests.

He found the normal course of study too simple for his acute mind, so he devoted himself to acquiring mastery of such subjects as the history of religions, Greek and Persian classics, Sanskrit, Egyptology, anthropology, ethnology, modern and ancient languages—particularly Egyptian, Arabic and Hebrew (because, he claimed, "Culture is polyglot, and the knowledge of many tongues is essential to an understanding of the world's intellectual and aesthetic achievements"), medicine and surgery (although he doubted that he could sufficiently depersonalize himself to become a doctor or surgeon), theoretical and experimental psychology (which became instrumental in getting him involved in crime and its detection), and the history of art and literature (he was a frequent contributor to student publications, and several of his drawings and paintings decorated the walls of the Harvard University Library).

After graduation, Vance traveled (later referring to it as "a bit of toddlin' round the world"), spending two years at Oxford (getting his M.A. with a thesis on Schopenhauer) and three years wandering through Egypt, Flanders, Spain, southern France, Holland, Italy, Switzerland, Monte Carlo, Greece, China, Japan (where he learned jiu-jitsu), India and Arabia.

World War I erupted while Vance was in Trichinopoly, in the south of India, and he returned to the United States to serve as a lieutenant in the army, earning the Croix de Guerre for his distinguished service in France.

Currie, the English valet who had accompanied Vance everywhere ever since he had been taken into service when Vance was at Oxford, also returned to his country to accept military duty. After the war, Vance located Currie and rehired him to look after his new home.

When Vance returned from France, he took one more trip, across the United States, before settling into a residence in New York City. He found an old mansion on East 38th Street, leased the upper two floors, supervising the remodeling himself, and constructed a hand-

E.M. Jackson portrays the student of Nietzsche, amateur psychologist, art aficionado, detective.

Vance as he appeared to E.M. Jackson in The Kennel Murder Case, *his last case with merit.*

some rooftop garden. Currie became valet, cook, and major-domo.

Vance also renewed his friendship with S. S. Van Dine, who had been a law student at Harvard while Vance was an undergraduate. Although temperamentally dissimilar, they had been inseparable companions at college, and only a sense of obligation to his father had prevented Van Dine from accompanying his friend on his travels. Instead, he became a clerk in his father's law firm.

With his new apartment established, Vance persuaded Van Dine to give up his junior partnership in Van Dine, Davis and Van Dine (located at 120 Broadway in the heart of the Wall Street district) to take on the financial and personal management of his affairs. Van Dine soon gave up his bachelor quarters in a West Side hotel and moved into the luxurious duplex.

Vance does not become a recluse, but he leads a quiet, self-contained life in his comfortable apartment. Much of his time and energy is devoted to further study in the arts and psychology. He finds time for sports, such as golf (his handicap is 3), tennis (which he also likes as a spectator, particularly at Forest Hills), polo, winter sports (traveling to Switzerland to indulge his hobby), horse racing (he once owned several race horses), and fox hunting (he breeds his own hunting dogs and also breeds Scottish terriers, keeping them in his kennels in New Jersey).

Another of Vance's favorite pastimes is attending antique exhibitions, searching for rarities to add to his already imposing collection. His apartment contains a collection of museum-quality Chinese antiquities, including a Ting-yao vase, one of the finest Chinese and Japanese print collections in the United States, paintings by Matisse, several Cézanne watercolors, a Picasso still life, a work by Michelangelo, numerous Egyptian treasures, miniature models of foreign architecture, Negro sculpture, a Renoir, which hangs above the mantle in the living room, and a fascinating assemblage of curiosities relating to games of skill and gambling.

Vance's library is to be envied. Van Dine once spent three months cataloguing the rare books and first editions but did not complete the task. Among the volumes contained in the cases which reflect an extraordinary catholicity of taste are a **Who's Who**, Remy's **Demonolatry**, the **New York Social Register**, works of psychology by Freud, Jung, Stekel and Ferenczi, the **Satyricon** of Petronius, a large selection of medical books, the **American Biographical Dictionary**, **The Evolution of the Dragon** by Elliot Smith, **Trattato della Pettura** by da Vinci, the **Life of Genghis Khan** and most of the important classics. He loves to read into the early morning hours, often turning to the Old Testament, of which he has said, "When I weary of the professional liter'ry man, I find stimulation in the prose of the Bible."

Music is also a passion of Vance's, and he is a fine amateur pianist; he also attends many concerts (preferring chamber music recitals to symphony orchestras) and operas (his favorite modern opera is **Louise**; his favorite Wagnerian opera is **Die Meistersinger**). Other interests include semi-precious stones, poker (he is unbeatable because of an uncanny knowledge of the psychological elements of the game), tropical fish (he raises several rare breeds), and long, relaxing drives in the country behind the wheel of his powerful Hispano-Suiza, which he bought shortly after World War I. He has a chauffeur, but prefers to drive himself to steady his nerves and clarify his brain.

It is on one of the bucolic sashays that Vance renews his friendship with John F.-X. Markham, the District Attorney for New York County

(Manhattan). A graduate of Columbia University, Markham had run for office on an independent reform ticket against Tammany Hall and won, serving only one four-year term. In his mid-forties while in office (during the Prohibition era), he is called the "watchdog" and is considered incorruptible. All of Vance's recorded cases take place during Markham's term.

Although they were friends for many years, sharing a mutual affection and respect that was profound, the idiosyncratic form of their relationship caused Van Dine to comment: "In the entire association between Markham and Vance I had never heard either of them pay the other a compliment of any kind. When one of them so much as bordered on a compliment, the other always broke in sharply with a remark which made any further outward display of sentiment impossible. To me it seemed as if both of them had a deep-rooted instinct to keep the intimate and personal side of their affection for each other disguised and unspoken."

During a conversation at the Stuyvesant Club, to which Vance, Van Dine and Markham all belong, Vance tells Markham he would enjoy accompanying him on one of his investigations. That casual remark, instigated out of a desire to satisfy idle curiosity, is to change Vance's life, giving him an interest to which he becomes more passionately devoted than art and literature.

The dramatic circumstances of violent crime give Vance the opportunity to study human psychology in a new environment, and he thoroughly enjoys it. He also solves a murder case which might otherwise have baffled the official police forever.

Vance makes no effort to disguise his contempt for police procedure, calling it "a masterpiece of absurdity," and he never changes his opinion of either law enforcement or the law itself.

To Vance, the law is an "elaborate invention of imbeciles" which he finds offensive to his sense of justice, denigrating it for its failure "to provide for the extermination of a dangerous and despicable criminal." It would be no surprise to him, he claims, to hear a judge in a courtroom confront a criminal and tell him: "I know, and the jury knows, that you committed the crime, but in view of the legally admissible evidence, I declare you innocent. Go and sin again."

Another criminal is not given a similar opportunity. When Vance discovers his plot to poison an innocent person, he does not cause the villain to be arrested—he switches drinks and calmly allows the criminal to be poisoned. District Attorney Markham is outraged at his friend's blatant disregard for the law.

Looking as effete as anyone could wish, Philo Vance is portrayed effectively by Clark Agnew.

"But it was murder!" bellows Markham.

"Oh, doubtless," replies Vance cheerfully. "Yes—of course. Most reprehensible...I say, am I by any chance under arrest?"

He is not, of course, getting away, in effect, with murder. His adherence to Nietzschean philosophy permits him to be indignant when it is suggested that he has done something not quite right.

"Don't be so righteous," he says. "Do you bring a rattlesnake to the bar of justice? Do you give a mad dog his day in court? I felt no more compunction in aiding a monster like———into the Beyond than I would have in crushing out a poisonous reptile in the act of striking."

His disaffection for the law, and for law enforcement officials, earns him the enmity of most members of the police department of New York City, particularly Sergeant Ernest Heath of the Homicide Bureau. Vance's arrogance, his humorous cynicism, his lectures on subjects of extreme esoterica, the general intrusion of the debonair dilettante, all combine to cause Heath

E.M. Jackson's illustration of a pensive Vance appeared in Cosmopolitan *(January 1933), which serialized* The Kennel Murder Case.

an acute agony in the lower back. As more cases are solved by the gifted amateur detective, however, Heath comes to accept his presence with greater equanimity, and he even eventually gives him undisguised respect and admiration.

Vance is unusual in the respect that he not only is an arrogant snob to the utmost degree, but he acts the part perfectly, and looks every inch of it as well. Every gesture, every sound he makes, heralds anew his personality.

Tall (slightly under six feet) and gracefully slim, he is extremely handsome, bearing some resemblance to John Barrymore. He is the Nordic type, his cold gray eyes set far apart, with drooping eyelids contributing to a somewhat languid, yet derisive, look. He has a long, sharply chiseled face; a straight, slender nose; a prominent, straight, narrow chin with an unusually deep cleft; an ascetic, apparently cruel mouth; and the full, sloping forehead of an artist.

His facial expression is sardonic, superior and cynical, which accurately reflects his character. He is reserved and aloof, seems ashamed of any display of emotion, and, although a man of some charm, is not gregarious, feeling generally uncomfortable in crowds. He is also, he admits, never truly happy. He is himself brilliant, and hates stupidity.

Despite his brilliance, Vance has his failings, the major intellectual one of which is that he has only partial use of those mental faculties until after noon. Consequently, he makes it a habit to rise late—never before 11 A.M. if it can be avoided. Shortly after arising, he has breakfast, which traditionally consists of nothing more than thick Turkish coffee and two Rēgie cigarettes, unless a special occasion requires a more elaborate meal, such as an omelette or other specialty prepared by Currie.

The Rēgie cigarettes are a trademark for Vance. Imported directly from an agent in Constantinople, these expensive Turkish cigarettes have rose-petal tips, but Vance nonetheless frequently uses a slender ivory cigarette holder with a platinum rim. He carries the cigarettes in a solid gold case, together with a gold lighter.

Vance also carries an appointment book, in which he takes frequent notes—but never in pencil; he prefers the gold fountain pen which he carries on his watch chain. He also carries a monocle in his waistcoat pocket, and sometimes carries a walking stick.

Always fashionably dressed, he favors rough tweed suits (even in July) and a soft Homburg, either black or a subdued green. He never wears a boutonniere. At home, he wears loose dressing gowns and robes, in a variety of bright colors, with sandals to match.

Because of his fondness for privacy and a reluctance to make personal or professional commitments of any kind, Vance spends a good deal of time at home, languishing in his dressing gown, engaging in studies of an aesthetic nature, and enjoying the company of his pets.

He considers his pet Scottish terrier bitch, "Miss Mac Tavish," more precious than his Cézannes. His affection for animals extends to his horses. When one of his stable of thoroughbreds has to be destroyed because of a broken leg, he is so upset that he sells the rest and is unable to look at a racing form again for a year. **The Morning Telegraph** has been, for a long time, the only newspaper he can stand to read.

Four-legged animals are not the only pets for which Vance has affection. The handsome Vance had had several romances in his college days, and his name was linked with a famous beauty of Budapest, but he seems genuinely to have lost his heart to only one woman: Zalia Graem, a young sportswoman and friend of Floyd Garden, whom Vance meets on the investigation later

In 1934, Warren Williams (center) portrayed Vance in The Dragon Murder Case, *one of the strangest films in the series. Williams also played in the Lone Wolf and Perry Mason series.*

Herbert Morton Stoops envisioned Philo Vance as a bit older and crueler-looking, than most of his fellow illustrators.

recorded as **The Garden Murder Case**.

Obviously smitten by the beautiful young woman, Vance is unable to hide his emotions. Van Dine notices his friend's reaction, and writes:

"I believe that the season [Spring], with all its subtle innuendoes, was the real explanation of the change that came over Vance himself during his investigation of the crime. Up to that time I had never considered Vance a man of any deep personal emotion, except in so far as children and animals and his intimate masculine friendships were concerned. He had always impressed me as a man so highly mentalized, so cynical and impersonal in his attitude toward life, that an irrational human weakness like romance would be alien to his nature. But in the course of his deft inquiry into the murders in Professor Garden's penthouse, I saw, for the first time, another and softer side of his character. Vance was never a happy man in the conventional sense; but, after the Garden murder case, there were evidences of an even deeper loneliness in his sensitive nature."

Vance's affection for the charming young lady, who reciprocates the emotion, is quite deep and sincere. When she becomes engaged to another man, he sets sail for Egypt, both heartbroken and relieved. He does not consider himself the type for marriage, claiming on two separate occasions that "A man's affections involve a great responsibility. The things a man wants most must often be sacrificed because of this exacting responsibility."

Vance doubts, and Van Dine agrees with him, "his capacity to make any woman happy in the conventional sense."

Even after the three month trip to Egypt, Vance is not cured of his emotional anguish. "To this day," writes Van Dine in 1935, "Vance has not lost his deep affection for Zalia Graem. He has rarely mentioned her name, but I have noticed a subtle change in his nature, which I attribute to the influence of that sentiment."

She marries someone else within a year.

Not long after, Vance is involved in the case he regards as his personal "favorite"—recorded as **The Gracie Allen Murder Case,** it constitutes his one patent failure as an investigator.

Vance retires to a villa outside Florence, Italy, soon after his unhappy experiences with Zalia Graem and the Gracie Allen case, and permits, at that time, the publication of his adventures by Van Dine.

S. S. VAN DINE (pseudonym of Willard Huntington Wright, 1888-1939) Born in Charlottesville, Va., Wright was educated at St. Vincent and Pomona Colleges, Harvard University, and studied art in France and Germany, using his extensive education to secure jobs as literary and art critic for various publications. Falling ill, he began to read detective novels, decided he could do better than the authors he was reading, and produced the outlines for three Philo Vance novels, all of which were aimed at a more intelligent, more cultivated reader than he supposed ordinarily read that type of literature. They were enormously successful, as were most of the other Vance novels, and Wright made a fortune—which he spent on the good life, dying with an estate valued at only $13,000.

BIBLIOGRAPHY

1926 **The Benson Murder Case** (Scribner's)
1927 **The "Canary" Murder Case** (Scribner's)
1928 **The Greene Murder Case** (Scribner's)
1929 **The Bishop Murder Case** (Scribner's)
1930 **The Scarab Murder Case** (Scribner's)
1933 **The Kennel Murder Case** (Scribner's)
1933 **The Dragon Murder Case** (Scribner's)
1934 **The Casino Murder Case** (Scribner's)
1935 **The Garden Murder Case** (Scribner's)
1936 **The Kidnap Murder Case** (Scribner's)
1938 **The Gracie Allen Murder Case** (Scribner's)
1939 **The Winter Murder Case** (Scribner's)

FILMOGRAPHY

1929 **The Canary Murder Case** (Paramount) with William Powell (as Philo Vance), Louis Brooks, James Hall, Jean Arthur; directed by Malcolm St. Clair.

1929 **The Greene Murder Case** (Paramount) with William Powell, Florence Eldridge, Jean Arthur, Ullrich Haupt; directed by Frank Tuttle.

1930 **The Bishop Murder Case** (MGM) with Basil Rathbone (as Philo Vance), Leila Hyams, Roland Young, George Marion; directed by Nick Grinde and David Burton.

1930 **The Benson Murder Case** (Paramount) with William Powell, Natalie Moorhead, Paul Lukas, William Boyd; directed by Frank Tuttle.

1933 **The Kennel Murder Case** (Warner Brothers) with William Powell, Mary Astor, Ralph Morgan, Helen Vinson, Jack LaRue; directed by Michael Curtiz.

1934 **The Dragon Murder Case** (Warner Brothers—First National) with Warren William (as Philo Vance), Margaret Lindsay, Lyle Talbot, Dorothy Tree; directed by H. Bruce Humberstone.

1935 **The Casino Murder Case** (MGM) with Paul Lukas (as Philo Vance), Rosalind Russell, Donald Cook, Alison Skipworth; directed by Edwin L. Marin.

1936 **The Garden Murder Case** (MGM) with Edmund Lowe (as Philo Vance), Virginia Bruce, Gene Lockhart, Benita Hume; directed by Edwin L. Marin.

1936 **The Scarab Murder Case** (Paramount; British) with Wilfrid Hyde-White (as Philo Vance), Kathleen Kelly; directed by Michael Hankinson.

1937 **Night of Mystery** (Paramount) with Grant Richards (as Philo Vance), Helen Burgess, Ruth Coleman, Roscoe Karns; directed by E.A. Dupont.

1939 **The Gracie Allen Murder Case** (Paramount) with Warren William, Gracie Allen, Ellen Drew, Kent Taylor; directed by Alfred E. Green.

1940 **Calling Philo Vance** (Warner Brothers) with James Stephenson (as Philo Vance), Margot Stevenson, Henry O'Neill, Ralph Forbes; directed by William Clemens.

1947 **Philo Vance Returns** (PRC) with William Wright (as Philo Vance), Terry Austin, Leon Belasco, Ramsay Ames; directed by William Beaudine.

1947 **Philo Vance's Gamble** (PRC) with Alan Curtis (as Philo Vance), Terry Austin, Frank Jenks, Tala Birell; directed by Basil Wrangell.

1947 **Philo Vance's Secret Mission** (PRC) with Alan Curtis, Sheila Ryan, Frank Jenks, Tala Birell; directed by Reginald Le Borg.

Lord Peter Wimsey

Because of an inflated affection for her detective, Dorothy L. Sayers has provided more information about Lord Peter Wimsey than is known about most detectives. Little is left to conjecture, seldom can inconsistencies be found, and only trivial gaps in his life remain unfilled, requiring hypotheses or fiction for clarification.

Apart from growing several inches (his height going from five feet, nine inches to just six feet in the course of his exploits), Wimsey's life follows a pattern of realism that gives the detective every appearance of being a real-life character. In some ways, of course, he is.

In all likelihood, Wimsey had more than one prototype. Of the first importance is Eric Whelpton, a tall, handsome, Byronic figure with whom the author was, for a time, passionately in love. Like Wimsey, Whelpton attended Oxford, served in World War I, and returned from it to face horrible nightmares, a victim of ravaged nerves. Also like Wimsey, he was an accomplished linguist, a gourmet, and generally familiar with, and attracted to, the good things in life. Since Miss Sayers was in love with Whelpton at precisely the time she created Lord Peter, it would be folly to suggest that he played no role in the development of the detective's formation.

Also offered as a possible model for Wimsey is author John Cournos, a "mystery man" in Miss Sayers' life. She certainly knew him well, and they may have been lovers (of which she had her share). His apparent intellectual similarities to Wimsey indicate that he must have contributed to the character to some degree.

Wimsey's intellect and personality follow a rocky path during his early years. Although admittedly brilliant when he is introduced in **Whose Body?**, he is also affected and obnoxious, with a sense of humor that would discredit a low-grade moron.

He constantly drops his "g"s, says "ain't" and generally appears to have attended the same school of speech as Reggie Fortune and Philo Vance—guaranteed to cause severe pains in the

Although physically unlike the titled amateur detective, Ian Carmichael has played him (on TV) more than any actor.

stomach, brain or lower back.

Wimsey takes nothing seriously, including murder. "I'm enjoyin' this," he admits at one point in the investigation, and he goes so far as to ad lib doggerel about the corpse: "We both have got a body in a bath/We both have got a body in a bath/For in spite of all temptations/To go in for cheap sensations/We insist upon a body in a bath."

Fortunately, Wimsey matures as the series of books about him progresses, and in the last story, "Talboys," he is a solid family man with a wife, three sons, and all his "g"s firmly in place.

His wife is Harriet D. Vane (the middle initial is as important to her as the "L" was to Miss Sayers) and no one disputes the theory that the true love of Wimsey's life is Dorothy L. Sayers herself, as she would have liked to be.

Of their many similarities, none is more pronounced than their mutual love for Wimsey. In **Busman's Honeymoon**, these lines appear:

"Oh, Peter...All my life I have been wandering in the dark—but now I have found your heart—and am satisfied.

"And what do all the great words come to in the end, but that?—I love you—I am at rest with you—I have come home."

The words are equally valid coming from the lips of Harriet Vane, or the pen of Dorothy Sayers.

Peter Death Bredon Wimsey was born in 1890, the second son of Mortimer Gerald Bredon Wimsey, the 15th Duke of Denver, and Honoria Lucasta Delagardie, who came from an old Anglo-French family.

Family relations were strained during Peter's childhood. His father was a bounder and, before he died, embroiled the family in scandal. Peter himself was a small child; in the words of his uncle, Paul Austin Delagardie, "a colorless shrimp" who horrified his father with his intense interest in art and music. The duke made no secret of favoring his first son, Gerald Christian Wimsey, later Viscount of St. George and the 16th Duke of Denver.

Following Gerald into public school, Peter at first gained acceptance with his ready wit and, later, it was discovered that he was "a brilliant natural cricketer."

"Plenty of Eton men," his uncle wrote, "will remember the 'Great Flim,' as Peter was known." It was also at about this time that his uncle Delagardie took Peter under his avuncular wing, teaching him the ways of a gentleman. Delagardie maintained that "however good the material one has to work upon, it is ridiculous to leave any young man's social education to chance."

In 1909, Peter earned a scholarship to study history at Balliol College, Oxford. It was here, his uncle reports, that "he became rather intolerable...he began to give himself airs. He acquired affectations, an exaggerated Oxford manner and monocle."

Prior to World War I, Peter fell in love with a young girl who, in the opinion of the Wimseys, "had neither brains nor character." The family opposition nearly prompted him to marry immediately, out of spite, until it was pointed out to him "that if he came back mutilated, it would be very unfair to the girl." He had not been gone very long when she married someone else.

In despair, Peter threw himself into the fighting with abandon. His men liked him and he made a good officer, attaining the rank of major and winning the Distinguished Service Order for "some recklessly good intelligence work behind the German lines."

Wimsey's World War I career came to an abrupt halt in 1918, when he was "blown up and buried in a shell-hole near Caudry . . . that left him with a bad nervous breakdown, lasting, on and off, for two years."

Although the war had cost him his girl and, temporarily, his health, it did gain him Bunter. Formerly his sergeant, Bunter was to become the perfect gentleman's gentleman.

Lord Peter moved into a second floor flat at 110A Piccadilly W. in London and, according to his uncle, "shut everybody out of his confidence...and became, in fact, the complete comedian."

It was the (unrecorded) Attenbury Emeralds case in 1921 that saved Wimsey from using his independent means to provide for himself a life of aimless dilettantism. Though not especially difficult of solution, the case gained him notoriety as "a noble sleuth" and furnished diversion for his active mind.

The case also was the occasion of his meeting detective Charles Parker, "a quiet, sensible, well bred fellow" who "has the valuable quality of being fond of people without wanting to turn

In the only motion picture based on a Wimsey novel, Robert Montgomery plays a low key, non-eccentric Lord Peter. Constance Cummings is the newly wed Harriet in The Haunted Honeymoon.

them inside out." During the course of Wimsey's criminal investigations, Parker (whose hobby is the study of New Testament commentaries) is first promoted to Detective-Inspector, then finally to Chief Inspector. Equally important, he also falls in love with and marries Peter's sister.

Wimsey's family plays a vital role, not only in his life, but in his cases. His first case is taken at the behest of his mother. His sister Mary (whom he calls Polly), a blue-eyed ash-blonde with a "brilliant" complexion, is an early suspect in Peter's second recorded case; his brother, the Duke, is actually tried for the crime in the House of Lords, but Peter saves him. He also has cases involving a nephew and, much later, his sons.

After the first two recorded exploits, Wimsey decided that detection was "legitimate work for society" and set up business as a more-or-less professional private detective, opening an office at 97 St. George's Square. His agency is manned (so to speak) by retired secretaries and similar maiden ladies under the capable supervision of Miss Alexandra Katherine Climpson, "a thin, middle-aged woman with a sharp sallow face and a very vivacious manner."

Although Miss Climpson has a vital, recurring role in the Wimsey saga, his most valuable employee is, without question, the exemplary ex-sergeant, Bunter. Wimsey calls him "my confidential and assistant sleuth." He is that, and much more. He runs errands for Wimsey which are invaluable in the investigations, uses his photographic skills on countless occasions, makes terrific coffee (which wins the plaudits of everyone who has ever had even a single sip), and has acquired sufficient bibliographic knowledge from his employer that he is trusted to attend book auctions and make purchases in his behalf. For these talents and efforts, along with the meticulous ministrations expected of any first-rate gentleman's gentleman, Bunter is

For the publication of "The Learned Adventure of the Dragon's Head" in Pearson's *magazine, Lord Peter is handsome and aristocratic.*

paid the princely sum (in 1923) of £200.

Books are perhaps the major interest of the "Sherlock Holmes of the West End." He collects them, reads them, and is the author of at least two monographs: **Collecting of Incunabula** and **The Murderer's Vade-Mecum.** He brings his writing gifts to an advertising agency, using his middle names, Death Bredon.

His literary tastes date back to his youth, and he took honors in both history and literature. He is an avid admirer of Dante. Music, too, interests him, and he is fond of playing Bach and Scarlatti on the piano with his long, wide, muscular, square-tipped fingers. Among Wimsey's other accomplishments are his abilities as a sportsman: he rides horses superbly, drives automobiles equally well, is a "skilled shot" when hunting partridge, casts "a mighty rod" and is a fine swordsman.

Another subject of which he is a student and practitioner is campanology, or churchbell change-ringing, which forms the cornerstone of one of his most famous cases. **The Nine Tailors** are, in fact, nine churchbells; "tailor" is a fen-country (East Anglian) corruption of the word "teller" (the toll of a bell to announce a death).

Virtually every hobby and interest, every physical feature, and more than a few personality traits identify Wimsey as an aristocrat. A member of the Marlborough and Egoists clubs, it has been said of him that his looks "caricatured him as a typical aristocrat."

His face is "long and amiable," with a long, beak-like nose, a long, narrow chin, and a long forehead with a receding hairline. His hair, brushed back and sleek, is described as straw-colored or tow-colored, and his eyes seem to change color from gray to "ice blue."

An aristocrat, he is properly referred to as Lord Peter. When someone mistakenly calls him Lord Wimsey, he explains, "But I'm not a peer, you know—that's my brother Denver. My name's Peter. It's a silly name, I always think, so old-world and full of homely virtue and that sort of thing. . . . But we always have a Peter after the 3rd Duke, who betrayed kings somewhere about the War of the Roses, though come to think of it, it ain't anything to be proud of. Still, one has to make the best of it."

Wimsey is prepared to make the best of almost anything, including most any case that happens to come his way. "Begone dull care!" he says. "Be at great pains . . . to cultivate a detached outlook on life. Take the example of the bloodhound, who will follow up with equal and impartial zest the trail of a parricide or of a bottle of aniseed."

A remark about his face gives rise to a typically self-deprecating description of his detective technique. "It's a silly kind of face, of course, but rather disarming, don't you think? I know it isn't the kind I'd have chosen, but I do my best with it. I do hope that it isn't contracting a sleuth-like expression, or anything unpleasant. This is the real sleuth, my friend Detective-Inspector Parker of Scotland Yard. He's the one who really does the work. I make imbecile suggestions and he does the work of elaborately disproving them. Then, by a process of elimination, we find the right explanation, and the world says, 'My God, what intuition that young man has.' " (Wimsey is thirty-seven at the time he makes this statement.)

Although Wimsey is a better detective than that, and he has great fun enthusiastically chasing criminals, he suffers mightily when he finally captures them, experiencing anew his childhood headaches and nightmares, and his war-time shell-shock symptoms. On his wedding night he actually cries at the news of the execution of a criminal whose apprehension he has engineered.

His wedding was to Harriet D. Vane, the mystery writer he met in 1930. The author of **Murder by Degrees** and **The Fountain Pen Mystery** is on trial for her life, accused of murder.

A "young woman of great ability," she was raised "on strict religious principles" and earned "her own living in a legitimate way, owing nothing to anyone and accepting no help." When she found herself in love with a writer by the name of Philip Boyes who was opposed to marriage, she found the strength to abandon her "strict religious principles" and lived with him "on terms of intimacy."

In June 1929, Boyes died of arsenic poisoning and Harriet was charged with the crime. Neither Wimsey, who is engaged to aid the defense, nor Miss Climpson, who coincidentally is on the jury, believes her to be guilty.

Perhaps the look of the young woman in the dock persuades Wimsey of her innocence. Her eyes are tired, no doubt from the rigors of the trial, and her skin is a trifle sallow, perhaps for the same reason. Slight and dark, she has "black brows fronting squarely either side of a strong nose a little too broad for beauty." Her mouth "was the mouth of one who has been generous and repented of generosity; its wide corners were tucked back to give nothing away." Her "curious, deep voice" attracts Wimsey.

It attracts him sufficiently for him to fall in love with her and propose marriage to her—sort of. "What I mean to say is," he stammers, "when all this is over, I want to marry you, if you can put up with me and all that."

Harriet refuses him because she "fears that their marriage may be unable to withstand the pressure of the debt she owes him for saving her life." Two years later, Peter tries again. Harriet discovers a corpse while out on a walk and calls Peter in to investigate. Once again asking for her hand at the conclusion of the case, Peter is given an encore of her initial rejection.

Drowning his sorrows in a love affair with an opera singer, Lord Peter does not see Harriet again for three years, when another investigation brings them together. A series of poison pen letters at the college at which she is in residence creates a major difficulty and Harriet attempts to resolve the mystery on her own. When she fails, she asks Peter's help, and he solves the case again. Again he asks her to marry him and, at long last, she accepts.

Eric Whelpton during the World War I era. Once passionately devoted to him, Dorothy L. Sayers used him as a partial prototype for Lord Peter, although she persistently denied the obvious.

Having achieved the success of romance, Wimsey becomes much less active as a detective. He matures nicely, and he and Harriet have three children, Bredon, Paul and Roger, who provide obstacles for Harriet's continued efforts to write mysteries. The eldest son, Bredon, shows some keen interest in detective work.

Having almost entirely vanished from public life, Peter's activities in later years remain largely unchronicled, shrouded more in the mystery of obscurity than of the sinister. It is rumored, probably correctly, that he has done some work for the Foreign Office, both in peacetime and on a dangerous war mission.

Whatever the exploits in which Lord Peter Wimsey was engaged, it is likely that he drew inspiration from the family arms: Sable, three mice courant, argent; crest, a domestic cat crouched as to spring, proper; motto: As my Whimsy takes me.

Perhaps a whimsical variant of the Wimsey motto, normally stated as being: "As my whimsy takes me."

DOROTHY L. SAYERS (1893-1957) The only child of the headmaster of Christ Church Cathedral Choir School, Oxford, Dorothy Leigh Sayers learned Latin by the time she was seven and spoke fluent French as well. She took top honors in medieval literature at Somerville College, Oxford, graduating (one of the first women to receive a degree) in 1915. She worked for an advertising agency, wrote the first novel about Lord Peter Wimsey in 1923, and quit writing detective fiction before World II, devoting herself entirely to her first passions—religion, medieval literature and philosophy. She lectured and wrote many pamphlets and articles on religion and spent nearly a decade translating Dante. Despite her zealous devotion to the church, she was rumored to have had more than a few lovers, and bore a child out of wedlock in 1924.

FILMOGRAPHY

1935 **The Silent Passenger** (Associated British) with Peter Haddon (as Lord Peter Wimsey), John Loder, Mary Newland, Austin Trevor; directed by Reginald Denham.

1940 **The Haunted Honeymoon** (MGM—British, British title: **Busman's Honeymoon**) with Robert Montgomery (as Lord Peter Wimsey), Constance Cummings, Robert Newton, Googie Withers, Leslie Banks; directed by Arthur Woods.

BIBLIOGRAPHY

1923 **Whose Body?** (Boni & Liveright)

1927 **Clouds of Witness** (Dial; published in 1926 by Unwin, London)

1928 **The Dawson Pedigree** (Dial; published in 1927 as **Unnatural Death** by Benn, London)

1928 **The Unpleasantness at the Bellona Club** (Payson)

1929 **Lord Peter Views the Body** (Brewer; published in 1928 by Gollancz, London)

1930 **Strong Poison** (Brewer)

1931 **Suspicious Characters** (Brewer; British title: **The Five Red Herrings**, Gollancz, London)

1932 **Have His Carcase** (Brewer)

1933 **Murder Must Advertise** (Harcourt)

1933 **Hangman's Holiday** (Harcourt; four of the twelve stories are about Lord Peter Wimsey)

1934 **The Nine Tailors** (Harcourt)

1936 **Gaudy Night** (Harcourt; published in 1935 by Gollancz, London)

1937 **Busman's Honeymoon** (Harcourt)

1940 **In the Teeth of the Evidence** (Harcourt; published in 1939 by Gollancz, London; two of the seventeen stories are about Lord Peter Wimsey)

1972 **Lord Peter** (Harper & Row; contains all twenty-one stories about Lord Peter Wimsey, including three previously uncollected; the first edition of this collection omits "Talboys," which was included in the second edition)

Nero Wolfe

Sherlock Holmes was not the first detective, but he was the first character to become more real than the flesh-and-blood personages of his time. The only other detective in literature about whom that is true is Nero Wolfe. A few other detectives may be greater in that they have solved more complex cases, and a few may even be more famous in distant regions of the world, and a few may sell more books, but none has achieved an emotional rapport with readers to equal that of Rex Stout's fat man.

In book after book, from 1934 to 1975, Stout wove a pattern of intricate detail that brought the eccentric detective and his tough, wise-cracking assistant, Archie Goodwin, to life. The old brownstone on West 35th Street exists, almost as clearly as 221B Baker Street.

Wolfe and Holmes follow paths that cross at more than one point. Much like the greatest detective of them all, Wolfe has inspired a devout fandom that speculates on unrevealed details of his past, combing books for evidence, filling in gaps with inferences, suffering frustration at the hands of an author who changed facts, dates, names and other elements of his detective's history to suit the exigencies of the newest book.

Still, more is known about Wolfe's life than about most other detectives, thanks to the narrative efforts of his assistant and chronicler, Goodwin, who represents (particularly in the early books) the dominant form of American detective fiction for many years, the "Hard-Boiled School," just as Wolfe represents the classic English form, the puzzle story solved by an eccentric armchair detective.

Archie is not merely a stupid, worshipful acolyte, employed solely to feed the ego of the detective and ask foolish questions for the benefit of dull readers. Archie is an excellent detective on his own, a tough, cynical man of action, able to do many things beyond the power of Wolfe, just as Wolfe's intellect towers over Archie's. In an unusual and healthy relationship, the talents of the two men complement each other to produce the best detective agency in New York—and the best dialogue in mystery fiction.

Wolfe, of course, is still the mastermind, and

Archie has no choice but to stumble blindly along, as much out of his depth as Dr. Watson or Captain Hastings. The difference is that Archie doesn't care for it very much, and takes no pains to disguise the fact.

He is not above calling Wolfe a "hippo" or a "rhinoceros," nor is he reluctant to quit when he has had too much. He once tells Wolfe, "You are simply too conceited, too eccentric, and too fat to work for!" Not the reaction of the typical Boswell of crime literature.

Neither Wolfe nor Archie age during the forty-one-year history of their affairs, nor do the other recurring characters who populate their world.

Stout was a fast writer, completing a novel in four to six weeks, and he did not revise. Although his prose suffered not at all, his hard facts sometimes strayed, which may account for the ambiguity of Wolfe's and Archie's birthplaces, some fuzziness about Wolfe's early years, and some characters' undergoing a name change from one book to another.

Other facts are deliberately, not inadvertently, obscured. They are not the lapses of Stout; they are the flummery of Wolfe himself, who prefers to remain reticent about his biography. Sometimes the confusion is Archie's, although it is impossible to deny that his memory is superb, and he is less susceptible to errors of omission or commission than Polton, Watson, Hastings or Dupin's anonymous chronicler.

Little is revealed about Wolfe's ancestry, for example, but that is not Archie's oversight so much as it is Wolfe's sense of privacy. There is some evidence, and a widely held belief, that Wolfe is the illegitimate son of a liaison between Holmes and *the* woman in his life, Irene Adler. Knowledgeable students of detective fiction will have no difficulty in noting the striking physical similarities of Wolfe and Holmes' older brother, Mycroft.

Like most other creators of memorable detectives, Stout did not intend for his books to undergo intense scrutiny, or to serve as subjects for profound scholarship. His purpose in writing the books was more noble. They were conceived to give pleasure.

"If I'm not having fun writing a book," he said, "no one's going to have any fun reading it."

There can be no doubt that Rex Stout had enormous fun writing his books about Nero Wolfe.

Every day, with a degree of constancy that does not fall short of incredibility, is a ritualistic agenda of small details, unwaveringly adhered to with a single-mindedness that borders on fanaticism, for the occupants of Nero Wolfe's New York City brownstone house. (The number, on Manhattan's West 35th Street, is either 506, 618, 902, 909, 914, 918, 922, 924 or 938, according to which of Archie Goodwin's chronicles one believes, though it is quite likely none of these, the various numbers serving to prevent an increase of traffic among idle tourists.)

For Wolfe, the day begins between 8 and 8:15 A.M., when his cook, Fritz Brenner, brings the breakfast tray to his room. The tray probably contains peaches and cream, eggs (but never fried), green tomato jam, and hot chocolate (never coffee or tea at breakfast).

Wolfe may eat in his bed (a large affair with a headboard of streaky enselmo, a black silk canopy and a matching coverlet), or he may pad barefoot in "half an acre" of bright yellow pyjamas across the room to a table by the window and eat there. While slowly eating, he reads two newspapers.

After dressing in a three-piece suit, tie, and yellow shirt (to be always fresh, he wears two shirts each day), he steps into his private elevator to the rooftop greenhouse which houses 10,000 orchid plants. Many of the plants are valuable; two (the famous Black Orchids), are unique. For the next two hours, Wolfe attends to the orchids (he calls them his concubines) with the assistance of Theodore Horstmann, the best orchid nurse alive but whose personality is suggestive of sour milk.

At 11:00, Wolfe takes the elevator down to the first floor and the combination office-sitting room, where he greets Archie the same way every morning: "Good morning, Archie, did you sleep well?" He places a fresh spray of orchids in the vase on his desk, then settles into "the only chair in the world he really approves of" and addresses himself to the requirements at hand, such as mail, germination records, etc.

Lunch is served at precisely 1:15, and it is a serious matter. Wolfe maintains that "a stomach long empty thins the blood and disconcerts the brain." There is little danger either of his blood's thinning or his brain's being disconcerted. Archie claims that one of Wolfe's major objections to atom bombs is that they might disturb people eating.

Edward Arnold (center) portrayed the corpulent private eye only in Meet Nero Wolfe. *Lionel Stander (left), usually cast as a villain, is Archie. Victor Jory is a nervous visitor.*

Following a comprehensive lunch, at which discussion of business is permitted only under critical conditions, Wolfe returns to the office until four, when he returns to the plant rooms for two more hours; then the day's business is concluded from 6 to 7:15, when dinner is served. Coffee is had in the office, where Wolfe is likely to begin a conversation (on anything, from the most commonplace to the importance of the new moon in Babylonian astrology) or read a book (sometimes three books at the same time, reading a few pages of one, then a few of the next). At midnight, he turns in.

If he had a choice, not only the typical day would pass that way—every day would, with nothing more urgent than conversation, reading, orchids, eating and drinking beer (he has cut down—to five quarts a day).

Responsibilities, however, intrude. Salaries for Archie, Fritz and Theodore, taxes and maintenance on the old brownstone, the orchids, expensive food and incidental costs require a minimum monthly income of $10,000 for Wolfe to survive. That is why he is a private detective.

Unlike Holmes, who accepts cases for the mental stimulation, or Philo Vance, who finds it

Since he leaves his brownstone only under extreme provocation, Wolfe in a topcoat is a rare sight.

good sport, or Philip Marlowe, who sees it as a noble quest, Wolfe allows himself to be hired so that he can earn enough money to maintain his lavish lifestyle. Despite the economic necessity of taking cases, Wolfe takes them reluctantly. He hates to work.

Goodwin recognizes this failing in his boss, and accepts the resonsibility of acting "as the thorn in the seat of Wolfe's chair"; Wolfe appreciates Archie's chore—and occasionally admits the need for it. Archie's prime occupation beyond prodding Wolfe is to act as his legs or, rather, his body.

The only part of his body that Wolfe generally needs to use is his brain. The function at which he excels is thinking. He does it better than anyone else, knows it and is excessively immodest about it.

Inspector Cramer, the long-suffering New York City policeman who handles the homicides in Wolfe's precinct and therefore has to endure the detective's arrogance, has told him: "You're the worst thorn in the flesh I know of, but you are also half as smart as you think you are, and that puts you head and shoulders above everybody else since Julius Caesar."

Wolfe's self-analysis approaches humility—for him. "I have no talents," he admits. "I have genius or nothing."

Being a genius, Wolfe can get away with a lot. One character describes him as "the most improbable combination of ignorance and knowledge on earth." When Wolfe asks about the business hours of the morgue, or the simple geography of the New York metropolitan area, Archie is embarrassed to answer in front of strangers. Any moderately competent private eye should know such things, he reasons.

The questions do not embarrass Wolfe. Eccentrics do not embarrass easily. And Wolfe is an eccentric of the first rank. He does not, for example, ever leave his house, except under extreme provocation or "to meet personal contingencies"; they are rare.

All machinery he regards as personal enemies, although he seems satisfied with his four-by-six-foot, $7,000 personal elevator. It requires many years of pressure to get Wolfe to agree to have the brownstone air-conditioned.

Nothing frightens Wolfe more than automobiles. They are demons, he says, capable of destructive "whims," and he trusts only Archie behind the wheel. Even then, he sits on the edge of the back seat of his car (he buys a new Heron sedan every year), clutching the strap, ready to leap for his life. He would sooner cut his throat than step into a taxi.

Wolfe does not move any more than absolutely necessary. He is not built for it. According to Archie, he weighs somewhere "between 250 and a ton," with the most common estimate being a seventh of a ton (about 286 pounds); he is five feet, eleven inches tall. He once decided that he was too fat and went on a physical fitness rampage to slim down. For exercise, he threw darts for fifteen minutes a day (calling them javelins).

For all his bulk, his movements are smooth and efficient, almost graceful. Wolfe's corpulence is an integral part of him; he fits it. When a desperate situation forces him to assume a disguise, he grows a beard and drops a hundred pounds, making him "unrecognizable." Even with his weight, he has been called handsome by women.

If Wolfe attempted to be a private detective in the ordinary sense, his near-immobility would make it impossible for him to function. But he needs only two elements to handle any case successfully, and he has them both—brains, and Archie Goodwin.

"I am not a policeman," Wolfe says. "I am a private detective. I entrap criminals, and find evidence to imprison or kill them, for hire." It is a highly specialized skill, and he admits that, in nine cases out of ten, Inspector Cramer's services "would be more valuable than mine." But in the tenth case, Wolfe has no peer. His genius transcends logic and deduction to encompass intuition and insight as well; Wolfe calls his talent "a feeling for phenomena."

Before he can begin to exercise his genius, however, Archie must locate and bring to him data. "I'm chiefly cut out for two things," Archie modestly says, "to jump up and grab something before the other guy gets his paws on it, and to collect pieces of the puzzle for Wolfe to work on."

To accomplish his tasks, Archie uses a variety of techniques. With women, his major weapon is his charm and good looks. Just under six feet tall, with broad shoulders and narrow hips, he has brown eyes and a pleasant baritone voice. One person compares him to Clark Gable, but he claims that "No one can say I resemble a movie actor, and if they did it would be more apt to be Gary Cooper." Whomever he looks like, he is attractive to the opposite sex. Wolfe pretends to believe that no woman under thirty can resist his assistant.

Archie is also able to use guile in his search for information. Wolfe has taught Archie that "We use a great many lies in this business, sometimes calculated with great care, sometimes quite at random." The secret of success, he says, is to "tell only useful lies, and only those not easily exposed." He has apparently taught the lessons so well that Archie has surpassed even Wolfe. "For barefaced lying," Cramer says to Archie, "I'd play you on the nose."

Although he doesn't use disguises, Archie has impersonated a personnel expert, a financial secretary, a florist, a photographer and, of course, a policeman. He has also pretended to be corrupt to gain a criminal's confidence.

Among other of his talents, Archie has successfully burgled more than one apartment, knows more than a smattering about fingerprints and locks, and says "there are very few blocks in Manhattan I don't know." He is also "exceptionally strong," according to Wolfe, and a good fighter—clean or dirty. His best punch is a right to the kidney.

He can also handle a gun, with a variety of medium-calibre revolvers and automatics at his disposal. Since an incident dating back to February 1935, Archie does not leave the house without arming himself if he is involved in a murder case.

When data have been gathered, Archie reports back to Wolfe. With practice, he has developed his memory to the point where he is able to provide mental pyrotechnics unique in criminal literature. Incredibly, he can repeat an hour-long conversation among five people verbatim, complete with inflections, gestures and facial expressions. "The only difference between me and a tape recorder," he says, "is that you can ask me questions." It is his goal to be so accurate and complete that questions are unnecessary. A good job earns Wolfe's favorite word of praise: "satisfactory"; a job of surpassing excellence merits "most satisfactory."

For additional information, Wolfe likes to question clients, witnesses or suspects in his office. It is here that Wolfe is at his best. To reach Wolfe's office, one has to locate the four-story building on the south side of West 35th Street, between 10th and 11th avenues (less than a half block from the Hudson River), climb the seven steps and ring the doorbell. Archie (or Fritz, in his absence) looks at the visitor through the one-way glass panel in the door.

One is then ushered into either the office or the "front room," which has windows facing 35th Street and is used as a waiting room. It is soundproofed (as is the entire first floor) and contains its own fireplace, a table, sofa with six velvet cushions, a piano and bench, and a checkerboard. It shares a lavatory with the office, and a door leads directly into the office, enabling Wolfe to play a shell game with the police if they happen to be hunting his client.

The office is spacious, high-ceilinged and lined with shelves. Those behind his desk contain books (1,200 volumes); the rest contain files and cabinets. The cherrywood desk has eight drawers. In the middle drawer Wolfe keeps the caps of the day's beer bottles so that he can keep track of how many he has had. A murderer once hid a poisonous snake in that drawer.

On top of the desk is a gold bottle opener (a gift from a grateful client), a vase for orchids, a paperweight (a block of wood once used as a murder weapon) and a bookmark—sometimes a counterfeit ten-dollar bill, sometimes a thin strip of gold. The bookmark is used only for the books Wolfe admires; bad ones are dog-eared. The letter opener is a horn-handled knife thrown at Wolfe by a man named Bua; Archie shot him. Into the desk is built a buzzer which Wolfe uses to summon Fritz, usually for more beer.

Behind Wolfe's desk is a picture (first of the Washington Monument, later of a waterfall) covering a panel through which one can see and hear everything that takes place in the office. The office also has facilities (rarely used) for electronic eavesdropping.

At right angles to Wolfe's desk, eight feet away, is Archie's desk, in which he keeps the guns and ammunition, and the letterhead stationery and calling cards used by the firm. On top of the desk is the telephone, a notepad and pencil, with which he takes down information in a shorthand of his own invention.

Also in the office is an old-fashioned, two-ton safe which contains important documents and petty cash—$5,000 in used tens, twenties and hundreds. There are a radio and a television set (Wolfe likes to turn them off). On the walls are hung Holbein reproductions, a wall clock, an engraving of Brillat-Savarin, a portrait of Sherlock Holmes and maps.

Although Wolfe rarely travels, he likes maps, and Archie sometimes finds him studying the atlas, possibly indulging in vicarious wanderlust, possibly thinking about the house in Egypt which he owns. For similar purposes, whatever they are, Wolfe uses the globe, custom-made by Gouchard at a cost of $500, which stands in the corner.

On the floor of the office is the fourteen-by-twenty-six-foot rug given to him by an Armenian. It is either a Keraghan or a Shirvan.

For guests there is a big yellow sofa, some straightbacked yellow chairs and, for the guest of honor, a big red leather chair. Cramer uses it, and so do clients. A small table of massaranduba stands close by, to facilitate the writing of checks by clients.

When someone occupies the red leather chair, Wolfe is probably preparing to work. He usually does not rise when someone enters his office (although his manners are, generally, impeccable), claiming that "engineering considerations" keep him in his chair. To acknowledge the entrance of a welcome guest, he nods his head curtly about an eighth of an inch; if he is being genuinely effusive, his head will incline a full quarter of an inch.

When Wolfe sits behind his desk and a visitor faces him from the red chair (or the scene may be more crowded), the stage is set for Wolfe's interrogation. It is an art, and Wolfe excels at it. Even the police sometimes ask him to question a particularly difficult witness. He is relentless and thorough. "When gathering eggs," he says, "you must look in every nest."

Engaged to clear a client of a crime, Wolfe invariably points out that he can accomplish that only by finding the guilty person. "Innocence is negative," he says, "and can never be established; you can only establish guilt."

Regardless of his objective, Wolfe has to think on a case and, when he does, he leans back in his chair and goes into what Archie calls his "lip act." With his eyes closed, Wolfe pushes his tightly closed lips out a fraction of an inch, then pulls them back in a puckering movement. Out and in. Out and in. It may last for a few seconds, or it may continue for hours. It is a sign that Wolfe has discovered the key to the investigation and he is deep in concentration, attempting to unravel the confused threads of the case. It is impossible to disturb Wolfe while he is thus engaged. When the lip act is concluded, the normal next step is what Archie calls "Wolfe's charade"—the gathering of all suspects, clients, witnesses and police in Wolfe's office for the denouement.

Only Wolfe knows what is planned at these gatherings. He prefers not to reveal too much information to Archie because, he says, he does not want to "strain Archie's powers of dissimulation," which outrages his assistant, who counters with: "When the day finally comes that I tie Wolfe to a stake and shoot him, one of the fundamental reasons will be his theory that...everything inside my head shows on my face."

The real reason he keeps everything secret until the last moment, Archie claims, is that "Wolfe likes to have the curtain go up revealing him balancing a live seal on his nose." He has never dropped the seal. The culprit is revealed and hauled off to jail, and he collects his fee, which is considerable (Wolfe has several times collected fees of $100,000; "I do not soil myself cheaply," he says).

He has come quite a distance, both geographically and socially, since his youth, which was spent in Montenegro (now part of Yugoslavia). Wolfe is now a citizen of the United States, but whether he was born in this country or Montenegro remains unclear. On several occasions he has stated that he was born in that small Balkan state (Lovchen, Monte Nero, the Black Mountain, for which he was named), but in 1938 he told an FBI agent that he was "born in this country."

Following Meet Nero Wolfe, *which was based on* Fer-de-lance, *only one other Wolfe film was made. Rex Stout was unhappy with them and refused to allow further cinematic productions.*

Wherever he was born, the event occurred sometime during the 1890s, and his entire childhood and beyond was spent in Montenegro. Here, he played with his dog and his best friend, Marko Vukcic, and climbed the Black Mountain for the first time at the age of nine. Wolfe says that he was an agent for the Austrian government "as a boy," but this seems to have been a few years before World War I, so he was not a young boy. When that war erupted, he turned against Austria, joined the Montenegrin army, and "starved to death" in 1916, when the Austrians attacked, and "fought machine guns with fingernails." Further heroics in the war included a six-hundred-mile walk to join the American Expeditionary Force, along which he claims to have killed two hundred Germans.

After the war, he returned to Montenegro and, in 1920 or 1921, adopted a three-year-old orphan girl, leaving her behind when he was forced to leave the country. In 1929, he returned again to attempt to see his adopted daughter, and was once more forced to leave the country.

He soon turned up in what was to become his permanent residence. "Coming to this country in 1930, not penniless," Wolfe recalls, "I bought this house."

If the information concerning the first thirty-five years or so of Wolfe's life seems vague or sparse, it is because he is personally reticent or deliberately contradictory about it. Archie explains it best when he says that Wolfe "has fifteen or twenty pasts."

Perhaps no point is more obscure than the question of Wolfe's married life, if there was one. When asked by the FBI if he had ever been married, he replies, "No. Married? No." On a different occasion, however, he obviously relished telling an anecdote about a woman who tried to kill her husband by cooling his brow with a rag soaked with poison. "The man on whom she tried this experiment," he says, "was myself." In all likelihood, this is probably the Montenegrin woman to whom Wolfe refers as the only person from whom he has ever "skedaddled, physically."

Montenegro and its politics continued to play a large role in Wolfe's life. In 1938, his long-lost adopted daughter reappears, using the name Carla Lovchen, teaching dancing and fencing in a New York salon. She is deeply involved in an international plot involving Nazis, Bosnian forest concessions and murder. Wolfe clears her, but their relationship is sporadic. She actually seems closer to Wolfe's friend, Marko Vukcic, and becomes a dedicated member, with Vukcic, of The Spirit of the Black Mountain, which exists to fight for the liberation of Montenegro from the rule of Tito's Yugoslavia.

This type of activism is characteristic of Vukcic, "the oldest and best friend Wolfe ever had," and the only man in New York to call Wolfe by his first name. According to Wolfe, Vukcic was "headstrong, gullible, over-sanguine, and naive." A big man with a swarthy complexion, "magnificent" white teeth, and a thick tangle of dark brown hair, Vukcic resembled nothing more than "a lion upright on his hind legs."

An outstanding chef, he came to New York in 1927 and founded the best restaurant in New York, Rusterman's. Commensurate with his stature, he is a member of "Les Quinze Maîtres," an organization of the world's fifteen greatest chefs. As much as he loved food, he loved women more.

Sergeant Purley Stebbins of the N.Y.P.D. articulated it vulgarly but accurately when he described Vukcic as a "chicken-chaser." Felix, one of the restaurant's employees who inherited Rusterman's (under Wolfe's trusteeship) on Marko's death, put it more tastefully when he said that Vukcic "had a warm eye for women."

Marko is murdered, and Wolfe fulfills a boyhood pledge by going to the morgue and placing gold dinars on his friend's unseeing eyes. As he attempts to track down the killer in the United States, Carla returns to Yugoslavia to carry on Marko's work with the resistance until she, too, is murdered. Incredibly, Wolfe breaks the habits of nearly a lifetime to pursue the villain to Europe. Archie accompanies him, stupefied by this new vision of Wolfe. "It's quite a shock," he says, "to see a statue turn into a dynamo without warning."

The adventure in Montenegro strains Archie's linguistic ability. He is limited to fluency in one language. Wolfe, however, is totally comfortable with eight (English, French, Spanish, Serbo-Croatian, Bari, Hungarian, Italian and Albanian). Wolfe's background required a thorough knowledge of various tongues. Archie's (in either Canton or Chillicothe, Ohio) did not.

Born in 1910 (or 1911, 1912, 1913 or 1914) to James Arner Goodwin (he once says his father's name is Titus, but he was probably joking), he has stayed in touch with his family. He has at least one sister, and his mother came to New York to visit him and Wolfe.

An outstanding athlete in high school, excelling at baseball and football, he graduated, he said, "with honor but no honors." Afterward, he "went to college two weeks," he recounts, "decided it was childish, came to New York and got a job guarding a pier, shot and killed two men and was fired, was recommended to Nero Wolfe for a chore he wanted done, did it, and was offered a full-time job." He has held it ever since.

Archie has remained a bachelor for a combination of reasons. The first, he explains, is that "I love to do a good job more than anything else I can think of, and I suppose that's what shorts the line." His job simply comes first with him. But it was not always that way. "The only girl I had ever been really soft on," he says, "had found another bargain she liked better. That was how I happened to meet Wolfe."

If he ever does marry, the girl will have to be Lily Rowan, a blue-eyed blonde who is the best dancer he knows. She is also very rich. Her father was a Tammany Hall Democrat who made millions installing sewers. He also used his influence to get Cramer on the police force. Lily used to live at the Ritz, but she now has a penthouse on East 63rd Street, a place near Katonah in Westchester County and a ranch in Montana. Archie has a key to her apartment.

Because of an incident that made her brag that she was "the only woman alive who has necked with Nero Wolfe," and that made Wolfe smell of *Houri de Perse* perfume, he pretends not to like her, calling her "rich, intemperate and notorious."

During World War II, Wolfe assisted the government in ferreting out domestic enemies, taking no pay for his work, and Archie, a major in G-2, was assigned to assist him for the duration.

In the late 1940s and early 1950s, Wolfe engaged in the greatest struggle of his career, matching wits with Arnold Zeck, a criminal mastermind in the tradition of Professor Moriarty and Ernst Stavro Blofeld.

He lives in Eastcrest, a "large, luxurious mansion" on "the highest hill in Westchester." Wolfe explains how Zeck makes ends meet. "He has varied and extensive sources of income," the detective says. "All of them are illegal and some of them are morally repulsive. Narcotics, smuggling, industrial and commercial rackets, gambling . . . blackmailing, political malfeasance," which is not an exhaustive list. Zeck, continues Wolfe, has an "unexcelled talent, a remorseless purpose, and a will that cannot be dented or deflected." Like other arch-villains, Zeck remains above suspicion by keeping several levels of underlings between himself and the actual perpetration of crimes, with only the very top men knowing of his existence.

Wolfe first learns of Zeck's activities in 1938 but, since his interests do not conflict with Zeck's, he does not pursue the matter. Five years later, on June 19, 1943, Zeck personally telephones Wolfe to offer advice on a case. A second telephone encounter ends with Zeck's veiled warning: "I have a strong admiration for you, but I admit I am much easier to get along with when I am pleased."

His interest piqued, Wolfe learns everything possible about the criminal, including the rumor that he "owns" twenty Assemblymen and six district leaders. According to Lon Cohen of the **Gazette**, a friend of Archie's and Wolfe's, if a newspaperman printed something unfavorable about Zeck, his body would be found "washed ashore at Montauk Point, mangled by sharks."

One encounter between Wolfe and Zeck results in gunmen's spraying Wolfe's plant rooms with machine gun fire, causing $40,000 worth of damage.

Of Zeck, Wolfe said, "He is the only man on earth that I'm afraid of. I'm not afraid he'll hurt me; I'm afraid of what he may someday force me to do to keep from hurting him."

In April 1950, the titans, each on opposite sides of the law, meet again, this time in a duel to the finish. With Zeck aiming his heaviest weaponry at the detective, Wolfe announces his retirement and disappears. "His will failed him," exults Zeck. But in June, a drastically changed Wolfe, now unrecognizable, returns, and meets Zeck face to face for the first time.

Goodwin also met Zeck, and recalled that their adversary was "nothing but forehead and eyes. It wasn't a forehead, actually, it was a dome, sloping up and up to the line of his faded thin hair. The eyes were a result of an error on the assembly line. They had been intended for a shark and someone got careless. They did not now look the same as shark eyes because Arnold Zeck's brain had been using them to see with for fifty years, and that had had an effect."

Engaging Wolfe in mortal combat dooms his foe, of course, and Zeck pays the ultimate price for his arrogance. Almost without a stir, the routine of the Wolfe brownstone resumes its normal undeviating pattern. Next to Wolfe himself, no one is more responsible for the smoothly running operation than Fritz Brenner, the major domo.

Neither Fritz nor Wolfe shares Archie's affection for women. Wolfe says, "You can depend on a woman for anything except constancy," and "the vocations for which they are best adapted [are] chicanery, sophistry, self-advertisement, cajolery, mystification, and incubation." Pressed on the subject, however he admits that women are "astonishing and successful animals," that his misogynist pose is "counterfeit" and that he carries his excessive fat "to insulate my feelings."

Fritz' objection to women is simpler; he fears they will upset his household. He lives in the basement of the brownstone with his framed menus, pictures of famous chefs, his collection of utensils and a pet turtle. In addition to the cooking, he is responsible for cleaning the entire house except for the office and Archie's bedroom (Goodwin's responsibility) and the plant rooms (Horstmann's).

A Swiss whose native language is French, he enjoys sitting in his stockinged feet, reading a French newspaper, but with slippers nearby "on account of things left on his toes and feet by the war to remember it by." He has a sweet smile, and is the only man Archie knows who can giggle without giving one doubts about his fundamentals.

As a cook, Wolfe rates Fritz just below the greats and he could easily work in New York's best restaurant (Rusterman's) at double his present salary (which exceeds $1,000 a month). When cooking, he is quite serious, wears a chef's hat and apron, and does not like to talk to anyone. He grows his own herbs in a garden in back of the house.

Fritz once tosses off an epigram ("Starving the live will not profit the dead") which Wolfe mistakes for Montaigne; he congratulates his cook.

Language is important to Wolfe. Archie says, "Which Wolfe loves most, food or words, is a tossup." He loathes clichés, says that "contact is not a verb under this roof," and is scrupulous about literal meanings of words, often sending

Archie to the dictionary for reference. Wolfe's dictionary is Webster's Second Edition; the third edition he found subversive for, among other transgressions, condoning the interchangeable use of "imply" and "infer"; he burned it. Profanity is used rarely, his favorite expletive, "pfui!", frequently.

Wolfe has considerable knowledge of legal terminology, but he relies on Nathaniel Parker (also referred to as Henry George Parker) when, as Archie says, "only the law will do." He has freed Wolfe and Archie from jail more than once, and may be depended upon "for everything except fee-splitting."

Even more indispensable to Wolfe's operations is Saul Panzer, a free-lance private detective he hires when Archie has too many chores to handle on his own. Goodwin calls him "the best operative south of the North Pole," and he demands (and gets) double the standard fee of other private eyes. He is worth it.

At trailing a suspect, he is a "nonpareil" and he literally never forgets a face. "I have developed my faculties," he explains. Saul is five feet, seven inches tall, 140 pounds, has a big nose that hides his "wrinkled little mug" that always looks as if he shaved yesterday, and has clothes that look similarly disheveled. The best poker player that Archie knows, partly because of a tender smile, Wolfe nonetheless trusts him "farther than might be thought credible."

Another free-lancer employed by Wolfe from time to time is Fred Durkin, a bear-like, "bald and burly," five foot ten, 190-pounder who can tail people better than anyone except Saul Panzer. Married to an Italian woman (they have four children), he has the map of Ireland on his face.

Archie said that Fred was "as honest as sunshine, but he wasn't so brilliant as sunshine." He is an effective private eye, however, because "he knows what to expect from his brains, which is more than you can say for some people with a bigger supply." Wolfe will not allow Fred to eat at his table because he "puts vinegar on things." Fred thinks Wolfe could prove "who killed Cock Robin" any time he had the notion to.

Wolfe's third choice for a free-lancer to help out is Orrie (for either Orville or Orvald) Cather, whose strong point is his ability to get people to tell him things. It isn't that he is a good questioner, Archie points out, but there is "something about his face makes people feel he ought to be told things."

A handsome, six-foot, 180-pound former professional football player who moves like a cat, he has a good singing voice, confident brown eyes, wavy lips, and was "born with the attitude toward all attractive women that a fisherman has toward all the trout in a stream." He has never found a reason to change, including his marriage.

Other operatives employed by Wolfe include John Joseph Keems, who looks like "a Princeton boy" and thought "it would be a fine thing for the detective business" if he got Archie's job; Theodolinda ("Dol") Bonner, who has her own detective agency, caramel-colored eyes, long curling lashes, and is considered "dangerous" by Fritz; Sally Corbett (also known as Sally Colt) who assists "Dol" and whom Archie thinks of as a younger sister; and the mysterious Mister Jones, seen by no one except Wolfe, who delivers (for cash in advance) information on the inner workings of the American Communist Party.

For more general information, Wolfe and Goodwin consult Lon Cohen, assistant to the publisher of the **Gazette**. An excellent journalist, he demands information in exchange for the information he supplies; he often gets it.

Paradoxically, Wolfe's most valuable information generally comes from his fiercest rival, the New York City Police Department, especially the Homicide Bureau and its head, Inspector L.T. (also referred to as Morgan) Cramer, a cigar-chewing, red-faced, irritable cop of thirty years whose talks with Wolfe range from helpful, good-humored sweetness to outright rage.

Wolfe is often willing to exchange the products of his thinking for the results of police investigation. "Mr. Cramer's indefatigable routine," concedes Wolfe, "does have its advantages." Nevertheless, Wolfe has his reservations and tells him, in a fit of pique, "your acceptance of your salary constitutes a fraud on the people of New York." In calmer moments, they drink beer together in Wolfe's office, and Wolfe once saves his career.

Archie, too, has ambivalent feelings about Cramer, once admitting that he is "by no means a nitwit" and on another occasion saying: "I wouldn't give an unconditional guarantee on his brains, but there is nothing wrong with his guts."

Of himself, Cramer says he is "not exactly a boob" and is proud of his honesty and good reputation. The only time he becomes physically violent in the brownstone results from Archie's suggestion that he is on Zeck's payroll. He earns $10,000 a year. Often exasperated by Wolfe and claiming to look forward to the day he can lift

Selected as one of the twelve great detectives of literature, Nero Wolfe adorns one of the commemorative stamps issued by Nicaragua for the fiftieth anniversary of Interpol.

his license, he admits that, over the years, "Wolfe has been better than square" with him.

Cramer's right-hand man is Sergeant Purley Stebbins, who is never at his best around Wolfe because, according to Archie, he is controlling his impulse "to see how many clips it would take to make Wolfe incapable of speech." Stebbins hates to visit Wolfe but does it anyway, rather than pass the buck to subordinates.

Lieutenant George Rowcliff is used mainly by Cramer to harrass Wolfe and Goodwin, both of whom hate him. Wolfe will never forgive him because he came to the house with a warrant and searched it. To Archie, he is just a jerk, so he torments him. Rowcliff stutters when he gets agitated, so Archie begins to stutter first, then accuses Rowcliff of mocking him.

Although both Wolfe and Goodwin have their differences of opinion with the representatives of the law, and occasionally flout the law (Wolfe drank bootleg beer during Prohibition; they often withhold evidence and hide suspects; Archie breaks and enters), they have strong codes of morality and ethics.

One of Wolfe's tenets concerns his substantial fees. "It is desirable that you earn your fees," he says, "but it is essential that you feel you have earned them. . . . Never collect or accept a fee that you feel you haven't earned; if you do, your integrity crumbles and your ego will have worms. With that one reservation, get all you can."

Despite that dictum, Wolfe considers himself a romantic and will often take a case because he feels a moral obligation, or as a gesture, with no prospect of a fee. On the whole, Archie shares the view, and is quite satisfied to work for a principle, rather than financial gain. It is one of the many traits shared by Wolfe and Goodwin. Although they fight often and bitterly (Archie calls Wolfe "pigheaded" and "childish"; Wolfe says to Archie: "Your head full of ideas? Even my death by violence is not too high a price for so rare and happy a phenomenon as that"), they have enjoyed one of the happiest and closest alliances of the many great detective teams in literature.

In a late published adventure of Wolfe and Goodwin, **In the Best Families**, Archie returns to the old brownstone, the door standing open, and finds a note announcing Wolfe's retirement. "If I actually had seen the last of Nero Wolfe," he says, "it was a damn sad day for me."

It was not the end then, but there will be no new adventures. It is a damn sad day for us all.

Robert Stanley depicted Wolfe in his pajamas for the Dell paperback of Too Many Cooks.

REX STOUT (1886-1975) Born in Noblesville, Ind., one of nine children, Rex Todhunter Stout was a child prodigy, reading the Bible twice by the time he was four, reading more than one thousand classics before he was ten, and being the state spelling champion at the age of thirteen. After dozens of diversified jobs, he invented a school banking system which earned him a small fortune, and gave him the leisure to write. He sold numerous tales to early pulp magazines, but his first novel was a literate psychological study, **How Like a God** (1929), which he wrote in Paris. **Fer-de-Lance**, the first Nero Wolfe book, appeared as a serialization in **The Saturday Evening Post** and as a book in 1934. Both it and the detective were extremely popular, and scores of books followed. Like the more notorious Dashiell Hammett, Stout was politically active in left-wing causes, particularly during the 1930s and 1940s.

FILMOGRAPHY

1936 **Meet Nero Wolfe** (Columbia) with Edward Arnold (as Nero Wolfe), Lionel Stander, Russell Hardie, Joan Perry, Victor Jory, Nana Bryant; directed by Herbert Biberman.
1937 **The League of Frightened Men** (Columbia) with Walter Connolly (as Nero Wolfe), Lionel Stander, Irene Hervey, Allan Brook, Eduardo Ciannelli; directed by Alfred E. Green.

BIBLIOGRAPHY

1934 **Fer-de-Lance** (Farrar & Rinehart)
1935 **The League of Frightened Men** (Farrar & Rinehart)
1936 **The Rubber Band** (Farrar & Rinehart)
1937 **The Red Box** (Farrar & Rinehart)
1938 **Too Many Cooks** (Farrar & Rinehart)
1939 **Some Buried Caesar** (Farrar & Rinehart)
1940 **Over My Dead Body** (Farrar & Rinehart)
1940 **Where There's a Will** (Farrar & Rinehart)
1942 **Black Orchids** (Farrar & Rinehart)
1944 **Not Quite Dead Enough** (Farrar & Rinehart)
1946 **The Silent Speaker** (Viking)
1947 **Too Many Women** (Viking)
1948 **And Be a Villain** (Viking)
1949 **Trouble in Triplicate** (Viking)
1949 **The Second Confession** (Viking)
1950 "Door to Death" (Dell)
1950 **Three Doors to Death** (Viking)
1950 **In the Best Families** (Viking)
1950 **Curtains for Three** (Viking)
1951 **Murder by the Book** (Viking)
1952 **Prisoner's Base** (Viking)
1952 **Triple Jeopardy** (Viking)
1953 **The Golden Spiders** (Viking)
1954 **Three Men Out** (Viking)
1954 **The Black Mountain** (Viking)
1955 **Before Midnight** (Viking)
1956 **Three Witnesses** (Viking)
1956 **Might as Well Be Dead** (Viking)
1957 **Three for the Chair** (Viking)
1957 **If Death Ever Slept** (Viking)
1958 **And Four to Go** (Viking)
1958 **Champagne for One** (Viking)
1959 **Plot It Yourself** (Viking)
1960 **Too Many Clients** (Viking)
1960 **Three at Wolfe's Door** (Viking)
1961 **The Final Deduction** (Viking)
1962 **Gambit** (Viking)
1962 **Homicide Trinity** (Viking)
1963 **The Mother Hunt** (Viking)
1964 **Trio for Blunt Instruments** (Viking)
1964 **A Right to Die** (Viking)
1965 **The Doorbell Rang** (Viking)
1966 **Death of a Doxy** (Viking)
1968 **The Father Hunt** (Viking)
1969 **Death of a Dude** (Viking)
1973 **Please Pass the Guilt** (Viking)
1975 **A Family Affair** (Viking)
1977 **Corsage** (James A. Rock)

Index